Approaches to
Teaching Baudelaire's
Flowers of Evil

Approaches to Teaching
World Literature

Joseph Gibaldi, series editor

For a complete listing of titles,
see the last pages of this book.

Approaches to
Teaching Baudelaire's
Flowers of Evil

Edited by

Laurence M. Porter

*A gift from the Sonia Raiziss Giop
Charitable Foundation helped
make publication of this book possible.*

The Modern Language Association of America
New York   2000

©2000 by The Modern Language Association of America
All rights reserved
Printed in the United States of America

For information about obtaining permission to reprint material from
MLA book publications, send your request by mail (see address below),
e-mail (permissions@mla.org), or fax (212 477-9863).

Library of Congress Cataloging-in-Publication Data

Approaches to teaching Baudelaire's Flowers of evil / edited by Laurence M. Porter.
p. cm. — (Approaches to teaching world literature ; vol. 64)
Includes bibliographical references and index.
ISBN 0-87352-751-8 (cloth) — ISBN 0-87352-752-6 (pbk.)
1. Baudelaire, Charles, 1821–1867. Fleurs du mal. 2. Baudelaire, Charles,
1821–1867—Study and teaching. I. Porter, Laurence M., 1936– II. Series.
PQ2191.F63 A67 1999
841'.8—dc21   99-052504

"Searching for Swans: Baudelaire's 'Le Cygne,'" by Richard Terdiman,
was adapted from a section of his book *Present Past:*
Modernity and the Memory Crisis and is used by permission
of the publisher, Cornell University Press.

Cover illustration for the paperback edition: *Baudelaire par lui-même*, 1863–64.
Album Baudelaire: Iconographie réunie et commentée, by Claude Pichois
(Paris: Gallimard–Bibliothèque de la Pléiade, 1974) 238. Background
photograph: *Le Pont-Neuf en 1852*, by Marville. Musée Carnavalet, Paris.
Used with permission of the Musée Carnavalet.

Published by The Modern Language Association of America
10 Astor Place, New York, New York 10003-6981

In fond and admiring memory of Anna Balakian,
an inspirational leader, teacher, and scholar

CONTENTS

Thematic Approaches

Cultural Studies

Gender-Based Approaches

Religious and Ethical Issues

Computer-Assisted Instruction

PREFACE TO THE SERIES

In *The Art of Teaching* Gilbert Highet wrote, "Bad teaching wastes a great deal of effort, and spoils many lives which might have been full of energy and happiness." All too many teachers have failed in their work, Highet argued, simply "because they have not thought about it." We hope that the Approaches to Teaching World Literature series, sponsored by the Modern Language Association's Publications Committee, will not only improve the craft—as well as the art—of teaching but also encourage serious and continuing discussion of the aims and methods of teaching literature.

The principal objective of the series is to collect within each volume different points of view on teaching a specific literary work, a literary tradition, or a writer widely taught at the undergraduate level. The preparation of each volume begins with a wide-ranging survey of instructors, thus enabling us to include in the volume the philosophies and approaches, thoughts and methods of scores of experienced teachers. The result is a sourcebook of material, information, and ideas on teaching the subject of the volume to undergraduates.

The series is intended to serve nonspecialists as well as specialists, inexperienced as well as experienced teachers, graduate students who wish to learn effective ways of teaching as well as senior professors who wish to compare their own approaches with the approaches of colleagues in other schools. Of course, no volume in the series can ever substitute for erudition, intelligence, creativity, and sensitivity in teaching. We hope merely that each book will point readers in useful directions; at most each will offer only a first step in the long journey to successful teaching.

Joseph Gibaldi
Series Editor

PREFACE TO THE VOLUME

Baudelaire's Significance

Charles Baudelaire's *Fleurs du Mal* may be the most influential, and perhaps the greatest, volume of lyric poetry in French literature. It has echoed widely abroad, in Australia, Japan, Southeast Asia, Latin America, and Senegal, in addition to Europe and the United States. Individual poems are continually being translated and anthologized in standard compilations such as Norton's *World Masterpieces* or St. Martin's *Western Literature in a World Context*.

Baudelaire's title implicitly dissociates ethics from aesthetics, culminating in the art-for-art's-sake movement initiated by Théophile Gautier. At the same time, in blatant contradiction to the moral detachment of his aestheticism, Baudelaire merges the didactic Augustinian and the apologetic Rousseauesque confessional traditions: he vehemently urges his general audience to learn from his superior moral insight, while imploring acceptance, understanding, and forgiveness from his select, idealized audience. His poet-persona is both preacher and penitent. His lyric cycle, which presents his spiritual autobiography, overshadows even Victor Hugo's similar collection, *Les Contemplations* (1856) and suggests a modern but sinful Dante or Petrarch. By dramatizing a tortured spiritual state, he helped prepare the international decadent movement, which lasted until World War I (see Porter, "Decadence").

The confessional sensibility remains strong in modern poetry. Teachers can readily find examples in many countries. Baudelaire's ambivalent attitude toward consciousness-altering drugs echoed Thomas De Quincey (*Confessions*) and anticipated debates today. Gifted with considerable psychological sophistication, Baudelaire more than once traces his attitudes back to childhood, foreshadowing psychoanalytic theories of infantile sexuality and its polymorphous perversity. *Les Fleurs du Mal* and the autobiographical prose writings offer feminist critics clear, abundant evidence of a male madonna-prostitute complex and of a keen if intermittent self-awareness regarding the poet's ambivalent relationships with women.

Rejecting Baudelaire's morbid, introspective subjectivity, the French Catholic renaissance during the first half of the twentieth century emphasized religious commitment, but it claimed Baudelaire as a precursor in reviving a religious sensibility. Later, existentialism opposed social and political commitment to Baudelaire's self-absorbed ethos: Jean-Paul Sartre was fascinated by Baudelaire as a supreme example of bad faith (meaning moral self-deception).

But Sartre failed to recognize Baudelaire's ironic dialogue with himself, most obvious in the several prose poems that rework certain verse poems. Baudelaire invented the modern prose poem, and it became the centerpiece of the ironic tradition, which had been inaugurated by Byron, Heinrich Heine, and Alfred de Musset and to which Tristan Corbière and Jules Laforgue contributed less powerfully. Baudelaire's ideal of self-sufficient and disabused detachment, illustrated by his figure of the dandy, flowed into the modernist and postmodernist worldview. From this perspective Francis Ponge's prose poems present an instructive contrast to Baudelaire's prose poems, and René Char's lyrics to Baudelaire's lyrics. In many ways, then, Baudelaire's poetry provides an ideal approach to nineteenth- and twentieth-century literature. Students can enjoy it because it is less nebulous than most Romantic verse but more accessible than much later poetry. Like Romantic poetry, it expresses intense feelings; but, like modernist poetry, it is grounded in urban reality. Baudelaire also preserves all the traditional sensuousness of lyric poetry—recurring sounds and rhythms—that today have taken refuge mainly in popular music.

Baudelaire's Morality and Aesthetics

Les Fleurs du Mal and the prose poems poignantly model social and moral awareness, using the moralizing *we* to ensure that we readers cannot disavow our responsibility for injustice and depravity. But first, like Montaigne before him, Baudelaire shocks us and compels us to listen by evoking the democracy of the body: our senses enjoy; then we must suffer and die. The rotting corpse awaits the perfect statue memorialized by art (for the sources of texts and translations used in this volume, see the first paragraph of part 1, "Materials"):

> Rien n'offusquait sa parfaite clarté,
> Et tout semblait lui servir de bordure.
> [. . . . .]
> La Maladie et la Mort font des cendres
> De tout le feu qui pour nous flamboya.
> ("Un Fantôme" 78–79)
>
> Nothing obscured her perfect radiance;
> Everything seemed to serve her as a frame.
> [. . . . .]
> Into ashes Sickness and Death reduce
> All of the fire that blazed for us once.
> ("A Phantom")

"Une Charogne" (58–62; "A Carcass") says the same.

Baudelaire's torment and his sense of superiority intersect in his hyperesthesia, a condition by nature incommunicable. Unlike T. S. Eliot, who supposedly said he used poetry to shield himself from emotion, Baudelaire cannot separate the two. He seems torn between torpor and hysteria, between a drugged or hibernating state (described in some of his happiest poems, such as "La Géante" or "L'Invitation au voyage") and the impulsive *acte gratuit* dramatized in the prose poem "Le Mauvais Vitrier." Inspired by Edgar Allan Poe ("The Black Cat," "The Telltale Heart," "The Imp of the Perverse"), the motif of the senseless act foreshadows later French novels treating destructive impulses, novels such as André Gide's *Les Caves du Vatican* and Albert Camus's *L'Etranger*.

Baudelaire seeks to balance hyperesthesia and torpor in the active passivity he finds through observing the rich spectacle of Paris (cf. Guillaume Apollinaire in "Zone"), as the stroller or flaneur inspired to what Ross Chambers baptized "loiterature" (*Loiterature*). The result is a split between the naive, still-hopeful self (e.g., in the verse "Le Rêve d'un curieux") and the disillusioned self (e.g., in the prose poem "L'Etranger"). These two figures meet as Jesus and Saint Peter in "Le Reniement de saint Pierre" and as speakers and audience in "Le Voyage," a story frame without a story. Baudelaire's lyric selves may attain disillusionment (knowledge that disables) but never enlightenment (knowledge that empowers). After defining the social role of the *poète maudit* ("the accursed poet") and the aesthetics of the lyric in the earlier poems of *Les Fleurs du Mal*, the lyric self (or, often, his surrogates) attempts desperately to distract himself from the existential agony of the human condition. By turns, he plunges into sexual, spiritual, and equivocal love. After an episode of profound clinical depression (the "Spleen" poems), he seeks renewed distractions in the Paris street scene, and then in drugs. Finally, despairing, he rebels against God but cannot escape death (for a contrasting and complementary narrativization of *Les Fleurs du Mal*, see the essay by Timothy Unwin, this volume). His tone suggests a Jansenist deprived of grace; Blaise Pascal's comments on *divertissements* in the *Pensées* explain well the adventure of Baudelaire's lyric self. Thus the trajectory of Baudelaire's spiritual odyssey distinguishes Baudelaire sharply from the optimistically prophetic poets Hugo, William Blake, and Novalis and announces the modern age.

But such conclusions, by themselves, risk being facile. To counteract an excessive insistence on Baudelaire's modernity and on the Paris scene by many contemporary teachers and critics, I sometimes end a course by resituating Baudelaire in relation to the origins of world literature. "Le Voyage," the final poem in the 1861 edition of *Les Fleurs du Mal*, has uncanny affinities of tone with the last three tablets of one of the oldest recorded literary monuments, the *Epic of Gilgamesh* (versions exist from 1700 to 100 BC). Horrified by the prospect of death after witnessing the decay of his best friend, Enkidu, Gilgamesh seeks immortality. The three persons he successively encounters each marvel at how his travels have emaciated him, seared him with cold, and burned him with sun—precisely the condition of the travelers in "Le Voyage." In the Old Babylonian version, a tavern keeper unsuccessfully urges Gilgamesh to enjoy the simple but attainable pleasures of food, dancing, children, and a wife. But Gilgamesh is doomed to remain discontented, and his quest must fail.

Why Poetry?

The publication of this volume marks an important moment in the life of the Approaches to Teaching World Literature series. It is the first volume devoted to a lyric poet who did not write in English, and it seeks to promote the study, teaching, and enjoyment of lyric poetry from outside the anglophone world. The meditative intensity of poetry affords a memorable, terse introduction to the sensibilities of others in cultures throughout the world. Ideally, as the first painter of Tom Sawyer's fence attracted others, the publication of this book will encourage future MLA volume editors and classroom teachers more often to treat figures such as Petrarch and Leopardi, Rilke and Heine, Hugo and Ronsard, Césaire and Senghor, Darío and Vallejo.

Can lyric poetry be relevant to our students' concerns? Most of our life is not dramatic but routine. And yet within routine we lodge our fantasies, our privileged moments of heightened awareness, and our stifled impulses. Every lawyer, Gustave Flaubert observed in *Madame Bovary*, bears the debris of a potential poet (364). Lyric poetry presents privileged moments direct, without a narrative frame. In the hot medium of print that requires active imaginative participation, such moments show us new paths through the routine and sometimes beyond it, including the paths of empathy (McLuhan; McLuhan and McLuhan). Poetry makes the inner life of fantasy—our wishes, lies, and dreams, the things we never told anyone—into a shared experience.

Many imagine lyric poetry to be esoteric, but we have only to listen to people attending a poetry reading to realize that our country abounds in enthusiastic amateur poets who are starved for good poetry. The humanities should help people better to understand others, to express themselves, and to enjoy. Poetry leads directly toward all those goals. And vicarious exposure to the imaginative freedom of the poet can inspire students in any later career.

Acknowledgments

I am indebted to Melissa Weber of the Michigan State University Fine Arts Library for guiding me into the music literature concerning the art song. I should like to thank my mother and remember my father for passing on their love of poetry, which both of them wrote and published. I am also grateful to my teachers for having shared their exceptional enthusiasm for literature. Among them, Roger Shattuck and Judd Hubert are represented in this volume. Serge Doubrovsky, Paul Bénichou, and the late René Jasinski and Herbert Dieckmann also made my school years memorable.

Anna Balakian said that Baudelaire, one of her first loves, was the catalyst for her career. She had finished the handwritten revisions to her introduction here only shortly before her sudden death in the summer of 1997. No one could see Baudelaire in a broader context than she; no one had more influence worldwide in promoting knowledge of French symbolist poetry. It is to her memory that these essays are dedicated, with deep affection and respect.

Laurence M. Porter

Part One

MATERIALS

Editions and Translations

French and Bilingual Editions

For French and English quotations from *Les Fleurs du Mal*, despite flaws in the translations I have chosen James McGowan's Oxford World's Classics bilingual edition (1993), because of its low cost, convenient format (the originals and the translations on facing pages), ready availability, and excellent long introduction by Jonathan Culler. Where McGowan's translation has been emended by contributors to the volume, that exception is noted. This bilingual edition uses the French text from Auguste Poulet-Malassis's 1861 version but also inserts in the places where they appeared in the 1857 edition the six poems legally condemned in 1857. A useful "Note on the Text" describes the 1857, 1861, and 1868 editions and provides a table showing the relative arrangement of the poems in the first two editions (xxxviii–xlviii). The book's contents are referred to by page number only. Quotations from works other than *Les Fleurs du Mal* come from Marcel Ruff's edition of the *Œuvres complètes*—chosen, again, because of its moderate cost—and are accompanied by our contributors' original translations. Occasionally other Baudelaire texts are used. All references besides the bilingual edition of *Les Fleurs du Mal* carry short titles.

For all-French texts in upper-division and graduate courses, our respondents favored the 1994 Garnier edition of *Les Fleurs du Mal* (ed. Adam), the less expensive Flammarion edition (ed. Dupont; *Charles Baudelaire:* Les Fleurs du Mal), or the cheaper but physically flimsy Classiques Larousse complete edition (ed. Semichon) based on Claude Pichois's text. Were cost not a factor, a plurality of respondents, and the editor, would prefer Pichois's two-volume Pléiade edition of the *Œuvres complètes* (1975–76). It is essential for serious scholarly work.

When they do not use selections from an anthology of French poetry or from a course pack, instructors of less specialized courses often choose bilingual editions of *Les Fleurs du Mal*, without evincing any strong preference. Some prefer to the McGowan edition the renderings by William H. Crosby in *From Flowers of Evil and* Paris Spleen, with an introduction by Anna Balakian. The Marthiel Matthews and Jackson Matthews version was cited without comment. Richard Howard's 1982 translations drew strikingly mixed reviews. Felix W. Leakey's translations of selected poems (*Charles Baudelaire, 1821–1867*) are noteworthy as a labor of love. I would strongly recommend another bilingual edition, which appeared too late to be noted by our respondents: Norman R. Shapiro's *Selected Poems from* Les Fleurs du Mal. Shapiro's translations achieve the tour de force of preserving equivalents of the French rhythms and rhymes, thus communicating Baudelaire's sensuousness. And lexically, they are the best I've seen.

English Editions and Anthologies

Several respondents suggested the notes and preface of Rosemary Lloyd's edition and translation of *La Fanfarlo* and the short prose poems as background in English (*Prose Poems*). The most commonly used English texts are in anthologies that survey all French literature. The perennially popular annotated collection *Poèmes, pièces, prose* edited by Peter Schofer, Donald Rice, and William Berg is organized by genre. The anthologies of nineteenth-century French literature compiled by Michael Bishop and by André Lagarde and Laurence Michard are used less frequently, the latter more often in secondary schools than elsewhere.

Courses and Course Designs

The survey responses show that, on average, in introductory courses in French literature the class spends a week or two on Baudelaire; in nineteenth-century survey courses it spends two to three weeks; and in graduate seminars on Baudelaire perhaps half the class time will be devoted to the verse poems. In order of popularity, the prose poems, critical essays, and confessional writings come next. Our sampling, of course, is self-selected, involving teachers with a particular liking for Baudelaire.

Eléonore Zimmermann ends her course Love, Self, and God in French Romanticism with Baudelaire. Excluding Alfred de Vigny, Stirling Haig contrasts the Romantics' divinization of nature with Baudelaire's cult of artifice. A course on modern French poetry or on modern poetry may begin with Baudelaire and spend two or three weeks on selections. Gretchen Schultz devotes to Baudelaire one quarter of a course for upper-division and graduate students on nineteenth-century poetry and gender issues.

Baudelaire may be included in a course on the varieties of love experience. A comparative course in confessional literature can proceed (among countless possibilities) from Augustine through Jean-Jacques Rousseau and Baudelaire (who combines the admonitory and the pleading modes of the confession) to Malcolm X, Sylvia Plath, and Diane Wakoski. Ronald Saint-Onge describes what could be the nucleus of a course based on the contrast of genres: "Introducing Poe's 'Poetic Principle' in connection with Baudelaire's 'Notes nouvelles sur Edgar Poe' often generates a polemic on the nature of literary genres and the relative merit of the short story as compared to the novel and [of] the lyric poem in contrast to the epic poem."

Norman Lewis, a respondent who teaches English literature, reports using Baudelaire, sometimes for only one class period, in Introduction to Literature and Introduction to Poetry in the lower division, courses required of majors. He uses Baudelaire to expose students "to a form of poetry that is not mimetic" and to illustrate the function of symbolism in a poem. Such a discussion can lead naturally to T. S. Eliot, for example; seminars on Baudelaire and Eliot are popular in courses on comparative literature and world literature.

For a year-long, team-taught senior honors seminar on symbolism, I have used Blake, Coleridge, Poe, Baudelaire, Mallarmé, Yeats, Valéry, and Rilke. I would add that it is useful to distinguish personal symbolism (e.g., in Baudelaire, the *gouffre*) from universal, the personal symbolism often being a crux of an author's originality.

The particular poems chosen by respondents vary widely, although "Au lecteur," "Correspondances," "Harmonie du soir," "L'Invitation au voyage," and the sections "Spleen" or "Tableau parisiens" are often assigned. "Le Cygne" remains enormously popular.

Close readings are frequently assigned as paper topics, although among other possibilities are evaluating a particular critical essay on Baudelaire; applying its methods to one of the poems; situating a particular poem in relation to the poet's life story (in order to illuminate his time); and making a case, with specific examples, for calling Baudelaire a Romantic, symbolist, or modernist *avant la lettre*. Projects for student reports and papers include close readings or explications of individual poems and an examination of motifs—the flaneur, exile, love, world-weariness, spleen, the search for the absolute, defiance of God.

More-ambitious projects can treat the gratuitous act, for example, a motif that links Baudelaire to Poe, Gide, Camus, Cortázar, and many others; or students can compare Baudelaire's privileged moments of special insight and revelation with those ranging from Saul's experience on the Damascus road (in the Acts of the Apostles) to the experiences of Blake and other Romantics, Joyce, Proust, and ironic modernists such as T. S. Eliot. To study Baudelaire's emphasis on fragmentation and on the artificial as opposed to the natural (i.e., as a defense against decay) leads into postmodernism. Brief selections from more recent poets offer students a wide range of literary experience and help them discover new favorites.

Why do our respondents choose to teach Baudelaire? "Baudelaire is the most important poet of the nineteenth century," Mary O'Neil claims in a typical reply, at least concerning the poets of France. Students find his poetry appealing. Susan Wolf observes that one would "be hard put to find another nineteenth-century poet to whom so many students can relate more completely or who is experienced as more contemporary. [His descriptions of ennui] remain some of the freshest, most psychologically apt, and remarkable in all French literature." His intimateness, irony, urbanity, and eroticism make him seem close to us. In pragmatic terms, poems by Baudelaire figure in the International Baccalaureate program and on the secondary school reading lists for advanced-placement French 4 and 5 (language) as well as 6 (literature).

The explanation by teachers "I've always loved Baudelaire" is characteristic. In an age where increasing urbanization is inevitable, more and more of us will hear this poet of the city speaking to our material condition. Regarding our emotional and spiritual condition, Baudelaire addresses the fundamental experiences of love, loss, and the sufferings of *Homo duplex* torn between good and evil. In love, his lyric self vacillates between dependence and nurturance, sensibility and sensuality. At other times it swings from exaltation to profound depression, and from inquisitive detachment (the flaneur) to yearning for a fulfillment more than human. The topics of visionary experience and of facing aging and death flow naturally from his cyclothymic (manic-depressive) emotional world. He raises the issue of sexual orientation in the lesbian poems. The relativity of beauty is suggested by the love poems to the mulatto Jeanne Duval (see Miller). Implicitly, both the verse and prose poems ask a question addressed at length in the moralizing essay *Les Paradis artificiels*: Can drugs enhance creativity? Unlike Hugo and Mallarmé, Baudelaire appeals to students because the identity of his lyric self is always at issue; "fitting in" (Ainslie McLees's phrase) is problematic. His tones of sincerity and irony also appeal to students: he does not seem to wear a mask or to adopt a pose. Only the poems where he lectures us ("Au lecteur"; "Le Voyage") are overblown.

Since Baudelaire addresses many current issues, since students enjoy him, and since—as our respondents tell us—class discussions can readily be generated from reading him, he is eminently suitable for courses not only in French literature but also in general humanities and world literature, such as the one James Lawler teaches in English to both undergraduates and graduates at the University of Chicago. One can use Baudelaire as a starting point for discussions of general questions too: What is art? beauty? depression? evil? morality? poetry?

Other Disciplines

Among other disciplines that can throw light on Baudelaire's poetry, history and art history are mentioned most often by respondents. Timothy Raser explains:

> I prefer a historical stance because both the signifieds and the referents of signs change, and an understanding of such change enables closer reading of poems. The historical method also allows generalizations about historical moments and the delimiting of historical periods, both of which are invaluable exercises that will enable students to read research of this kind more critically. Within the historical perspective, I use a semiotic method.

Baudelaire's poetic descriptions of works of art and discussions on aesthetics within *Les Fleurs du Mal* point clearly to opportunities to apply art history and theory in approaches to Baudelaire's work. Instructors may also refer to architecture, urban planning, photography, and psychoanalytic theory. Swedenborgianism as well as Catholicism may be used as background for the nineteenth century, and a socioeconomic approach may compare the social critique of Baudelaire with more recent belief systems, such as neo-Marxism. Critical theory (a congeries of disciplines) and psychoanalytic theory seem less prominent now than in the recent past, although Sigmund Freud and Jacques Lacan—and more recently Nicolas Abraham and Maria Torok—still provide starting points for some instructors' analyses. Explorations of depression can also relate Baudelaire's poetry to students' experiences. No respondent seems to advocate using any particular critical method exclusively, and those few who label their method say it is eclectic. A simple, effective assignment mentioned by more than one respondent is to have students choose illustrations from art books and explain why the illustrations are appropriate. This method induces students to look at many reproductions of paintings and drawings, which in turn give them a feeling for the times.

Pedagogical Challenges

Vocabulary is more of an obstacle than we like to admit, as Eléonore Zimmermann shows us with devastating wit in this volume. Students quickly become aware that lyric poetry is a language within a language. Inversions of word order, formal rhetoric, Latinate vocabulary, archaisms, and rare words create problems, several instructors remark. As Timothy Raser puts it, "It's hard to argue that this book is still about us when its language is not that taught in Composition and Conversation." The widespread use of inexpensive bilingual editions masks this difficulty but does not decisively help students recognize nuances of tone, particularly the ironic and the comic. Students also need to be helped in exploring the concepts of the allegorical and of the poetic. Sonya Stephens and Thomas Vosteen suggest "synesthesia exercises" ("Describe something that tastes like X smells . . ."). A discussion of how students perceive the differences between the poetic and the prosaic might be a good opening move.

Several respondents mention students' lack of historical background and cultural knowledge pertinent to mid-nineteenth-century France (see Richard Terdiman's essay, this volume). In any course, guiding students at first with a highlighted text and by modeling, we can ensure that they know how to scan an alexandrine sonnet correctly. Few first language speakers of French, even with a *licence* in literature, can manage that. It's important to feel the rhythm. In seminars on Baudelaire, students can write their own regular, Baudelairean sonnet and correct it until they get it right.

Baudelaire's misogyny—springing perhaps from a patent mother fixation and resulting in a madonna-prostitute complex—and his powerful eroticism, with sadistic elements, can make him difficult to teach, particularly to younger students and to women, many respondents say. *Grosso modo*, love, sex, and drugs (including alcohol, with which Baudelaire, like some students, is fascinated) readily stimulate interest. But "Baudelaire tends to have a polarizing effect on the class," William Olmsted reports. "Men finding him 'natural' and 'telling it like it is,' [. . .] women curious but uneasy and sometimes [. . .] viewing him as a pure chauvinist and [exploiter] of women." The trial of Baudelaire for immorality and the suppression of six poems (they were literally ripped by government censors from the copies on sale) allow one a ready comparison with the recent controversies over funding for the National Endowment for the Arts, ratings of films, and pornography on the Internet. The condemnation of the six poems was officially rescinded only in 1949.

"The emphasis on death and the attraction of evil—the very double posture—proves difficult in dealing with idealistic adolescents," Haig observes, and Lawler says something similar. Raser points out the traditional decorum of a classroom as an obstacle: it may be socially (if not morally or legally) acceptable for our students to do certain things that it is not acceptable for them to talk about in a group mixed by gender and by generation. The students do accept, he adds, "the analogy I occasionally make between Baudelaire and bad-boy rock stars."

A broader, underlying problem is students' limited exposure to religion, in particular, Catholicism (see the essays by Olmsted and by Culler, this volume). Even an experienced critic may not realize that the sequence "encensoir [. . .] reposoir [. . .] ostensoir" ("censer," [. . .] "portable altar," [. . .] "monstrance") in "Harmonie du soir" refers to the unfolding of an outdoor mass as it passes through the stages of initial purification of the sanctuary with incense, the retelling of Christ's self-sacrifice, and the climactic Elevation of the Host, suggesting our hope for resurrection (which the monstrance recalls in static form). The poem title "Réversibilité" (the doctrine of the transfer of supererogatory merit from the saints to those otherwise unworthy to be saved) remains opaque to many readers. Those moments in *Les Fleurs du Mal* that evoke the second stage of sin in Catholic theology—morbid delectation, brooding on the possibility of a sinful act before committing one's will to performing it—also elude many readers. Selected paragraphs from *The New Catholic Encyclopedia* and from the Gospels (e.g., to gloss "Le Reniement de saint Pierre") can help.

Although most of our students have gone to a place of worship, what Baudelaire and his contemporaries learned in school is far different from what our students learn. In the nineteenth century, traditional higher education in the Western world included rhetoric, French, Latin, and Greek. For at least seven years, schoolboys like Baudelaire pored over a corpus centered on Vergil's *Aeneid*, Horace's *Odes*, and Ovid's *Metamorphoses*. Citing such works, we can discuss with students Baudelaire's Latin and Greek titles ("De profundis clamavi"; "Duellum"; "Héautontimoroumenos"; "Moesta et errabunda"; "Sed non satiata"; "Semper eadem"), Latin tags (Te deum [26]; de profundis [150]; esto memor [162]), mythological references, and his Latin poem, "Franciscae meae laudes"—not to be pedantic but to show how these reminiscences of Baudelaire's schooldays locate the crystallizations of obsessions. For Baudelaire, Latin evoked an earlier personal as well as an earlier historical time. Our students may initially dismiss the Latin in Baudelaire as affectation or distracting ornament, but those phrases open a royal road to the emotional childhood that Baudelaire's genius rediscovers at will. We can ask students which early memories *they* dwell on and invite them to trace those memories back to the students' still-living past. Schofer reports good success in having students write original prose poems in French, based on Baudelaire's verse, and in having them elaborate contrasting interpretations of one Baudelaire poem: for example, "Parfum exotique" can be treated as both "a love poem and as a poem of escape from the woman."

Recommended Readings

Bibliography

The critical, selective bibliography compiled by James S. Patty, Laurence M. Porter, and Cassandra Hamrick covers Baudelaire studies up through 1989. For 1990 on, I would recommend the MLA online bibliography (MLAIB) accessible through the Internet and through computer terminals in major libraries—often connected to a printer. Better yet, on some electronic resource servers, searches of the MLAIB, *ProQuest* (which has superseded ACAD, the *Academic Index*), and *Linguistics and Language Behavior Abstracts* (LLBA) can be combined. The *American and French Research on the Treasury of the French Language* (ARTFL) database from the University of Chicago omits many essential texts by Baudelaire but allows one to make and download keyword-in-context searches in nearly two thousand French literary works. The *Bulletin baudelairien* from Vanderbilt is more complete. *The Year's Work in Modern Language Studies* includes evaluations but appears late and is uneven both in coverage and in the quality of its reviews. Otto Klapp's annual *Bibliographie der französischen Literaturwissenschaft* lists book reviews as well as dissertations (dissertations also appear in MLA).

Background Materials

Several respondents cited Gordon Wright's *France in Modern Times* for historical background. Several use poems by Théophile Gautier, Hugo, Alphonse de Lamartine (specifically, the *Méditations poétiques*), and Paul Verlaine for contrast. Pichois and Jean Ziegler's biography *Baudelaire* (1987; translated and abridged in 1989) is popular, as is Sartre's unsympathetic overview, Jerome Thellot's *Baudelaire: violence et poésie*, and the rich mine of information in Terdiman's *Present Past*). As a group, Richard D. E. Burton's several books situating Baudelaire in his cultural and historical context (*Baudelaire and the Second Republic*; *Baudelaire in 1859*; *Context*)—which Terdiman's book also does—were often mentioned.

General Introductions

Peter Broome and Graham Chesters's *The Appreciation of Modern French Poetry, 1850–1950* was suggested by several as an introductory overview. Also mentioned were Hugo Friedrich's rich, lucid (although overstated and obsolescent) survey of modern poetry; Marcel Raymond's classic study relating Baudelaire to surrealism (first published in 1933); and Suzanne Bernard's history of the French prose poem.

Critical Studies

Walter Benjamin was the overwhelming favorite among Baudelaire critics (see Works Cited and also the special section devoted to Benjamin in Patty, Porter, and Hamrick 798–800). Leo Bersani's speculative psychoanalytic study *Baudelaire and Freud* follows in popularity. Also recommended, each by several respondents, were the studies of Baudelaire by Erich Auerbach, T. S. Eliot, Alison Fairlie (*Baudelaire*, "Reflections"), D. J. Mossop (on reading *Les Fleurs du Mal* as a tragic plot), Porter (*The Crisis of French Symbolism*), and Michael Riffaterre ("Response," *Semiotics*). Barbara Johnson's essays, as a group, were cited often. As a body of work, Chambers's essays are preeminent, and we can only hope that he will someday favor us with a volume devoted to Baudelaire.

The Instructor's Library

Pichois and Ziegler's two-volume edition of the *Correspondance* has proved useful to some instructors. I would add Anna Balakian's *The Symbolist Movement* as a possible literary history and Chesters's *Baudelaire and the Poetics of Craft* as a reference for versification. *The New Oxford Companion to Literature in French*, too recent to be mentioned by respondents, greatly improves the earlier version, offers a valuable desk reference for the instructor, and should also be recommended to graduate students. Otherwise, suggestions range so widely that one can only point to "Further Reference Materials" at the end of this volume, culled from our respondents' replies.

Audiovisual Materials

Several audio- and videocassettes presenting readings of Baudelaire's poems are listed at the end of "Further Reference Materials." Surprisingly, no respondent mentioned using art songs by Alban Berg, Emmanuel Chabrier, or Claude Debussy (*Ariettes, Cinq poèmes,* and *Songs*) based on the texts of Baudelaire's poems. Hearing them sung in a tenor voice (such as Hughes Cuénod's) can bring to life the poet-persona in Baudelaire and convey the moods of languor and of anguish often reflected in the texts. Period music by

Hector Berlioz (*Symphonie fantastique*), Debussy (*La Mer* or *L'Après-Midi d'un faune*), or Richard Wagner (*Lohengrin, Tannhäuser,* or *Der fliegende Holländer*) is sometimes played; one can save time by using it during the few minutes when students enter and get settled or prepare to leave class.

In the visual arts, slides of paintings by Eugène Delacroix and by Edouard Manet were the most popular. Jean-Baptiste Corot's paintings, Gustave Courbet's paintings, Honoré Daumier's caricatures, Michelangelo's sculpture (*Night* and *The Slave*), Auguste Rodin's sculptures inspired by Baudelaire's poems, Charles Meryon's etchings, and Nadar's photographs are sometimes represented as well. I strongly recommend the use of an opaque projector (or self-made slides) to show the class images of the Paris street scene and paintings or sketches by other artists—notably, Constantin Guys. In addition to books of photographs by Nadar, Eugène Atget, and the like, four volumes, specially focused on Baudelaire, provide a splendid source of slides. Two of these are used by our respondents: Pichois and Jean-Paul Avice's *Baudelaire/Paris* and Pichois and François Ruchon's *Iconographie de Charles Baudelaire*. Two others, apparently, are not known, but they should be: *Baudelaire: Petit Palais, 23 novembre 1968–17 mars 1969* and Pichois's *Album Baudelaire*. There is of course much overlap among these volumes. At some colleges and universities you can obtain from instructional media centers the free use of a camera, booth, and stand, with film and processing provided at cost: an hour of your time and about five dollars can give you three dozen slides—enough, with your commentary, for a whole class.

Some instructors find slides or music a distraction, but a projected transparency allows the class to see textual features and relations (between a verse and a prose poem, between a French text and an English text) in colors. As the cost of color printing comes down, we can anticipate including such pages in course packets.

Part Two

APPROACHES

Introduction

For this volume, I have particularly encouraged essays on teaching Baudelaire in the secondary schools. Faculty at such institutions have been underrepresented in the Approaches to Teaching World Literature series, although their students are numerous and their world literature curricula often broader than many university course syllabi. Essays on computer-assisted and multimedia learning were sought as well, and two can be found here, but in this domain much groundwork remains to be done before sophisticated multimedia programs created by scholars become widely available for teaching literature.

One preliminary issue: Should the *mal* in Baudelaire's title be capitalized? A minority of critics disagree; one even considered the capital *m* a symptom of Americanizing cultural imperialism. But since Baudelaire himself appears to have written *Mal* perhaps ninety percent of the time and since that spelling is true to the allegorizing tendencies of his work, I, like Marcel Ruff, have adopted it.

In the introductory overview, Anna Balakian distills half a century of teaching and research experience to examine the contrast between an undisciplined life and a disciplined art, and to show how Baudelaire is at once our timeless contemporary and supremely representative of his period.

We then proceed to particular institutional settings and the special problems that they pose. Adopting a comparative literature framework, Laurence Risser uses creative role playing to help International Baccalaureate students experience intense involvement with the poems through cooperative, dramatic reenactments. Ainslie McLees shows how to exploit individual learning styles in advanced-placement French 4, 5, and 6 and how to turn resistance to poetry to the teacher's advantage. And William Olmsted tells us how to steer between the reductionism of a purely secular approach and the dogmatic excesses of doctrinaire Christianity in the honors college of a church-related university, while studying a poet in whom the religious and the worldly are intricately confused. He recuperates the truly blasphemous virulence of *Les Fleurs du Mal* in a Catholic context.

The section on text-based approaches begins with Roger Shattuck, who shows us how to ground ourselves in direct observation of specific texts before succumbing to the lure of "flights of higher interpretation," which can fragment our understanding among urgently competing critical approaches. He adopts the strategy of inviting students to comment on "anonymous" verse selections from Baudelaire. In contrast, emphasizing the lexical particularity of the poet, Eléonore Zimmermann wittily dramatizes the difficulties even assiduous students confront as they struggle with Baudelaire's unusual, often esoteric vocabulary. Judd Hubert adopts a New Critical approach to translation that can help create a space for the play of pedagogy between the original text and its derivatives. Peter Schofer teaches sensitivity to how prosody can reinforce and inflect meaning. Timothy Unwin critically examines the idea of the "story" of *Les Fleurs du Mal* to lead us to an understanding of how narrativity ultimately breaks down under the fundamentally opposed constraints of the poetic. And Sonya Stephens tries to reduce students' sense of alienation from poetry by approaching verse poems through prose texts that are either their doublets or treat similar ideas.

In the thematic section, J. A. Hiddleston shows how to teach a rich, original typology of memory, which constitutes not a "secret architecture" of a tragic psychodrama but an authentic mode of unity in the collection. Like Richard Terdiman, he pursues a modernized phenomenological approach, whereas in the preface I insist on recuperating a coherent narrative from *Les Fleurs du Mal*, before explaining how that narrative then voids itself. Deborah Harter examines how Baudelaire's poetry affects our memory: the collection's extraordinary, brutal, and often subversive panorama of images forces us into radical insights concerning suppressed but familiar regions of our psyche.

Terdiman interweaves the political, personal, and social implications of "Le Cygne" for Baudelaire and his contemporaries. He demonstrates how the hard scholarship of a cultural studies approach can enrich and transform our understanding of texts that had previously seemed overly familiar.

In the two gender-based approaches of this volume, Susan Wolf's psychoanalytic approach explores how, through inversion, the poet's sadomasochistic, murderous impulses toward his phantasmal mother are staged as encounters with his murderous wives, lovers, or mothers, particularly in the "Spleen" poems, where mourning can mask matricide. Gretchen Schultz shows how the emerging discipline of gay and lesbian studies can illumine Baudelaire, and how the passive lesbian can stand in for the poet.

Treating religious and ethical issues, Jonathan Culler exposes the contrast of Baudelaire's "strangely archaic rhetoric" with critics' "resolute modernization" of the poet. He writes that what he takes to be Baudelaire's wager that a mode of allegorical action in which the Devil along with other figures are the principal actors is the best way to explore our bizarrely modern condition. And Edward Kaplan teases out the "ethical irony" with which the poet feigns a cruel or otherwise immoral position in order to provoke ethical self-examination and self-criticism in the readers.

A section on computer-aided instruction begins with Rosemary Lloyd's telling us, with many precise examples, how to use CD-ROM technology to teach poetry and the other arts. Eugene Gray, designer and director of two language laboratories, draws on his extensive experience in computer-literacy workshops and program development to explain how to use a hypertext environment to combine text, sound, graphics, and films to introduce image-oriented students to the extensive background materials essential for understanding Baudelaire.

Ross Chambers's concluding essay argues for creating permeable boundaries between the classroom (teaching *about* life) and life itself. "Thus we can teach (poetry as) both the utopian desire for another and better world and the dystopian consciousness that we inhabit a world of pain, in the understanding that those two impulses (the aesthetic, the critical) aren't incompatible but allied, having in common their deviational structure." Conformity, he warns, can teach only submission. He helps us reflect on how to make the classroom not the adversary but the ally of poetry.

Prologue: Baudelaire, a Contemporary of Us All

Anna Balakian

It is one of the anomalies of nature that undisciplined human behavior can be coupled with impeccably disciplined performance in the arts. Such is the case of the nineteenth-century French poet Charles Baudelaire, who found himself dysfunctional in society and at the same time became a central figure at the crossroads of several developments in poetry and poetics.

The lack of coordination between the life and the work becomes a problem for today's readers, who have better understanding of psychological analysis than of the process that turns the ordinary reality of a life into an extraordinary harvest in the arts. The life that reads like a clinical case is not hard for moderns to understand: a young man reared in the upper middle class, destined by his military stepfather, General Aupick, for an army career of social and financial distinction but abandoning such a rosy prospect to try his chances in belles lettres. By way of background, let us recall that shortly after Baudelaire's birth (1821), in Paris, his mother became widowed from a marriage of convenience with a much older man. Overprotective of her son, Charles, she indulged him in his growing years, was disappointed when he chose to pursue an uncertain life as a poet over a military career, yet kept letting herself be coaxed into making handouts to tide him over his successive gaps in bare sustenance. Mme Aupick was intermittently resistant then yielding, while her son's most regular though meager income came from his art criticism and translations from literature in English. Baudelaire little realized that this critical work and translations of Edgar Allan Poe and Thomas De Quincey were to give direction to his notions of realism and expanded reality and win him recognition as a modernist and forerunner of the symbolist movement and of surrealism.

In step with his erratic life, he changed domiciles fifty-six times and came to know the gamut of Parisian life from many perspectives. In one of his most famous and much-imitated poems, "Le Cygne" (172–76; "The Swan"), he deplores, overlooking the Tuileries, the changes that are taking place on this historic site that holds so many memories for him. What would he have said if he had seen the pyramid that dominates the Tuileries today? The swan poem starts as an allegory and ends in a broader symbolism that demonstrates his progression from Romanticism to the symbolist movement. The presence of this graceful bird in the midst of demolition makes it the archetype of other creatures on alien soil. In the first line Baudelaire evokes the classical persona of Andromaque the refugee, which the readership of his time would recognize as the dispossessed heroine of classical mythology. The widow of Hector, who was the fallen hero of the Greco-Trojan war, refused to be assimilated in the new order represented by the Greek warrior Pyrrhus, who proposed marriage to her and then offered her prominent relocation in the world of the invaders. Thus with the image of Andromaque, Baudelaire evokes the implied violation of the familiar Paris landmark by the intrusion of barbaric new structures and particularly of a new arch on the Carrousel grounds. His style at the beginning of the poem reminds us of Victor Hugo, to whom indeed the poem is dedicated. Then in free associations Baudelaire proceeds from one figure of exile to another, all allegorically associable with the swan. But from the descriptive narrative of the first part of the poem he leads us to a wider range of associations; they invite us to enter a sphere of meanings of which the swan figure is only a trigger. The swan becomes transformed into images that mitigate the anguish of all disoriented people for whom the vision of exterior change reflects the inner sense of personal exile: "A quiconque a perdu ce qui ne se retrouve / Jamais, jamais!" (176) ("whoever has lost what is never to be found again, never, never" [trans. mine]).

The swan was to remain a familiar figure well into the twentieth century. It emerged from a limited emblem of allegory to an international signet, recognized and evoked by many poets as the metaphor of estrangement and, in Latin American poetry, even as an evocation of colonial invasions. It was also appropriated by composers such as Camille Saint-Saëns and Jean Sibelius to suggest the separation of all artists from the rest of the world in the fin de siècle climate of the symbolist movement.

From his many domiciles Baudelaire had many vistas of urban poverty juxtaposed with overviews of salon society. He observed animals rotting in the streets, along with alcoholics, drug addicts, ragpickers loitering in the gutters. He had empathy for the same *misérables* immortalized by his contemporary Hugo, although Baudelaire put more emphasis on the urban character of their condition. But unlike Hugo, who in his voluminous work *Les Misérables* translated his compassion for the poor and the besieged into a social indignation against the phenomenon of unwarranted misery, Baudelaire presented each social fact just as the vaudeville artist does when he throws darts that pierce the surface of the phenomenon to demonstrate that there is a deeper reality. The impoverishment is part of a broader chancre that gnaws at the skin of being. These poems (and also proses) of poverty are the work of a Parisian, but their Paris is reflected in New York or Calcutta, anywhere in this world where poverty flourishes, because it is written by a poet who seeks escape "anywhere out of the world" (the title, in English, of a Baudelaire prose poem in *Le Spleen de Paris*; *Œuvres* [Pichois] 356) and who knows that the instrument of such escape lies within and not outside him.

The most powerful of Baudelaire's poems, however, were those on love and sexuality. Personally he was attracted by two opposite types of women, the sensual and the spiritual, the physically attainable and the ungraspable. He knew the prostitute; he cherished his mulatto mistress, Jeanne Duval; he adored the ideal woman beyond physical reach; he was compassionate toward the lesbian "sisters" in search of levels of sensuality as yet unknown. Several of his most erotic poems were condemned by court censor and deleted from *Les Fleurs du Mal*; this censorship gave an infamous reputation to the entire collection when it appeared in 1857.

Baudelaire died ten years after the first publication of *Les Fleurs du Mal*, from the consequences of syphilis, which at that time was an incurable fatal disease, as dreaded as is AIDS today. At forty-six he was aphasic, homeless, unrewarded, as he thought, for his extraordinary talents by a readership that went for the trendy and the conventional—the standard Romantic poets of the day—and that recognized him for his notoriety rather than for his writings.

Yet, ironically, this disturbed, tormented individual, succumbing to what in our time would be an early death, left a work that in its density and variety has become a cornerstone of world literature and, more broadly speaking, of a modernism that anticipates each new wave of modernism. There are many approaches to Baudelaire, but no single perspective will do justice to his multifaceted poetry, although from whatever window one looks at him, there is illumination and the sheer pleasure of reading his verse. If you are not French, you may develop an urge to translate him into your language, as if the better to embrace him and make him your own. Indeed the greatest poets in the world have tried to translate what seem his simple lexicon and uncomplicated grammatical structure. But no one quite succeeds in preserving his resonances and rhymes; the clustering of words that creates associable meanings; the ominous voice with its sonorities, whispers, and whimpers, its provocative sexuality, its repenting and rebellious religiosity, its diabolical threats and angelic serenity. What manipulator of language can create the seductive liaison of the refrain of "L'Invitation au voyage" ("Invitation to the Voyage"): "Luxe, calme et volupté" (108)? Indeed, composers have had better luck in setting to music this idealized voyage.

Let us look at the various aspects of his art. He uses many of the subjects of the contemporary Romantics: voyage, memory, love (attainable and unattainable), dread of death, fear of *le néant* (a word meaning "nothingness," but some have aptly associated it with "the chasm" [243]), defiance of God, attraction to the Devil, melancholy, the declining process in seasons and hours. But where other poets centralize these states and sites in their ego—or turn them into a polarization between good and evil, material and spiritual—Baudelaire plunges beyond the layers of the conscious and the unconscious into a pattern of imagery open to his readers' experiences as well as to his own.

You could read the 160 poems of Baudelaire and spotlight all those that make him a standard Romantic, whom he identifies in the image of the albatross. Masterfully the albatross cruises the skies but awkwardly drags his giant wings when he drops to earth. Or you can peruse Baudelaire again and find him the perfect example of the art-for-art's-sake poet, who contemplates exterior reality in its motionless perfection and in sharp contrast to the poet's turmoil. "Je hais le mouvement qui déplace les lignes" (38; "La Beauté") ("I hate movement that displaces the line" [trans. mine]), he explains in contemplation of immobile, immutable beauty. You can return to the same collection of poems and find enough evidence to make of Baudelaire a naturalist in his materialistic, sensual descriptions of the poor, the little old ladies on the brink of

death ("Où serez-vous demain, Eves octogénaires, / Sur qui pèse la griffe ef-
froyable de Dieu?" [186; "Les Petites Vieilles"]) ("Where will you be, octoge-
narian Eves, / As over you heavily hangs the frightful paw of God?" [trans.
mine]), the criminals loitering on street corners, and all the other members of
the subculture that Emile Zola was to make the center of his writing a few
years later.

If Baudelaire with his versatility had done nothing more than write in the
various accepted modes of his time, he would be recognized today as a repre-
sentative French poet of the mid-nineteenth century. But there was much
more to him. As he said in one of his most passionate love poems, "Le Balcon"
("The Balcony"), "Je sais l'art d'évoquer les minutes heureuses!" (74) ("I know
the art of evoking happy moments" [trans. mine]). Indeed, the art of evocation
that was to become the matrix of the symbolist movement claimed Baudelaire
some years later as its catalyst. This transformational quality affects all his vi-
sions and all his states of mind. There lies Baudelaire's modernism. He comes
into the literary world at the junction of Romanticism, aestheticism, and a bur-
geoning naturalism and makes use of all three modes, rhetorically and philo-
sophically. Without pretending to be a *chef d'école*, he established a new
manner of poetic communication. His curiosity about the expansion of the
power of the senses was intensified by his reading and translation of Thomas
De Quincey's *Opium Eater*. He came to the conclusion that "artificial par-
adises" gave you no more than what your sensory apparatus had the capacity to
sustain (*Œuvres* [Pichois] 399; "artificial paradises" is the title of a prose text
that contains a translation of De Quincey's work). The artist, therefore, should
pursue "the natural dose of opium" that heightens the imagination. "Each man
carries in him a natural dose of opium, incessantly secreted and replenished,"
which can transport him on trips unequaled by any physical journey (*Œuvres*
[Pichois] 303; the prose poem "L'Invitation au voyage").

This power of transformation can be observed in the most humble artists on
the Paris scene: the acrobats, the mimes, the comedians. Baudelaire was per-
haps the first to use the figure of the saltimbanco (a circus acrobat) as a medi-
ator between the real and the fantastic. Stéphane Mallarmé, Rainer Maria
Rilke, Pablo Picasso, and the surrealists were to follow suit. The comedian, in
the larger sense, placed on the stage that is the world, as Shakespeare per-
ceived it, knows how to give a twist to reality that changes our relation to it. The
comedian's object is to make us laugh when we really want to cry.

The first inkling one has of the difference between Baudelaire's way of see-
ing and writing—whether in verse or in prose poems—and the modes of writ-
ing of his contemporaries is in a simple early sonnet called "Correspondances"
(18; "Correspondences"). The poem begins with an array of the standard im-
ages that demonstrated what the English Romantic poet William Wordsworth
earlier called intimations of immortality: natural landscapes that have their pu-
rified counterparts in heaven, parallels between the here and now and the tran-
scendental that awaits us on another level of existence. Swedenborgian

philosophy, a popular form of Christianity at the time, is the frame of reference for the sonnet's quatrains; but then comes the sestet that expands the original perspective. It introduces the new art of suggestion that stretches into an infinity of variations what is in effect restricted totally to the material world: "Ayant l'expansion des choses infinies" (18) ("Having dimensions infinitely vast" [19]). The sestet offers a choice of words that moves the reader from one sensual stimulus to another, mingling touch with smell, taste with sound; and it offers visual images that amalgamate all the other sense perceptions. This synesthesia or profound unification of the senses is stimulated not by emotion or drugs but by the concerted efforts of the mind and the senses, both human capacities of material dimensions. *Esprit* in French means both "mind" and "spirit," but it is clear that Baudelaire is here referring to the mind and not to otherworldly, spiritual powers. Yet how often have translators distorted his artistic innovation by using the word *spirit* and returning his art of evocation back to the Romantic mode. Swedenborgian vision had its basis in allegory, that is, a one-to-one facing of the material and its counterpart in the moral or spiritual, whereas symbol is the image infinitely transferable from one viewing to another, in the associative power of its ambiguity. Symbol also becomes a bridge between one being and many others and suggests the ultimate universal bonding of human beings.

Many of Baudelaire's most compelling poems, which often are among the least biographically obvious ones, are fashioned through the linguistic mastery of the symbol. Much has been written in our time about stream of consciousness and its power to create free verbal and sensory associations as they affect literary imagery. But if indeed the associative quality of Baudelaire's poetry and of poets who followed in his footsteps is spontaneous and automatic, it is presented in very deliberate, contrived language that creates an intentional ambiguity. The reader's imagination is offered an open rather than closed circuit, invited to make many interpretations.

In a later poem, "Harmonie du soir" (96; "Evening Harmony" [trans. mine]), this difference can be more fully and explicitly noticed: Baudelaire balances states of mind with the effects of a parallel vision he establishes between religious imagery (the censer, the altar, and the monstrance) and the natural imagery of evening landscapes: the vaulted sky, the flowers that evaporate into their scents, and the light of the setting sun. The three invisible religious objects, metaphorically projected into the physical surroundings, stimulate the sensory organs into spiritual meditation. The censer diffuses its perfume, the altar spreads the silence, and the monstrance kindles illumination. But the mediator between these two sets is the poet in a meditative state. His subjectivity is no longer overt, as in Romantic poems of this genre, but has penetrated material reality: it has become the coagulated blood of a sunset. The heart that cries has taken the form of wood shaped into a violin that trembles—what one descendant of the symbolists, T. S. Eliot, was to call "the sacred wood." Baudelaire foresaw the goal of the symbolists: how to be subjective without eternally referring to the "I" and how to grasp the mystical dimension of human sensibility without having recourse to heaven. And he found the language to capture the pleasure of the mind and the senses without describing details of personal emotions. No single circumstance need be identified with the turning of anguish into spiritual harmony. That is the power of the symbol, self-referential and at the same time intimately referential to each individual reader.

Perhaps the best examples of the innovative poetics that hides specific reality beneath a protective ambiguity are the two poems about condemned women ("Femmes damnées" [238–46]). Only one of them caught the eye of the public censor, and an obscenity trial brought about its expurgation from *Les Fleurs du Mal*. Which of the two poems? It was the one conventionally written, although its content was controversial. It explicitly describes the movements and attitudes of two women designated by classical names (Delphine and Hippolyte), caught in specific situations and reprimanded by the poet in moralistic terms for their behavior. The other poem by the same name escaped the censor because of its more dense and less explicit form and because of its larger perspective, dealing not only with the notion of transgression of sexual codes but also with any break with acceptable patterns of living. Here lesbians are classed, namelessly, with all other groups of daring minds that are contemptuous of common reality. They are associated in Baudelaire's perception with those who search for the infinite, in the particular meaning the poet attributed to that word, suggesting not the void or depth or paradise but what is new, what has not yet been fathomed, what through the complexity of its connotations challenges the imagination. Out of the notion of the cursed women a symbol emerges that could be fanned out to refer to an infinite number of other situations and circumstances to be supplied by each successive reader. Note that the word *l'Infini* is one of the most ambiguous in Baudelaire's vocabulary. Sometimes it has the daring character of preastronautic voyagers; at other times it is an equivalent of the *gouffre*, relating everything to nothingness. But Baudelaire's personality did not disappear from his poetry into abstractions. And without the magnetism of that personality, his theory of evocation and his ever-widening field of associations might not have given him the poetic leadership he was to command after his death.

Among the subjects that had the power of fascination and that were intrinsic characteristics of his personality were his sexuality, his haunting fear of the passage of time, his immense sense of solitude before the cosmos, his combative religiosity. His passionate love of woman is a conflagration like the hot coals burning in his fireplace in "Le Balcon." It is the luminous radiation of light from his lover's eyes to his, the perfume of her blood that evokes past memories in haunting refrain as the lovers whisper in the declining light and he lies in rapture between her knees. In another erotic poem, "La Chevelure," the aroma of her hair evokes voyages to exotic lands and the mane of an animal in heat. In other poems, the woman is compared to cats in her sinuosity. T. S. Eliot was not the first to juxtapose the sensuality of cats with that of the movements and postures of woman. In other love poems, the intensity of passion boils over into sadism. Yet in still other poems, such as "L'Invitation au voyage," love is spiritualized, purified into innocent childhood companionship, in a cyberspace where sensuality is coupled with serenity. Although conveying his own pleasure and ecstasy, Baudelaire is enough of an artist not to let us feel that the women, whether sultry Jeanne Duval or some of the more pristine ladies whom he evokes, are just objects of his love. Reciprocity is fashioned not out of statement but through suggestive overtones.

Similarly, the terror of the *gouffre*, that pit or black hole that Hamlet characterized as "the bourn from which no traveler returns" (3.1.79–80), is not in Baudelaire's poetry a pre-Sartrean philosophical meditation on nothingness. It has both attraction and revulsion for Baudelaire, and this philosophical vacillation is conveyed in very personal tones. The *gouffre* is the challenge to infinity, which he views from all his windows: the unknown out there, the only voyage worth contemplating. His personal entrapment between belief in an afterlife and the terror of nothingness is mirrored in his recurrent, chilling image of emptiness, which in poems such as "Le Goût du néant" (152; "The Taste for the Abyss" [trans. mine]) awaits him and gives him his vision of the dynamics of the void, that power of nothing that physicists are exploring in our own time. His obsession with the devouring capacity of Time also marks his poetry with a personal stamp. In such poems as "L'Horloge" (160–62; "The Clock"), Time devours him minute by minute as, realizing the fragility of his life, he desperately tries to suck what he calls the gold out of the dimensions of Time.

Perhaps hardest for modern readers to understand is the ambivalence of Baudelaire's religious attitude. He finds himself caught between good and evil. But what are good and evil? First of all, they are encrusted in the Christian code of morality and sin in which he was reared and against which he rebelled often but from whose frame of reference he never escaped, even when he praised Satan over God and sided with Cain over Abel. His obsession with sin is particularly poignant in the poem "Un Voyage à Cythère" (254–58; "A Voyage to Cythera"). Cythera had been forever associated with Venus, the goddess of love, and by extension with the paradise of lovers. Baudelaire's boat, however, lands in an arid place that becomes focused on a branch of a dried tree, where hangs a dead and ravaged prey. Corruption in the physical sense moves to the moral level as the hanged creature's rotting flesh assumes the semblance of the poet's own being, putrefied by sin and repressed guilt. Antiquity's symbol of serenity, the happy isle, becomes the locus of an agonizing confessional and cry for atonement: "— Ah! Seigneur! donnez-moi la force et le courage / De contempler mon cœur et mon corps sans dégoût" (258) ("Oh Lord, give me the force and the courage / To contemplate body and heart without disgust" [trans. mine]).

Yet carnal sin is not the only form of *mal* for Baudelaire. The flowers he associates with *mal* have a broader meaning, untranslatable in English and incomprehensible unless taken in the context of the era in which Baudelaire lived. *Le Mal*, which can mean illness, evil, sin, in his day pointed beyond the personal sense of morality to the disquietude of the age: the aftermath of the French Revolution. This historical period, which began with abstractions about liberty, equality, and fraternity, ended in violent fratricide and an insipid restoration of a worn-out system of government. The revolution was to leave France politically unsettled and its population emotionally restless for the remainder of the nineteenth century. Particularly for the generation born after the French Revolution, rebellion was followed by apathy, boredom, dejection, a sense of hopeless movement toward a bottomless pit. All these states of mind and soul were to be expressed by Baudelaire as an unmarried, disengaged spectator of human catastrophe, constantly irritated by the foggy winter atmosphere that aggravated the depression that he called his spleen. In "Spleen (4)," "le ciel bas et lourd pèse comme un couvercle" (148) ("low and heavy sky weighs like a lid" [149]). In "La Cloche fêlée" (144; "The Cracked Bell"), spleen stifles his voice, as if he were crying out from under a heap of dead soldiers on a battlefield.

Still, strangely, his *mal* can take the form of flowers, the semblance of the beautiful. That is because his verse squeezes the quintessential from despair and transforms it into a cluster of gems that casts its reflection on each future reader according to the more recent forms that anguish has taken and that the concept of beauty has assumed. Thus one of the seemingly most horrible descriptions of material decomposition Baudelaire gives in his famous poem "Une Charogne" (58–62; "A Carcass") becomes human triumph over material reality. Its last line transforms through poetic alchemy the scum into gold, translated as nearly perfectly as possible by William Crosby:

> Then, O my beautiful, repeat this to the worm
>   Whose kisses eat your face away:
> That I preserve the sacred essence and the form
>   Of all my loves as they decay!   (*From* Flowers 69)

Baudelaire assumes many postures. Sometimes he looks like a priest, sometimes like the Devil, a Faustian devil tempting humans. Sometimes he becomes the dandy in exquisite gear, who, when he wants to touch up his graying hair, has the dye turn it green, making him look like a clown. Sometimes he is the melancholy prince, a Hamlet incarnate, morose, quivering between life and death. And, as in his introductory poem, addressed to the reader, "Au lecteur," he is whispering in our ear: "mon semblable,—mon frère!" (6) ("you who read me, don't pretend you are better; you are like me, my brother" [trans. mine]).

Should we then name him our contemporary? We would clip his wings. No, he has stopped with us only a moment on his long trajectory leading him to future contemporaries. Baudelaire will never become a postmodern, because each generation of readers will find something new in his perception of self and of the universe, in his relationship to others, in his battle with the void, in his manner of manipulating his readers with his sorcery and the multiplicity of his approaches to life and to art. What a supreme and frightening lover—yet wise enough not to have attempted to become a spouse. What a painter of his time, acutely observant but never circumscribed in the scenes he depicted. Let us call him not our contemporary but the contemporary of every new generation that encounters him and calls him modern, seeing with each new reading another aspect of that "something new" for which he searched in his existence as in his poetry. "Plonger au fond du gouffre, Enfer ou Ciel, qu'importe? / Au fond de l'Inconnu pour trouver du *nouveau*!" (292) ("To plunge into the abyss, Hell or Heaven who cares? / Into the unknown to find something new" [trans. mine]) is the way he ends his poem "Le Voyage" ("Voyaging"). The voyage is really an antivoyage. Voyages will neither unveil mysteries nor produce true revelations. The boundaries of the ultimate quest are interior ones.

Baudelaire has that provocative quality and diversity of communication that gives to all generations of readers worldwide the impression that he is not only ahead of his time but also ahead of theirs.

Teaching Baudelaire to
Advanced High School Students

Laurence Risser

Before plunging into the icy waters of Baudelaire with high school students, one must consider whether it is appropriate to introduce them to an author so controversial in his apparent celebration of all that is corrupt and perverse. Curriculum selection is a complex matter: the academic merits of one author must be weighed against those of others, and the social and cultural biases of the wider audience of parents and community must also be considered. Teachers must determine where lines will be drawn in the curricular sand for the coming year. Baudelaire may stir up the sand, but he deserves to be a contender.

The study of Baudelaire's work offers teachers an opportunity to synthesize Edgar Allan Poe's evocative and melodramatic presentation of the dark side of human nature (Poe was Baudelaire's mentor); Alexander Pope's rhetorical use of antithesis to shock, satirize, and enlighten; and T. S. Eliot's gift of the existential J. Alfred Prufrock. Other authors can readily be studied in connection with Baudelaire. Furthermore, the swiftness with which he moves from anticipation to despair mirrors the adolescent temperament: Baudelaire may in fact be more accessible to young people than to many adults. Finally, a study of Baudelaire may diversify the range of literary selections, incorporating a French author and the opportunity to examine the problems of a work in translation.

Baudelaire is conveniently introduced through reference to Edgar Allan Poe, an author familiar to virtually all high school students. Nudging students beyond Poe's plots and masterful development of suspense, I draw attention to his motifs, his imagery and assessment of human nature. The preoccupation with death; the cast of obsessive, driven characters; the crafting of language to establish emotional intensity; and a fascination with the paradoxical pleasure of pain can be found in both authors.

The Flowers of Evil presents students with an opportunity to search for answers to fundamental questions: What is it that gives life meaning? How do we respond to disillusionment? I ask students to study a few poems carefully and to discuss whether they reflect a quest for a more perfect world, an embittered yet persistent hope that beyond despair and evil there is an ideal to be discovered, or whether they represent pure cynicism, a self-indulgent wallowing in all that is debased. While teenagers lack the life experience of Baudelaire, some may find his appraisal of life refreshingly honest and see his work as part of the journey toward a positive truth.

To introduce Baudelaire's thought and writing, I focus on two poems, "Hymn to Beauty" and "Voyaging." The modest length of "Hymn to Beauty," its direct thematic posing of the question of whether beauty's origin is divine or infernal, its conclusion that the question itself is of no significance, and its controlled form of alexandrine quatrains in the French make it an appropriate sample of Baudelaire's work. Before exposing students directly to Baudelaire's work, however, I ease into his troubled world with the following, somewhat lighter, lines from Lord Byron:

> Lines Inscribed upon a Cup
> Formed from a Skull
>
> Start not—nor deem my spirit fled:
> In me behold the only skull,
> From which, unlike a living head,
> Whatever flows is never dull.
>
> I lived, I loved, I quaff'd, like thee;
> I died: let earth my bones resign:
> Fill up—thou canst not injure me;
> The worm hath fouler lips than thine.
>
> Better to hold the sparkling grape,
> Than nurse the earth-worm's slimy brood;
> And circle in the goblet's shape
> The drink of Gods, than reptile's food.
>
> Where once my wit, perchance hath shone,
> In aid of others' let me shine;
> And when, alas! our brains are gone,
> What nobler substitute than wine?
>
> Quaff while thou canst: another race,
> When thou and thine like me are sped,
> May rescue thee from earth's embrace,
> And rhyme and revel with the dead.

Why not? since through life's little day
Our heads such sad effects produce;
Redeem'd from worms and wasting clay,
This chance is theirs, to be of use. (154)

Byron offers smooth passage into a mind torn between attraction and aversion to death. Byron and Baudelaire share a fascination with the ultimate reality of death; both find wine the companion of choice to enhance the pleasure and ease the pain of too much life-consciousness. While Byron shares Baudelaire's romantic quest for experience that transcends the bland, suffocating existence of ordinary mortals, he has not plumbed the depths of Baudelaire's cynicism; he thus plays a useful role as an entree to Baudelaire.

After reading, discussing, and savoring Byron's satirical commentary on the vacuity of ordinary human wit and wisdom and Byron's resignation to accept the end of life, we turn to Baudelaire's "Hymn to Beauty." Here I use a standard approach for explicating a short literary work with an International Baccalaureate or other advanced literature class. We read the selection aloud; we take time to discuss first impressions and to identify questions to pursue in understanding the poem. Then students delve into it with the colored-pencil approach. This simple technique helps them sort out recurring literary devices, thematic threads, and tonal qualities. One color is used to underline similes and metaphors; another, lines that juxtapose sharply contrasting imagery or language; another, words relating to death and depravity; another, words of joy and divinity; and so on. Some words may be underlined in more than one color. The result is an aerial map of the poem, which highlights topics for discussion and analysis.

Instead of the customary small-group analysis and reporting, I prefer a full class discussion of the introductory "Hymn to Beauty." Baudelaire's shocking, suggestive language quickly engages students and leads to observations on his characteristic use of vivid, sharply contrasting imagery:

Beauty, you walk on corpses, mocking them;
Horror is charming as your other gems,
And Murder is a trinket dancing there
Lovingly on your naked belly's skin.

You are a candle where the mayfly dies
In flames, blessing this fire's deadly bloom. (45)

In addition to noting his intense language, I call attention to the rhetoric Baudelaire employs in his progression of thought. The opening apostrophe to beauty, "O Beauty! do you visit from the sky / Or the abyss?," launches the commentary of the poem with a question, the question that permeates his work: Is life divinely or demonically inspired? The question is rephrased in the third stanza, "Are you of heaven or the nether world?" However, it is lost in a shrug of the shoulders at the end of the poem in an answering question, "What difference, then, from heaven or from hell, / O Beauty, monstrous in simplicity?," and, "Angel or siren, spirit, I don't care [. . .] ." The poem is rich enough by itself to provide a miniature unit on Baudelaire, but I like to use it instead to prepare for further study.

The major focus in this limited study of Baudelaire, his long poem "Voyaging" (283–93), takes the reader on an odyssey from youthful curiosity to cynical ennui. The poem, written in numbered sections, each with a clearly delineated subject, provides convenient divisions for small-group analysis and large-group presentation. I divide a class of twenty-five students into five groups and assign the poem in units (by sections 1, 2, 3–4, 5–6, and 7–8). After reading the poem aloud with the students and discussing it just enough to see how it compares and contrasts with "Hymn to Beauty," where "Voyaging" is going, and what areas in it require further exploration, I turn it over to the small groups to work up their presentations. In the beginning it is helpful to identify students who have had several years of French. They can single out parts of the poem that do not translate readily into English and advise the groups on problematic lines.

Groups need at least a full class period to prepare their commentary. Explanatory notes from the James McGowan translation of *The Flowers of Evil* are furnished to students. As groups present their sections, I check to make sure they have noted the major points. If they have not, I lead the group toward those points through the following topics:

Section 1: *Types of voyagers* (283)

> The different types of travelers identified; the true voyagers
> The effect of opening the poem with reference to a "wide-eyed Child"
> The first clue that the voyage's discoveries may be unsatisfying
> The effect of juxtaposing contrasting language ("How grand [. . .] How petty," "Fire in the brain, / Heavy great with rancour," "scars of kisses")
> The significance of the last line of the second stanza, "Berçant notre infini sur l'infini des mers," which may be translated, more literally than McGowan does, as "Cradling, rocking our infinity on the finite seas"
> The voyagers' state of mind at the end of this first section

Section 2: *Human nature; the pursuit of empty dreams* (285)

> The effect of the simile comparing human beings to toys in the first stanza
> The contrast between what is imagined and what is real
> The effect of references to inebriation
> The degeneration of voyager to tramp

Section 3: *An appeal to other, more seasoned voyagers* (285–87)

> Raising expectations, the imagery of treasures, jewels, riches, stars
> The contrast between the would-be travelers and the noble voyagers

The rhetorical effect of the question

Section 4: *The response, the voice of experienced voyagers* (287–89)

The contrast in language between the visual imagery of places visited and the blunt confession "we are bored" (and "which left us unfulfilled and insecure")

Section 5: *Impatient eagerness to hear it all* (289)

The sense of incompleteness; the compulsion to experience vicariously

Section 6: *What travel has revealed* (284–91)

The effect of the opening address, "O Childish dupes!"
Characterization of men and women in stanza 2
Religious references to martyrs, saints; the preoccupation with brutality
Generalizations about mad humanity versus the "bold demented ones" who find their escape in opium
Satiric irony in stanza 4, line 3: "Indulge their lusts with hairshirts, or with nails"

Section 7: *The conclusion* (291–93)

"Ourselves," the destination of all travel
The significance of the metaphor "that sad oasis in ennui"
The enemy Time; the gladiator
How the cry "Onward ho!" in stanza 4, line 2, parallels but contrasts in tone with section 1, stanza 5, line 4: "We're off!"
Allusions to death and intoxication

Section 8: *The next voyage* (293)

Personification of death; recognition of a new captain
Irony in stanza 1, line 4: "you know our hearts are full of sunny rays!"
A question of interpretation: Is the concluding desire "To fathom the Unknown, and find the *new*!" an expression of despair or of the hope and curiosity that opened the poem? After students have responded to this question, I distribute copies of "Dream of a Curious Man" (281), have them skim it, and then pose the question again.

Just as I borrow Byron from other parts of the curriculum to introduce Baudelaire, so I find follow-up activities important to put Baudelaire back in context, since there is the possibility that he can be a black hole, sucking all energy and light into a soulless domain. Instead of giving the usual introductory sketch of the author, I like to have students compose their own profile of the man after they read his work, drawn not from notes and sources but from his writing. I caution them that biographical criticism is full of hazards; the relation between an author and the author's work is always tenuous, yet even so it is revealing to explore the connections. I have students tell me what kind of childhood they think Baudelaire had, how he got along with his parent(s), what his school years were like, how successful he was academically, whether he used drugs, and so on. After we have a good time assembling his portrait from the shadows, I give them a sampling of biographical facts: He was born in 1821; his father died when he was six; his mother then married a military man whom he detested; he was a rebel, was expelled from school, but passed the exams; his family sent him to India, but he returned to France to claim his share of his father's inheritance; he spent lavishly, squandering his money, had a love affair, took drugs, was put on a small allowance, and spent the rest of his life dodging bill collectors; he translated Edgar Allan Poe into French, published two short stories, and wrote his major work, *The Flowers of Evil*. The book was seized in 1857 and republished in shortened form in 1861 to appease the censors, who had judged six of the poems to be obscene. Baudelaire died in his mother's arms in 1867, at the age of forty-six.

In addition to learning to appreciate the author as an individual, students need to make the literary connections that Baudelaire's work invites. I offer extra credit to a student or group of students who lead a class discussion on the similarities between the voyagers of Baudelaire and T. S. Eliot's existential protagonist J. Alfred Prufrock.

For stylistic comparison and contrast, I like to introduce students to the satiric, cerebral writings of Alexander Pope. *The Rape of the Lock* works nicely. Canto 3 alone will suffice, if time is short. Pope's juxtaposition of antithetic elements has a coincidental counterpart in Baudelaire. Consider these lines:

> Here Britain's statesmen oft the fall foredoom
> Of foreign tyrants, and of nymphs at home;
> Here thou, great [Queen] Anna! whom three realms obey,
> Dost sometimes counsel take—and sometimes tea [. . .].   (3.5–8)

> The hungry judges soon the sentence sign,
> And wretches hang that jurymen may dine [. . .].   (3.21–22)

> Not louder shrieks to pitying heaven are cast,
> When husbands, or when lapdogs breathe their last [. . .].   (3.157–58)

Pope may seem formulaic and soulless in comparison with Baudelaire; but they both derive considerable dramatic effect from the jarring shock of contrasting references. While Pope presents his barbs in pure, grammatically balanced antithetic form, Baudelaire is more blunt and direct. Consider Baudelaire's lines:

> Horror is charming as your other gems,
> And Murder is a trinket dancing there [. . .].

The panting lover bending to his love
Looks like a dying man who strokes his tomb.   ("Hymn to Beauty" 45)

How grand the universe by light of lamps,
How petty in the memory's clear sight.
[. . . . .]
The gnawing ice, the copper-burning sun
Efface the scars of kisses and of lies.   ("Voyaging" 283)

The often rueful Rue de Baudelaire is marked not only by the muddy foot-prints of disconsolate travelers but also by glistening puddles that reflect shards of a better world. If your class has empathized with the tortured souls of Oedi-pus, Medea, Raskolnikov, Hamlet, and Ophelia and if your senior students suf-fer from their own ennui, you may find that a unit on Baudelaire is just the thing to rouse their sullen souls. No one has waged a more intense battle against the antagonist Ennui than Baudelaire. He has looked the enemy in the eye and taken him on with a life and literature that will challenge any disaf-fected, intellectual, contemporary student slouching through your halls.

NOTE

In writing this essay, I wish to express my gratitude to Ronald Chastain of Lingua Franca (the translation service, not the journal) of Minneapolis and to Henry Kalb of the College of Saint Catherine.

Engaging with Poetry in AP French: Fragmentary Perceptions

Ainslie Armstrong McLees

After twenty-three years of teaching in college, I decided several years ago to turn to high school teaching, feeling a duty to help students enter college with a grasp of French language and literature more profound than just verb conjugations and useful expressions (e.g., *Tiens!*). It was fortunate for me that a new public high school program, the Governor's School for Government and International Studies, in Richmond, Virginia, was being developed as a regional high school (grades 9–12) for the gifted and talented (students having national verbal and math scores at or above the eighty-fifth percentile and one or more additional test-demonstrated areas of giftedness or talent; see N. Johnson 14–19), who come from eighteen counties ranging from urban to rural. Because of the school's international-studies focus, foreign languages play an important role. There is a minimum graduation requirement of four years in one of nine languages and two in another. Many students enter with two years of foreign language study and continue through level 6. The French program is thriving, with over ten percent of our student body currently enrolled in French levels 4–6. We offer three advanced-placement courses, and it is here that Baudelaire comes into play.

Engaging high school students with poetry requires of the teacher imagination and creativity as well as a strong literary background. Students often come to an AP French class after having had negative experiences with poetry since seventh or eighth grade. They often fear the genre. Lecture classes or empty discussions in which any questions posed by the teacher assume one correct answer fail to introduce students to the ambiguity on which poetry rests. The seemingly random, condensed style that typifies lyric poetry makes students balk. Having given "wrong" answers in the past, they do not trust their hunch that a poem is polyvalent. Many educators teach students well and early that giving a "wrong" answer is not desirable. As a result, students seek to avoid failure by shunning poetry. To cope with the students' resistance, teachers use research or question-and-answer assignments rather than methods that engage students actively with the genre. Or teachers skip poetry altogether. It is a vicious circle: teachers' response to negative student reception cripples the methodology of their classroom. In short, students train their teachers, and they very often train their teachers not only how to teach them but also what to teach them.

But our students have much to teach us about poetry. Inexperienced students of literature approach its study with just the "innocent eye" described by John Ruskin in relation to art in *The Elements of Drawing* (22), with a freshness of perception unencumbered by theoretical frameworks. As Roger Shattuck points out, for teachers "complete naivete is impossible, but one can learn to put aside many categories of thought and provisionally to meet a work of art on its own terms" (417).

The thought occurred to me several years ago that the student resistance to poetry could be turned to the teacher's advantage. The teacher could explore the naive perspective of students, observe their world, hear their desire to grasp deeper meaning in their studies, and introduce the elliptical, metaphorical thought of poetry while encouraging students to trust their intuitive grasp of poetry's meaning without resorting to sequential logic. Several questions sprang to mind. What is the world these students experience? How can a teacher guide students to a deeper understanding of that world and the poetry of a nineteenth-century poet whose work was rejected at the time of its publication? How can the necessary bond of trust between students and teacher help recapture that fresh viewpoint students may offer?

An experienced teacher will notice that students have different learning styles. Much of what teachers have observed about those styles coincides with the findings of recent neurological research (Calvin; Kimura; Toga and Mazziotta). In relicensing courses, high school teachers learn pedagogical approaches that apply this knowledge (Campbell, Campbell, and Dickerson; Gardner). A visual learner internalizes information when it is associated with visual images; an auditory learner internalizes material when it is heard or accompanied by music; a sensorial learner needs concrete, hands-on experience with the work studied; and a kinetic learner acquires information most effectively when the learning involves movement. The more senses stimulated during a lesson, the more successful the lesson is likely to be (Stevenson and Palmes; Nisbet; Schmeck). Not too distant from the multisensory technique of teaching is Baudelaire's use of synesthesia to heighten effects and convey meaning. Outside the classroom, advertisers, news reporters, and political candidates are attuned to this methodology; they apply it readily in the media through visual imagery and sound bites.

I present here a teaching methodology developed in response to the reality of diverse learning styles, using as a point of departure six Baudelaire poems on the AP French reading list at the Governor's School ("Correspondances" ["Correspondences"], "L'Irrémédiable" ["The Irremediable"], "Chant d'automne" ["Autumn Song"], "Spleen (4)," "Hymne à la Beauté" ["Hymn to Beauty"], "L'Invitation au voyage" ["Invitation to the Voyage"]).

First, a few thoughts about the world our students experience, a world where the visual image—not the printed word—reigns. Newspapers in the nineteenth century introduced the first visual presentation of unrelated pieces of information, in print, aimed at the general reading public. A headline on a national political issue might appear, with its text in smaller print, beside *faits divers* on any number of subjects. This montage of fonts began to shape our tolerance for finding random bits of information adjacent to one another. In the twentieth century, radio news juxtaposed different items, delivering them in the auditory rather than the written mode. Film and television combined the auditory with the realm of rapidly changing visual images that were just as unrelated to one another and distanced in time and space from one another as a newspaper's varied articles. Along with the randomness of the material came an ever-decreasing emphasis on print and on length. The world in which our students have grown up is a world of rapidly changing visual and auditory images.

Whether we like it or not, it is the sound bite, a catchy image for a thought in a brief utterance, that typifies the culmination of this process of reduction and acceleration. *Sound bites*, a term generally implying shallowness, serve as a point of departure for examining the world students experience. Adopted by advertisers, news reporters, and politicians in video clips, headlines, and radio newscasts, sound bites capture the essence of an idea concisely. This multimedia technique, reducing information to a brief, picturesque combination of words often accompanied by visual images, duplicates certain characteristics of poetry. Contrasting sound bites with poetic lines or verses allows teachers to demonstrate that all brief utterances need not be shallow. For example, in "Chant d'automne" Baudelaire combines a typical nineteenth-century experience, anticipating the arrival of winter ("J'entends déjà tomber [. . .] / Le bois retentissant sur le pavé des cours" [116]) ("Already I can hear [. . .] / The thump of logs on courtyard paving stones" [117]) with a personal association ("avec des chocs funèbres") ("a dismal sound"). Indeed, phrases crafted by a master may express a profound insight, capturing the essence of a human experience in few words. Pedagogically speaking, the technique draws on more than one mode of learning (auditory and visual): a methodological synesthesia. A poem's metaphors and similes have the immediate force and powerful attraction of media sound bites but also have a beauty and depth all their own.

Now from theory to practice. To convey a sense of Baudelaire's style, themes, and imagery to my students, before analyzing an entire poem with its difficult linguistic and stylistic complexities I select approximately twenty verses that display strong visual or auditory imagery or dramatic contrasts; these verses provide a window into Baudelaire's originality and his desire to shock. The fragments of poetry kindle the class's curiosity and imagination without overwhelming students. Groups of three to five receive a set of four selections, each selection typed on a separate sheet of paper. One set might include:

1.

Quand la terre est changée en un cachot humide,
Où l'Espérance, comme une chauve-souris,
S'en va battant les murs de son aile timide
Et se cognant la tête à des plafonds pourris [. . .].   (148)

When earth is changed into a sweaty cell,
In which Hope, captured, like a frantic bat,
Batters the walls with her enfeebled wing,
Striking her head against the rotting beams [. . .].   (149)

2.

De Satan ou de Dieu, qu'importe? Ange ou Sirène,
Qu'importe [. . .]?   (44)

Angel or siren, spirit, I don't care [. . .].   (45)

3.

Il est des parfums frais comme des chairs d'enfants,
Doux comme les hautbois, verts comme les prairies,
— Et d'autres, corrompus, riches et triomphants,

Ayant l'expansion des choses infinies [. . .].   (18)

Odours there are, fresh as a baby's skin,
Mellow as oboes, green as meadow grass,
—Others corrupted, rich, triumphant, full,

Having dimensions infinitely vast [. . .].   (19)

Fragment 1 presents concrete imagery both visual (bat, walls, wing, head, ceiling) and tactile (hitting, banging, rotted) to illustrate the abstract concept of hope. Fragment 2 moves toward the abstract, first introducing Satan and God, concrete figures representing evil and good in Christian theology. Angel and siren mix Christian and pagan imagery; however, the importance of each lies in the figure's use of language (the angel's message; the siren's song), not just in its physical form. Fragment 3 attributes both concrete and abstract qualities to scents through synesthesia, raising the physical to the spiritual level.

I give no titles of poems, so as not to predetermine the students' reactions. Drawing again on the visual mode, I vary print fonts for verses from different poems to reinforce the rhythm, tone, and imagery and to suggest the depth and breadth of Baudelaire's poetic content.

Since the goal of this introduction to Baudelaire's poetry is to provide a hook, capturing the students' interest and engaging them in the study of complete poems, the poetic fragments need to suggest the whole poetic collection by representing themes of spleen, the ideal, boredom, revolt, and escape. Once the class has analyzed the verses for tone (the apparent attitude of the lyric self toward the subject or the audience or toward both) and theme (the evaluation of the subject as good, bad, or neutral), the students may brainstorm in small groups of three to five to generate a list of recurrent words, ideas, images, and moods. As each group finishes, a group representative writes the list on the board or on a transparency, clearly emphasizing the three things the group finds most significant. Each group reports to the class as a whole and justifies its three choices by citing examples from the texts. The contrasts of the two key concepts of spleen and the ideal emerge when I ask a student to create an undulating line on the board or transparency and members of each group place each recurrent element along the line according to whether the element falls into the category of spleen or the ideal. In the following group of verses, olfactory-based images will be placed along the serpentine line:

1.

Les plus rares fleurs
Mêlant leurs odeurs
Aux vagues senteurs de l'ambre [. . .].   (108)

The rarest of blooms
Would mingle their scents
With amber's vague perfume.   (109)

2.

Tu répands des parfums comme un soir orageux [. . .].   (44)

You pour out odours like an evening storm [. . .].   (45)

3.

Les parfums, les couleurs et les sons se répondent.   (18)

So perfumes, colours, sounds may correspond.   (19)

4.

Un damné descendant sans lampe,
Au bord d'un gouffre dont l'odeur
Trahit l'humide profondeur,
D'éternels escaliers sans rampe [. . .].   (158)

A damned soul fumbling down steps
Of an infinite stair without rails
At the edge of a gulf, with a smell
Betraying the clammy depths [. . .].   (159)

The order in which the images emerge will depend on the class and teacher. Fragments 1 and 3 are both positive and mysterious, suggesting the transcendence of the ideal. Fragment 4 is clearly negative and will be placed at the bottom of the line. Fragment 2, not as negative as 4, will appear along the descending line. The graphic configuration is shown in the figure below:

The Ideal: Les plus rares fleurs (108)
        Les parfums [. . .] se répondent. (18)

        Midway: des parfums comme un soir orageux (44)

                Spleen: Au bord d'un gouffre dont l'odeur
                Trahit l'humide profondeur   (158)

Further discussion of each item on the continuum deepens the students' understanding of Baudelaire's concepts of spleen and the ideal in emotional, aesthetic, and intellectual terms. A natural extension of this visually based exercise is a discussion of the idea of a *fleur du mal* riddled with moral and aesthetic paradoxes, since sources of evil along the continuum may generate images of beauty or images of beauty may generate evil. The concluding stanza of "L'Irrémédiable," where a dance of images vacillating between the spleen and ideal leads to the powerful "La conscience dans le Mal!" (160) ("Evil aware of itself!" [161]), provides a good example of the dialectic at play between the two concepts.

I often weave theoretical approaches into the discussion of the elements that the students identify. For example, a serpentine continuum may lead to a discussion of Marcel Ruff's suggestion that oscillation in Baudelaire's works is symptomatic of the heightened perception of the junction of the spiritual and material (*Baudelaire* 51). Furthermore, serpentine associations convey a clear visual sense of certain themes important to Baudelaire: the waves of the sea with its ebb and flow, the pulsing of circulating blood, the movement of walking, dancing, the play of shadow and light, the alternation of ecstasy and despair, and the human duality of body and spirit. On its descending and ascending lines the serpentine accommodates those themes that are neither the ideal nor spleen but that lead to ennui. The midway location denotes the monotonous, repetitive, common, stable, inert. Placement above the midway point attributes a positive (closer to the ideal) value; below, placement indicates a negative (closer to spleen) value. Students must always justify their placement of a theme on the line as an exercise in both analytic thinking and moral reasoning. When students impose a twentieth-century view on the poetry or poet, a discussion of the differences in morality and culture between the nineteenth and twentieth century adds depth to the students' understanding, opening a window onto French cultural history.

Having begun the discussion from individual images and continued it through stylistic devices; themes; and the concepts of duality, aspiration for the infinite through the ideal, and the looming possibility of the monotonous (ennui), students may tackle a complete poem. I start with poems that they can relate to other disciplines they know, namely, religion and literature ("Correspondances," "L'Irrémédiable"). Keeping in mind the Baudelairean notion that music and poetry are inseparable, we listen to a recording of the poem and then repeat it; each student also reads a line or two with background music by Franz Liszt or Richard Wagner, composers whose music Baudelaire admired (Hyslop 68–91). The students' oral reading touches the auditory mode within a rhythmic setting. The varied voices with their differing inflections—and distortions—allow for a second auditory take of the poem, which leads into a discussion of the formal elements of meter, rhyme, and rhythm, along with the necessary clarification of any vocabulary terms or cultural contexts that students may not understand. Before broaching the problems of vocabulary, style, or meaning, students give their first impressions of the poem from the reading by responding to open-ended questions. For one example: What words do you remember most vividly? Invariably, after listening to "Correspondances," students have apprehended the closing word or words of each line: the nouns *piliers* ("columns"), *paroles* ("spoken words"), *symboles* ("symbols"), *unité* ("unity"), *clarté* ("brightness"), *prairies, l'encens* ("incense"), *sens* ("senses"); the verbs *se confondent* ("intermingle"; the reflexive pronoun reflecting French usage as opposed to English), *se répondent* ("call and respond"; the reflexive pronoun denoting reciprocity); and the adjectival expressions *familiers* ("familiar"), *d'enfants* ("baby's"), *riches et triomphants* ("rich and triumphant"), *infinies* ("infinite"). Of all the words, *familiers* is the only one that routinely eludes classes.

To help students focus on the specific themes and motifs they may expect to encounter when they study the poem in depth, I ask them to develop categories for the end-of-line words. A brainstorming session will generate categories of themes (spirituality, religiousness, purity, innocence), sensory perceptions (colors, scents, sounds), and interactions (spoken words; echoed sounds; profound unity; mutual responses of sounds, scents, and colors). To work toward producing an awareness of the intertwining of themes, emotions, and motifs throughout (a complexity imaged in the prose poem "Le Thyrse" ["The Thyrsus"]), I ask the students to consider the interactions between people and things and between different realms of experience that suggest either past or present. Another visual paradigm, drawn this time from Baudelaire's translation of Poe's "Principles of Poetry" and presented in "Projets de préface" ("Preface Plans") for *Les Fleurs du Mal*, reinforces the idea that Baudelaire was both critic and poet. An image is created by the superimposition of angles resulting from the combination of horizontal and vertical lines and zigzags that represent the poet's conscious construct of perception through word choice — often oxymorons (Ruff, *Baudelaire* 142). The interdisciplinarian may suggest that students construct a geometric form with mathematical relations to represent the key ideas gleaned from the sum of words in the different categories. By attributing a positive or negative degree value to each theme, emotion, or motif, the student constructs a three-dimensional representation of the poem. The representation reflects the multifaceted nature of each element as it interacts with the others, and it allows the student to apprehend the depth of the poem's meaning. With luck, a prism may result, opening a discussion of light refraction and polyvalence as it relates to Baudelaire's poetry and nineteenth-century art.

As students go through the poem as a whole, they work in small groups again, having specific tasks to accomplish. First they read the entire poem together once more, clarifying vocabulary. Second, each group selects one image that it likes the most and justifies that choice orally to the class. Third, the groups create a chart of stylistic devices: meter, rhyme scheme, alliteration and assonance, most commonly used letter or sound. In a second chart they list particularly evocative adjectives, nouns, or verbs, similes and metaphors. Once these tasks are accomplished, we discuss the students' findings as a class and I gently adjust any misconceptions.

Having analyzed the elements present in the poem, we proceed to those absent: the abstract concepts that emerge from the concrete through the juxtaposition of certain words (e.g., *vivants piliers*) and through the synesthesia that weaves together the sensual fabric of the third stanza of "Correspondances." Working backward from the last stanza, students trace the themes of infinite expanses through the senses of smell, sight, and touch (amber, musk, benjamin, and incense). This exercise emphasizes the opposition, in the minds of many Americans, of sensuality and spirituality. The goal is to reveal the relations among the parts of the poem and between the spiritual and material. Again the collaborative efforts of teacher and students disclose the poem's depth.

A final discussion of each poem examines how Baudelaire combines the material and the spiritual, the quotidian and the unknown to create poetry of extraordinary originality. I have found that in a world of constantly shifting visual images, many students consciously or unconsciously draw visual images in their mind to accompany the studied poems. The mental tableau is not only an effective mnemonic device for content, it also enables students to experience the poem concretely. The leap from this natural tendency of students to pedagogy is easy. To gain an understanding of the students' idea of the poem, I ask students to illustrate a specific image or a full poem. "Autumn Song," part 1, with its combination of concrete visual and auditory imagery (falling chunks of firewood, a coffin, the spreading shadows, the cold sun) and with the emotions of anger, fear, and horror that lead the speaker to equate his spirit to a crumbling tower, provides a rich field for illustration. Parts 1 and 2 of the poem contrast sharply; in part 2, visual images evoking light and love lead to the finality of death and offer another take on the harsh auditory imagery of the final stanza of part 1. From the students' artwork, the teacher may introduce discussion topics, such as the marriage of abstract and concrete language to create the total effect of the poem or the traditional significations of autumn and its death symbolism. Drawings will vary from highly detailed and literal to abstract, giving the students the opportunity to explore how to move from the literal interpretation of a line of poetry to its abstract, generalized meaning. To promote discussion and thought about the poem, the teacher may encourage class members to pose questions to the student artist: Why did you place the falling woodblocks in the distance to illustrate stanza 1? Why did you make the woodblocks prominent in stanza 3, when the allusion to them is only in one line? How do the visual images of death in stanzas 4 and 7 compare and contrast?

As a closing activity, following their own inspiration, students individually create a visual representation of the connections within a poem. Representations that the students have created based on "Correspondances," "Spleen," "L'Irrémédiable," "Chant d'automne," or "Hymne à la Beauté" feature color-coding words by theme and emotion expressed; creating a graphic image that shows the connections through lines; making a collage of reprints of nineteenth-century art that illustrates the poem; producing an original artwork that reacts to the poem; creating an architectural model of a forest temple with Baudelairean accoutrements; giving a series of icons that reiterate the poem's themes through visual rhyming; and creating a violin score that attempts to convey the value of sounds and themes within the poem through musical counterparts. Several students wrote original poetry rather than create a visual project. One student's reading of "Correspondances" accompanied by a simultaneous American Sign Language rendition by another student is by far the most moving of the projects to date. Students present their work to the class with a justification of its appropriateness, answering Baudelaire's plea for impassioned, highly personal criticism, as stated, albeit in reverse, in *Salon de 1846*: "Le meilleur compte rendu d'un tableau pourra être un sonnet ou une élégie" (229) ("The best critique of a painting may be a sonnet or an elegy").

Finally, a word about engaging students in the synthesis of several of Baudelaire's poems. To compare and contrast content, formal elements, and personal reactions to the poem—or, in a more sophisticated setting, to compare and contrast theoretical frameworks—my students complete a Venn diagram, two or more overlapping circles with a rectangular rubric bar above each. The diagram allows students to place elements of similarity between the poems in the overlapping regions (preferably shaded) and contrasting elements—that make each poem original—outside the overlapping regions, in the circle that represents that poem (Froman). Teachers may provide as much or as little guidance as they wish, either by stating categories that must be included or by allowing students to include the elements that they find the most compelling. Using the diagram's contents as a point of departure, students may complete a written comparison of two or more poems, following a traditional explication de texte or the suggested AP poetic analysis format.

By harnassing the visual and auditory trends of twentieth-century media; by benefiting from the scientific research that is helping educators understand how students acquire, store, and retrieve knowledge through the play of sensory experiences; and by engaging students in an interactive study of Baudelaire's poetry, teachers may overcome resistance to poetry and awaken in students a more profound understanding of the complexity of creativity and human existence.

Powers of Evil: Teaching Baudelaire at a Church-Related University

William Olmsted

> The death of Satan was a tragedy
> For the imagination.
> > —Wallace Stevens, "Esthétique du Mal"

My students are undergraduates in an honors humanities program, housed in its own college within a comprehensive university affiliated with the Lutheran church, Missouri synod. Most of them are Lutherans of one denomination or another, although there is a large Roman Catholic minority, a few agnostics, the occasional devout atheist. Exceptionally bright and hardworking, these students preferred a church-related school to other topflight alternatives. By the time they take one of the courses in which I teach Baudelaire, they have typically had a course in Christian theology and one in non-Western religion. Often conservative but rarely fundamentalist in their beliefs, they incline toward that heroic or virtuoso religiosity that the sociologist Max Weber opposed to the commonplace religiosity or gnosticism of the "religiously 'unmusical'" (287). They are almost ready for *Les Fleurs du Mal*.

In any broadly humanistic education, of course, the book merits an important place. Not only is the text a major poetic achievement but it also helped shape the modern literary tradition. *Les Fleurs du Mal* presents challenges that require students to develop sophisticated reading skills and interpretive approaches. It is also an age-appropriate text, well suited to college students confronting the problematics of their "uses of pleasure" (Foucault) and struggling to deal with the religious and political consequences of newly acquired "cultural capital" (Bourdieu 2). Despite its appropriateness, *Les Fleurs du Mal* puts heavy demands on the instructor. One obstacle that crops up in any setting, church-related or no, is students' pronounced cultural dualism, a kind of mental split that makes it hard to convey the peculiarities of what might be called Baudelaire's religious sensibility.

Like most of their peers, whose religious background is vague or nonexistent, my students will defend a sharp separation between the categories of the secular and the religious. Indeed, it's sometimes easier to alert nonreligious students to the Christian aura of Baudelaire's poems by the simple expedient of having them read selections from the Bible, especially those that emphasize the distance between a jealous God and his chosen people: Genesis 1–4 (the fall of mankind, the knowledge of evil, the death of Abel); Psalm 22.1 ("My God, my God, why hast thou forsaken me?"); Matthew 10.34 ("not to send peace, but a sword"). Some students immediately grasp the connections between such texts and the religious symbolism that inhabits poems like "L'Irrémédiable" ("The Irremediable") with its

— Emblèmes nets, tableau parfait
D'une fortune irrémédiable,
Qui donne à penser que le Diable
Fait toujours bien tout ce qu'il fait!   (160)

Pure emblems, a perfect tableau
Of an irremediable evil,
Which makes us think that the Devil
Does well what he chooses to do!   (161)

But other students, invoking the by now sacred notion of the play of the signi-
fier, will deny to Baudelaire's Devil any ontological status comparable to the
Evil One of the Hebrew Scriptures. Instructors willing to confront their classes
on the differences between real and intertextual demons would, I suggest, cre-
ate a rather lively discussion.

It's possible to set aside the question of Baudelaire's personal beliefs and to
examine how the poetry deployed a religious vocabulary still familiar to an in-
creasingly secularized French readership. This tactic, since it shifts classroom
attention away from matters of dogma to the stuff of literature, has much to
recommend it. Today, however, the vocabulary in question is often arcane. Lau-
rence M. Porter suggested to me that a good test of students' religious literacy
pertinent to Baudelaire would ask them to explain the sequence *encensoir . . .*
reposoir . . . ostensoir ("censer" . . . "altar-cloth" . . . "monstrance") in "Har-
monie du soir" (96; "The Harmony of Evening"). I suspect the failure rate
would be high, particularly since the post–Vatican II simplification of Catholic
liturgy (and, by extension, the liturgies of Lutherans and Anglicans) has all but
eliminated the censer and the monstrance. Barring a visit to a nearby cathedral,
it's always possible to borrow from the nearest Catholic or Anglican church a
catalog (well illustrated, in my experience) from a liturgical supply company.
Simpler yet, you can recommend browsing through the *New Catholic Encyclo-*
pedia. With the use of such visual aids I've found it easier to help students un-
derstand how Baudelaire, as in the example of "Harmonie du soir," moves the
reader back and forth from representational imagery (at once religious and
erotic) to an incantational harmony of pure sounds.

Since the religious aspect of Baudelaire's poetry is reducible neither to the
merely contingent appropriation of a traditional vocabulary nor to the poeti-
cizing of preexistent dogma, it's worth reminding students not just that France
has been a Catholic country but also that even nonbelievers were steeped in
the liturgy, imagery, ritual, and sacred texts of Catholicism. Although historians
make this clear (Driskel; Kselman; Zeldin), perhaps a more effective way of es-
tablishing the context is by reading a short story such as Honoré de Balzac's "La
Messe de l'athée," in which a freethinking doctor pays for (and even attends) a
memorial mass for one of his patients. Baudelaire himself, of course, liked to

cultivate similar puzzles and asymmetries. His friends included militant anti-clericals such as Gustave Courbet and staunch Catholics such as Jules Barbey d'Aurevilly. His journals reveal him as a believer in the power of prayer (Baude-laire, *Œuvres* [Ruff] 641–42; "Mon cœur mis à nu"), but he was also ready to defend (on behalf of Poe and Nerval) the rights to self-contradiction and sui-cide (in "Edgar Poe, sa vie et ses œuvres" [*Œuvres* (Ruff) 340–41]; "Lettre à Jules Janin" [652]; and "Réflexions sur quelques-uns de mes contemporains" [488]). On four occasions he published "La Rançon," with its straightforward argument for salvation by works of art and love: "L'homme a, pour payer sa rançon, / Deux champs au tuf profond et riche, / [. . .] / L'un est Art, et l'autre l'Amour" (316, 318) ("To pay his ransom, Man must take / Two fields of tufa, deep and rich, / [. . .] / One field is Art, the other, Love" [317, 319]). Yet this poem was omitted from Baudelaire's selections for the 1857 and 1861 editions of *Les Fleurs du Mal* in order to allow his religious pessimism fuller sway, as in a poem such as "Le Rêve d'un curieux" ("Dream of a Curious Man"), where the speaker imagines the revelation following death in these terms:

> J'étais mort sans surprise, et la terrible aurore
> M'enveloppait. — Eh, quoi! n'est-ce donc que cela?
> La toile était levée et j'attendais encore.   (280)

> Yes, I was dead, and in that dreadful dawn
> Was wrapped. —And what! That's all there is to tell?
> The screen was raised, and I was waiting still.   (281)

When read in conjunction with Samuel Beckett's *Waiting for Godot*, this poem can be discussed to reveal how nonclosural forms lend themselves to critical questioning of doctrines concerning the afterlife and the apocalypse.

Organizing readings and discussions to foreground the problematics of Baudelaire's religious sensibility encourages student participation. Once the in-structor has opted to avoid the usual reductions (Baudelaire the symbolist, Baudelaire the already deconstructed, Baudelaire the misogynist), there re-mains another set of hazards, of a kind all too frequently encountered in a church-related academic setting. Even the most sensitive religion-and-litera-ture approach to Baudelaire runs the risk of becoming a covertly doctrinaire assessment of his orthodoxy. M. H. Abrams, for example, could find in Baude-laire nothing more than the simple dualism of a life-denying Manichaeism (445). This kind of view, unhappily reinforced by publishers' recourse to illus-trations like the Carlos Schwab painting *Spleen and Ideal*, can't be sustained against a reading of complex poems. Consider how an allegory such as "Un Voyage à Cythère" ("A Voyage to Cythera") unfolds a relation between re-morseful disgust and the hope for composure that elevates self-knowledge into a spiritual vocation:

Dans ton île, ô Vénus! je n'ai trouvé debout
Qu'un gibet symbolique où pendait mon image . . .
— Ah! Seigneur! donnez-moi la force et le courage
De contempler mon cœur et mon corps sans dégoût!   (258)

Venus, in your black isle not one thing was erect
But the symbolic tree whereon my image hung.
Ah, Lord! I beg of you the courage and the strength
To take without disgust my body and my heart!   (259)

Blaise Pascal believed that all religion begins in self-hatred. This Jansenist maxim helps locate a drive toward transcendence that can be felt even in the darkest of the "Spleen" poems, when the anguish of spiritual defeat is heightened by awareness of a lost or unattainable alternative. On such a contrast is built "La Cloche fêlée" ("The Cracked Bell"):

Bienheureuse la cloche au gosier vigoureux
Qui, malgré sa vieillesse, alerte et bien portante,
Jette fidèlement son cri religieux,
Ainsi qu'un vieux soldat qui veille sous la tente!

Moi, mon âme est fêlée [. . .].   (144)

Blessed is the bell of clear and virile throat
Alert and dignified despite his rust,
Who faithfully repeats religion's notes
As an old soldier keeps a watchman's trust.

My spirit, though, is cracked [. . .].   (145)

Closer to Byron's gloom than to William Wordsworth's "egotistical sublime" (Jones), Baudelaire's poetry follows what he called the "tendance essentiellement démoniaque" of modern art—exemplified by Ludwig van Beethoven, Charles Maturin, Edgar Allan Poe—that sheds light on the "Lucifer latent qui est installé dans tout cœur humain" ("Œuvres [Ruff] 483; "Réflexions sur quelques-uns de mes contemporains") ("The essentially demonic tendency [. . .] the latent Lucifer who is installed in every human heart").

For the most part, although not exclusively, Baudelaire's demonology catalogs the devils within, who are themselves empowered by "la perversité primordiale de l'homme" (347; "Notes nouvelles sur Edgar Poe") ("the primordial perversity of man"). These inner promptings to perilous, evil actions are the subject of many prose poems (e.g., "Le Mauvais Vitrier" or "Assommons les pauvres!") and Baudelaire was inspired to construct an entire theory of the comic based on the premise that laughter is a satanic exulting in the misfortunes of others ("De l'essence du rire"). Despite critical efforts to elevate Baudelaire's sadism, misanthropy, and satanism to Holocaust-inspiring proportions, the powers of evil as Baudelaire sees them are lacking in grandeur. As "Au lecteur" ("To the Reader") puts it,

> Si le viol, le poison, le poignard, l'incendie,
> N'ont pas encor brodé de leurs plaisants dessins
> Le canevas banal de nos piteux destins,
> C'est que notre âme, hélas! n'est pas assez hardie.   (4)

> If slaughter, or if arson, poison, rape
> Have not as yet adorned our fine designs,
> The banal canvas of our woeful fates,
> It's only that our spirit lacks the nerve.   (5)

Henry James ("a great deal of lurid landscapes and unclean furniture") and Ferdinand Brunetière ("Ce n'est qu'un Satan d'hôtel garni, un Belzébuth de table d'hôte" ["This is only a Satan for a furnished room, a boarding-house Beelzebub"]) complained about the pettiness of Baudelaire's diabolism (qtd. in Baudelaire, *Œuvres* [Ruff] 37). Their judgment was not so much wrong as sentimental, a Romantic hankering for heroic evil and Miltonically proportioned Satans. Hannah Arendt, a careful post-Holocaust reader of Baudelaire, pointed out that "the trouble with Eichmann was precisely that so many were like him" (253). And as "Le Crépuscule du soir" ("Dusk") notes, even the demons of the night conduct themselves like sleepy businessmen: "Cependant des démons malsains dans l'atmosphère / S'éveillent lourdement, comme des gens d'affaire, / Et cognent en volant les volets et l'auvent" (192) ("Meanwhile, corrupting demons of the air / Slowly wake up like businessmen / And, flying, bump our shutters and our eaves [193; modified]). A strong ethical sense prevents Baudelaire from locating evil anywhere but in our own neighborhood, gazing back from our own mirrors.

T. S. Eliot, an author who can be taught profitably alongside Baudelaire, once expressed the worry that his French "semblable" ("kindred spirit") seemed to be trying to reinvent Christianity ("Baudelaire" [1964] 373). But this assumes too much naïveté on the part of Baudelaire, whose book was indicted not just for obscenity but for blasphemy as well. Baudelaire expressed astonishment when despite poems such as "Le Reniement de saint Pierre" ("St. Peter's Denial"), he was acquitted of the charge of outraging religion. What, after all, are we to make of a poem that begins with the speaker's asking, "Qu'est-ce que Dieu fait donc de ce flot d'anathèmes / Qui monte tous les jours vers ses chers Séraphins?" (264) ("What, then, has God to say of cursing heresies, / Which rise up like a flood at precious angels' feet?" [265]), and that ends, after the speaker's assessment of the Crucifixion, with this resolution?

— Certes, je sortirai, quant à moi, satisfait
D'un monde où l'action n'est pas la sœur du rêve;
Puissé-je user du glaive et périr par le glaive!
Saint Pierre a renié Jésus . . . il a bien fait!   (266)

—Believe it, as for me, I'll go out satisfied
From this world where the deed and dream do not accord;
Would I might wield the sword, and perish by the sword!
Peter rejected Jesus . . . he was justified!   (267)

When students read the corresponding story in John 13–19 and Matthew 26, the peculiar blend of homage and rejection in the poem emerges clearly. Matters can be complicated further by their looking at the evasive, sarcastic note that preceded this poem in the 1857 edition, where Baudelaire declared himself a perfect actor shaping his mind to every sophism and denied that he personally wished for "notre Sauveur Jésus-Christ, pour la Victime éternelle et volontaire, le rôle d'un conquérant, d'un Attila égalitaire et dévastateur" (*Œuvres* [Ruff] 127) (for "our Lord Jesus Christ, for the eternal, voluntary victim, the role of a conqueror, of a devastating, egalitarian Attila"). Sincere or not, Baudelaire has written a poem that challenges with brutal directness the Christian legacy of pacifism.

No discussion of the religious dimensions of *Les Fleurs du Mal* would be complete without scrutinizing certain love poems. Women are angelized, as in "Hymne" ("Hymn"):

A la très chère, à la très belle
Qui remplit mon cœur de clarté,
A l'ange, à l'idole immortelle,
Salut en l'immortalité!   (300)

To the dearest, to the most lovely
Who lights the heart in me,
To the angel immortal, the idol,
Praise to eternity!   (301)

or demonized, as in "Le Vampire" ("The Vampire"):

Toi qui, comme un coup de couteau,
Dans mon cœur plaintif es entrée;
Toi qui, forte comme un troupeau
De démons, vins, folle et parée [. . .].   (64)

You invaded my grieving heart
Like the sudden stroke of a blade;

You came like a powerful band
Of demons, wild and adorned.   (trans. mine)

This "erotic religion," as Pierre Emmanuel has brilliantly argued, is at the same time a "spiritual abyss" (72) in which the combat with woman mirrors a combat with God (167). But from a different perspective, one that examines the sociological consequences of religious beliefs, Baudelaire's polarizing of women lends itself all too easily to the substitution of discipline in place of love, of reward and punishment in place of acceptance. As "Le Revenant" ("The Ghost") concludes, "Moi, je veux régner par l'effroi" (132) ("Myself, I want to rule by fear" [133]). Do we still live under a cultural regime where women are assigned and reassigned to the roles of madonna and prostitute? By reading poems such as "A une Madone" (118–20; "To a Madonna") and "Une Charogne" (58–72; "A Carcass"), students can explore such issues and discuss the ties between Christianity and misogyny.

And in examining *"L'Héautontimorouménos"* (154–56; *"Heautontimoroumenos"* [the self-torturer]), it's possible to extend this discussion to the very limits of our ability to grasp how a religiously driven self-hatred can provoke sadomasochism. Baudelaire's honesty about such matters makes for uncomfortable reading, a discomfort perhaps felt more acutely in church-related schools. Many of these institutions originated from their founders' wishes to preserve an ethnically centered religiosity while preparing young believers for entry into the dominant middle class. In bolder relief than elsewhere these schools display the copresence of conflicting attitudes: a commitment to progress and a belief in the fallen, sinful, or demonic nature of the social world. The second attitude strikes many of my students as old-fashioned, despite their familiarity with Martin Luther's great hymn and its reminder that "still our ancient foe / Doth seek to work us woe" (*Handbook* 192). But even the most career-minded student will pause when confronted by Baudelaire's insistence that "Le commerce est satanique, parce qu'il est une des formes de l'égoïsme, et la plus basse et la plus vile" (*Œuvres* [Ruff] 639; "Mon cœur mis à nu") ("Commerce is satanic, because it is one of the forms of selfishness, and the basest, vilest one of them"). What Baudelaire set against the modern drive for wealth and status was by no means a sense of his own moral superiority, as "L'Examen de minuit" ("Midnight Examination") makes clear:

Nous avons blasphémé Jésus,
Des Dieux le plus incontestable!
Comme un parasite à la table
De quelque monstrueux Crésus,
Nous avons, pour plaire à la brute,
Digne vassale des Démons,

Insulté ce que nous aimons
Et flatté ce qui nous rebute [. . .].   (334)

We have blasphemed Jesus, the most
Incontestable of all Gods!
Like a parasite at the feast
Of some monstrous profligate,
We have, to please the brute,
That worthy vassal of Hell,
Insulted what we love,
And flattered the one we scorn [. . .].   (335)

As the rhymed opposition of *Jésus/Crésus* emphasizes, Baudelaire's religious sensibility includes a lively sense of the difference between aspiration and action, between the desired good and the accomplished evil (see Rom. 7.19). Baudelaire's solution to the problem of human sinfulness does not seem to have been religious faith in the ordinary sense, and he may have never put aside his ambiguity (Emmanuel 157). Yet as a poet he considered himself an alchemist of a fallen world and its debased language. The fragments of an epilogue for the second edition of *Les Fleurs du Mal* call on the angels to witness that

[. . .] j'ai fait mon devoir
Comme un parfait chimiste et comme une âme sainte.

Car j'ai de chaque chose extrait la quintessence,
Tu [Paris] m'as donné ta boue et j'en ai fait de l'or.   (*Œuvres* [Ruff] 129)

I have done my duty
Like a perfect chemist and a saintly soul.

Since I've extracted from each thing the quintessence,
You [the city of Paris] gave me your mud and from it I've made gold.

Baudelaire appeals to my students because he exemplifies the difficulty in which they sometimes find themselves: they are uneasily aware of the powers of evil within them and their world, and they have no tools other than faith and their own flawed imaginations to set about the work of transformation.

TEXT-CENTERED APPROACHES

Baudelaire as an Unknown
Roger Shattuck

The culminating exercise in the inorganic chemistry course I took many years ago was the distribution to each student of an "unknown" solution in a test tube for analysis and identification. We began with smell, taste, color, and texture and moved on to more sophisticated chemical tests and reactions. Most of us found it marvelous that the innocent-looking liquid would follow the rules of nature and yield evidence of its hidden ingredients to our clumsy procedures.

But in literary studies, we rarely read an "unknown." The works assigned in a literature course always come with the labels already attached—author's name, genre, historic period, literary school, critical reputation. We may or may not respond accordingly, but the excitement of discovery is diminished by information provided in advance.

For present purposes, I ask the reader to imagine two fairly straightforward courses. One is an introduction to French literature of the nineteenth and twentieth centuries. In the opening weeks the students have read works by Mme de Staël, Stendhal, and Victor Hugo. The other is a two-year core course in the humanities, with a general lecture and two discussion sections each week. Students have read in the first three semesters representative authors of antiquity, the Middle Ages, non-Western traditions, the Renaissance, the Enlightenment, and Romanticism. At this point in both courses students receive copies of three unidentified poems in French; in the humanities course they also receive two different English translations of each poem. Nothing is said about the poems, not even to suggest they are typical or great or inferior. The assignment is to read attentively, both silently and aloud, and to be prepared to comment on all aspects of the poems, from the most immediate and descriptive elements (sound, versification, rhythms, vocabulary, division into parts, literal situation and meaning) to questions of interpretation (motifs, figures and symbols, tone, personal and social attitudes) and of the placement of the poems within the development of literary conventions and traditions in modern Europe and the Americas. Students are urged not to waste their time trying to identify the author but to apply themselves instead to the poetic qualities of the selections, in the broadest meaning of the word *poetic*.

Now the instructor, who knows the information withheld from the students, must encourage full engagement with the poems by abstaining from leading comment. And the instructor may perform a careful explication of one of the poems to encourage a truly exploratory reading of the others. The hope is that the students, by themselves and in minimally guided discussions, will respond to all aspects of the works—sensuous, musical, imaginative, social, philosophical, and spiritual.

Here are the titles and opening stanzas of the three unknowns I would choose for the two courses described:

L'Albatros

Souvent, pour s'amuser, les hommes d'équipage
Prennent des albatros, vastes oiseaux des mers,
Qui suivent, indolents compagnons de voyage,
Le navire glissant sur les gouffres amers.   (14)

The Albatross

Often, when bored, the sailors of the crew
Trap albatross, the great birds of the seas,
Mild travellers escorting in the blue
Ships gliding on the ocean's mysteries.   (15)

Harmonie du soir

Voici venir les temps où vibrant sur sa tige
Chaque fleur s'évapore ainsi qu'un encensoir;
Les sons et les parfums tournent dans l'air du soir;
Valse mélancolique et langouroux vertige!   (96)

The Harmony of Evening

Now it is nearly time when, quivering on its stem,
Each flower, like a censer, sprinkles out its scent;
Sounds and perfumes are mingling in the evening air;
Waltz of a mournfulness and languid vertigo!   (97)

Une Charogne

Rappelez-vous l'objet que nous vîmes, mon âme,
   Ce beau matin d'été si doux;
Au détour d'un sentier une charogne infâme
   Sur un lit semé de cailloux [. . .].   (58)

A Carcass

Remember, my love, the object we saw
   That beautiful morning in June:
By a bend in the path a carcass reclined
   On a bed sown with pebbles and stones [. . .].   (59)

A few questions could help the students' investigations without limiting their responses. What aspects of the verse and the sound appear most suggestive to you? Does the poem divide into parts, or does it form a seamless whole? Identify two or three key words. What pointers would you give to a person planning to read the poem aloud for an audience? Does the poem contain allusions to conventional literary themes and to other works and events? A poem, read closely and deeply, yields so much evidence about itself that one is never reading blind.

With a minimum of guidance from the instructor, a good discussion could bring out many important aspects of these works. The four quatrains of "L'Albatros" are built of sonorous, mainly end-stopped lines with alternating rhyme. Three stanzas tell the simple story of a magnificent bird taken captive on shipboard and prevented from walking on the deck by its immense dragging wings. The fourth stanza, attached like the moral of a fable by Aesop or La Fontaine, compares the bird to a poet. The exceptional powers that allow both to soar, literally or figuratively, to great altitudes above the earth also condemn bird and poet to the condition of a crippled giant when they are condemned to exile on the ground. The association of poetic genius with avian flight forms one of the conventional figures of Romantic poetry in Goethe, Shelley, Hugo, and many others. The author of this poem brings out the underside of that figure and treats the grounded poet-genius as a pathetic specimen who will be mocked and victimized by ordinary mortals. The last line sums up the paradoxical predicament in a highly quotable formula: "Ses ailes de géant l'empêchent de marcher" (16) ("He cannot walk, his wings get in the way" [trans. mine]). Though the poem may be based on an incident from the author's experience, it reads like a well-executed exercise in classic alexandrines on the assigned subject of an albatross. To read this poem aloud effectively enough to elicit pity requires an expressive voice but no great subtlety of interpretation. A polished poem of minor accomplishments.

"L'Harmonie du soir," also composed in quatrains of end-stopped alexandrines, relies deeply on surface qualities of sound, repetitive and contrasting.

That swaying pattern of sound evokes both an expansive Romantic landscape of sunset and an implied sequence of the mass being celebrated. After the suspension points, the last line breaks away from the description of a poetic landscape and carries us toward events looming in the poet's mind. But that breakaway line is held firmly in place by the versification, particularly by the two repeated rhymes, -ige and -oir, a shrill, acute sound contrasted with a subsiding lament. Those insistent sounds knit together the entire poem, otherwise formed out of nearly random lines. The final line fails to close the poem by repetition as one expects, even though the sounds conform to the pattern established. How does one read this oddly dispersed yet tightly constructed poem? Two words give us a clue. *Tournent* (line 3) connects powerfully with *vertige* (line 4, prepared by all the other *v*-sounds in the stanza, particularly *valse*) to convey the sensation that we ourselves are drawn into the turning motion of these lines. For they are describing the sunset, the magic moment in which the shifting alignment of our eyes with sun, horizon, and the abyss of the skies may give us vertigo. We ourselves are turning with the earth, and suddenly we can feel it. We could almost fall off. The patterned sounds, the religious imagery connected to the rhyme -oir, the sense of quiet fulfillment usually associated with sunset—these elements tend to lull us into a surrender to nature and even to death. But the last lines startle us, both with the unprepared welling up of a memory and with a moment of terror caused by the revelation of the earth's naked and palpable rotation beneath our feet.

Reading "Harmonie du soir" requires a masterful command of poetic effects in order to create a ground of monotony and fascination against which the final lines will declare both self-affirmation and physical fear. This poet has written a lullaby that metamorphoses into an obsessive vision of our precarious existence on the surface of the globe.

CHAROGNE From the hideous word used as title until the last line celebrating "mes amours décomposés!" (62) ("my decomposed loves" [trans. mine]), the twelve stanzas of "Une Charogne" mock the traditions of Romanticism that provide the motifs of the first two poems. Even the versification, which alternates the sonorities of the alexandrine with the more familiar beat of the eight-syllable line, undermines any sustained effect of sublimity. The first stanza rhymes *âme* ("soul," here used as a lyric form of address to the poet's beloved) with *infâme* ("infamous," a strong pejorative linked to exposure and decomposition). And the rhyme gives birth to the word that will appear in the next stanza: *femme* ("woman"), rudely brought down from the idealism of *âme* into the humiliation of *lubrique* ("lubricious"). Spurning all ideals, these lines obliterate the conventions of romantic love, the beauty of woman, the attractiveness of natural landscape, the mystery of life. In the first nine stanzas, the spectacle of a stinking, vermin-infested animal carcass infects the rest of the world around it with decay and horror. The Arcadian delights of a walk in the country with one's lover are overcome by a hideous vision of death in life, where the only "flower" in the landscape (st. 4) is the bloated carcass itself with its putrid stench. The woman nearly faints out of disgust.

Almost superfluously, stanzas 10 and 11 rub in the anti-Romantic moral of the tale. The poet speaks directly to his lovely companion and declares, in effect, "This is what you will soon look like, my lovely angel." Sarcasm drains the endearments of their usual meaning. Then, in a reversal that can also be read as sarcasm directed at the very act of writing a poem, the last stanza appeals to the ancient immortality topos. The poet says cajolingly that his mistress may die and disappear, but these immortal lines of poetry will allow her fame to live on. By now, the disenchanted Romanticism and cynical explicitness of the earlier descriptive stanzas make it difficult to locate the tone of the last stanza. Does it ridicule poetry? Or does it redeem poetry in the face of the most hideous physical decay?

The seventh stanza uses the term *étrange musique* ("strange music") for the poem's precarious posture between beauty and corruption. And, given the situation of French poetry at mid-nineteenth century, these twelve stanzas make a truly strange music. Written in highly formal verse based on a classical tradition of balance, order, convention, and control, the lines also introduce a rowdy gang of words utterly alien to that kind of poetry. The poem seems to be written on a wager about using the very term *charogne*, along with other outcasts such as *suant* ("sweating"), *putride* ("putrid"), and *ordure* ("filth"). Rhyming *Nature* with *pourriture* ("rottenness"), and *passion* with *infection* can be read as a poetic sneer at nature and at passion. The music in this iridescent poem is so strange and alternating that it deserves two or three different oral performances to test its attitudes toward nature, love, death, beauty, and poetry itself. Both the German poet Rainer Maria Rilke and the French painter Paul Cézanne found a source of exaltation and inspiration in this perverse pastoral.

Read blind in this fashion, the three poems will, I believe, strike students as fairly different from one another in subject, form, treatment, and quality. Some students will never respond to them, especially students who have to use the English versions and cannot hear the music of the French. Similar experiments I have made in literature courses lead me to predict that most students will attribute the three poems to different authors and will be surprised to learn that they are the work of one poet. In both the courses imagined, the small introduction to French literature and the large lecture-discussion course in humanities, the blind consideration of the poems could provide the most challenging and rewarding part of the Baudelaire segment. What then, in the time remaining, would one want to tell students about this mid-nineteenth-century French poet?

If the students have read well and listened deeply to Baudelaire's strange music, it will be possible to tell them, even to show them, that he changed the course of European poetry, that he is the pivotal figure for French, English, Spanish, German, American, and even Russian poetry. The first step in this demonstration is to point out Baudelaire's inventiveness and influence in two other domains: he was a strong partisan critic of literature, the arts, and the spectacle of modern life in Paris at its apogee; he was the principal inventor and practitioner of the new intermediate genre, the prose poem. If possible, students should now read the beginning and the end of "Le Salon de 1846," including "L'Héroisme de la vie moderne" (*Œuvres* [Ruff] 227); "Notes nouvelles sur Edgar Poe" (346; Poe's ideas on pure poetry made a deep mark on Baudelaire); and selections from "Le Peintre de la vie moderne" (546). Of the prose poems, "Le Confiteor de l'artiste" (149), "L'Invitation au voyage" (159), and "Le Mauvais Vitrier" (151) will exhibit the variety of that collection of experimental writing.

With these additional readings, the instructor has a more solid basis on which to point out the degree to which Baudelaire, like many great artists, is a poet of contradictions. No wonder the three poems, read blind, do not seem to belong to one poetic sensibility. Baudelaire will not cohere in his entire work, which covered almost three decades, even though individual essays and poems attain a strong unity of effect. It is finally worth listing the conflicts and contradictions that weave through Baudelaire's works, because every attentive reader will find a different set. One can find a quotation in Baudelaire to demonstrate his support of both sides of the following set of opposites. Sometimes he changed his mind. Sometimes he understood that a full-grown sensibility can embrace and employ both terms. Sometimes he was simply torn between two attitudes and alternated between them. The following list of opposites represents a rash simplification of subtle ideas and feelings in Baudelaire's works, but it has some pedagogical usefulness as a basis of discussion:

Traditional versification employed with vigor and resourcefulness. Nontraditional subjects reinforced by shocking vocabulary and imagery

Bitter hatred of the pettiness of his contemporaries. Jubilant observation and celebration of "the heroism of modern life"

Close association of art with moral standards (*la morale*) and social usefulness. Separation of art from moral standards and social usefulness (art for art's sake)

Poetry as honest revelation of even the most atrocious truths. Poetry as the deceitful product of devices and ruses practiced by a consummate actor, even a charlatan

Poetry as the record of cultivating one's most intimate suffering. Poetry as the rare flower that triumphs over suffering and despair

Attentiveness to nature as the living symbol of the cosmos. Scorn of vulgar nature as inferior to the refinements of the artificial and the artistic

The infinite and elevating charm of women. The hideous and paralyzing baseness of women

The profound truth of the Christian doctrine of original sin. A strong attraction to blasphemy, satanism, and a reluctance to renounce sin and evil

Far from exhaustive or even satisfactory, such a catalog suggests the multiple dimensions and long reach of Baudelaire's thought.

After surveying the variety and intensity of Baudelaire's works, a student is better prepared to appreciate Baudelaire's influence on European literature, both on poets and on critical opinion about modern poetry and the arts. Only extensive reading in a great number of languages can convey a full awareness of Baudelaire's presence among us in poetry, painting, art criticism, and aesthetics. A survey of translations provides a parallel index of his influence. For the two imaginary courses I have described, I would suggest that the instructor summarize the work of three critics and urge interested students to look at their essays: T. S. Eliot, Jean-Paul Sartre, and Erich Auerbach. All three write out of deep personal conviction about the notion of poetry and the figure of Baudelaire in modern culture. And they write also as if they were responding directly to one another in a lively discussion.

Calling him a counter-Romantic and "a fragmentary Dante," Eliot respects Baudelaire's sense of sin and evil as evidence of his "unsuccessful struggle toward the spiritual life" ("Baudelaire" [1932] 336, 339). Honesty and sincerity in facing suffering qualify Baudelaire as "man enough for damnation" and worthy of his "high vocation" (344).

In a strongly polemical two-hundred-page introduction to Baudelaire's work, Sartre refuses the poet any claim to honesty and sincerity. Too weak to redraw the boundaries of the world to fit his temperament as a true existentialist would do, Baudelaire accepted the authority of bourgeois-Christian morality without trying too hard to live up to it. "He preserved the Good in order to be able to do Evil, and, if he did Evil, it was in order to pay tribute to the Good" (99). Such alleged hypocrisy on Baudelaire's part provokes Sartre's most damning denunciation: bad faith. This form of hypocrisy successfully deceives itself and leads the soul to hide from itself "by perpetual flight" (100). Sartre's relentless psychological analysis quotes Baudelaire's writings not as poetry deserving literary interpretation but as pure biographical self-revelation and self-degradation.

A German scholar who had to flee the Nazis and came to the United States, Auerbach had read Sartre's introduction and answered it in an essay entitled "The Aesthetic Dignity of the *Fleurs du Mal*." Leaving aside Eliot's concern with Baudelaire's spiritual life and Sartre's harsh psychological verdict, Auerbach discusses the resources of Baudelaire's mixed poetic style and the authenticity of his self-dramatization in a tradition going back to Petrarch. In the light of a "crisis of our civilization" that Auerbach sees after World War II, he affirms the value of *Les Fleurs du Mal* with all its horrors. "It is his unswerving despair which gave him the dignity he has for us" (224).

Obviously, in a course or seminar whose announced topic is Baudelaire, the device of using unknowns, of reading blind, will not lend itself readily. But an equivalent discipline can be adopted as a means of encouraging close and careful reading of the works themselves before the introduction of biographical and historical considerations. The order of events in teaching concerns all of us.

I also recommend that any course spend whatever time can be afforded on examining and commenting on portraits of Baudelaire, painted and photographic. Almost all of them are reproduced in black and white in the excellent *Œuvres complètes* edited by Marcel Ruff. Above all, students should see slides of and meditate on the differences between the portraits, each executed in two versions, by two major painters who were Baudelaire's friends and close associates. Edouard Manet's 1862 etching and the small background figure in *La Musique aux Tuileries* (1862) show Baudelaire as a jaunty, top-hatted dandy in an elegant social setting. Gustave Courbet's intensely painted oil portrait of the poet (1849) and the corresponding figure in the immense allegorical composition *L'Atelier* (1855) show Baudelaire intently reading a book, smoking the pipe of the imagination, and letting his left hand dangle downward into a half-defined area of luminous ruddiness. Here is another pair of embraced opposites: the posed and costumed social being and the self-absorbed, meditating man of letters indifferent to the world around him. These two double portraits, once seen, make it impossible to remain blind toward Baudelaire as a coruscating sensibility and a physical presence on the scene of modern literature.

Let's Start with Words

Eléonore M. Zimmermann

> O toison, moutonnant jusque sur l'encolure!
> —"La Chevelure"

A. She said that these poems are short and that we really have to know all the vocabulary. Did you look at "La Chevelure" ("Head of Hair") yet? It's assigned for tomorrow, and already in the first line there are three words I don't know. Do you know the meaning of *toison*?

B. No, and it's not in the *Mini Larousse*. They have *TGV* in really big characters, but no *toison*. We'd better look it up in a bigger dictionary.

A. My *French-English Concise Larousse* [*Larousse Dictionnaire*] lists "1. [*pelage*] fleece," and "2. [*chevelure*] mop of hair." The second meaning makes some sense. But do you know what *pelage* means?

B. Nope.

A. Do you know what *fleece* means?

B. I'm not sure. In my *HarperCollins College Dictionary* [*Collins First Harper*] they also give "fleece" as the first translation of *toison*. So we'd better be sure about the exact meaning of *fleece*. Here we are: my *Webster's Collegiate Dictionary* defines *fleece* as "the coat of wool covering a sheep or similar animal."

A. So Baudelaire replaces "la chevelure," the mop of hair, with a word that really applies to animals?

B. It sure seems that way: the HarperCollins puts "de mouton"—that means "of sheep," doesn't it?—in parentheses before giving "fleece" as the translation. And look at the first line of the poem! The word after *toison* is *moutonnant*. That must be related to *mouton*.

A. Well, before we get into that, let's make sure about *toison*. Let's use my roommate John's *Le Robert and Collins French-English, English-French Dictionary*. John swears by it. Here we are: "a) [*mouton*] fleece." So that's the same word as in the other dictionaries. And it is again linked to sheep. But on the next line—this is interesting—this dictionary has "La Toison d'or," which is translated as "The Golden Fleece." You remember that story about Jason from the mythology course . . .

No such conversation has, of course, ever taken place: students do not have a whole collection of dictionaries in their rooms. However, while it may stretch our imaginations, it nevertheless illustrates what problems the conscientious student who wants to understand "La Chevelure" (50–52) might face. Let us go one step further and assume there are students who are even more conscientious and do what most of their teachers ask them to do, namely, use a French-French dictionary. New problems will arise. In *Le Petit Robert* (1968) they would find under *toison*, first, "pelage laineux des ovidés, ensemble des poils mêlés de suint de ces animaux" ("woolen coat of the ovine races, whole of the hair mixed with suint of these animals"). This confusing vocabulary may prompt them to close the book. Should they find the courage to read on, they would be rewarded by an allusion to "La Toison d'or" and then discover that the first line of "La Chevelure" is quoted, preceded by the information that in the middle of the nineteenth century the word *toison* could mean "Chevelure très fournie ou d'apparence laineuse" ("very thick or woolly-appearing hair"). *Le Petit Larousse illustré* (1991) would inform them, more succinctly and less confusingly, that *toison* means "(1) Laine d'un mouton; pelage abondant d'autres animaux. (2) Chevelure abondante" ("wool of a sheep; thick coat of other animals; rich hair"). "La Toison d'or," however, is not mentioned and can be found only in the second part of the dictionary.

Should the students then go on to look up *moutonnant*, the second difficult word in the first line of "La Chevelure," they would not find it in any of the English-French dictionaries except the *Robert and Collins*, where "[*mer*] flecked with white horses; (*littér.*) [*collines*] rolling" may strain both their knowledge of English idiom and their imagination. *Nonchaloir* will bring worse trouble.

This illustrates a fundamental difficulty in teaching *Les Fleurs du Mal* that students always mention: the vocabulary presents a real obstacle to their understanding of the poems. For French-speaking teachers, such a complaint may at first seem surprising: if asked to come up with the name of a writer using an extensive vocabulary, they would think of Victor Hugo rather than Baudelaire. Yet, obviously, the problem of vocabulary must be dealt with in Baudelaire before we can hope to proceed further. To me, the solution can never be to give the students a translation of the text, because the impact of the poem in French, once lost, is almost impossible to recover. Various other possibilities suggest themselves. Depending on the level of the class, vocabulary sheets could be distributed with the assignment, or the poem might be read in class with some explanations before it is assigned as homework. The instructor might also choose to use an anthology such as André Hurtgen's *Tous les poèmes pour le cours avancé*, where difficult words are either translated or explained in the margin, and the marginal notes could then be expanded on or corrected by the instructor.

This difficulty on the level of vocabulary need not, however, be only a vexing problem. As we help our students to understand and, we hope, to appreciate the richness of Baudelaire's poetry, focusing on vocabulary can serve as a starting point to alert them to one essential feature of literature, and of poetry in particular, namely, semantic density.

Thus, as a first step, the various translations or explanations of a word allow the instructor to point out that words in poetry frequently have more than one meaning and to stress that it would, in fact, be contrary to the nature of poetry to reduce them to only one. "La Chevelure" is particularly well suited to make such a point. The complexities of its vocabulary, as illustrated by our brief imaginary dialogue, might discourage students if we start with this poem; but those complexities might fascinate them if we introduce it later in the course.

Because of the language barrier, but also because of changes in our daily lives, education, and general frame of reference since the nineteenth century, students will need a little help with this poem. Even if they are lucky enough to find an allusion to the Golden Fleece in their dictionary—and happen to know what it means—it would take a very unusual student to inquire whether this allusion might be relevant to the meaning of the first line of "La Chevelure." Today's students will not have gone through the experience, still common a generation ago, of waving white handkerchiefs to friends departing by train or boat, and consequently the last line of the first stanza, "Je la veux agiter dans l'air comme un mouchoir!" ("I'll shake it like a kerchief in the air!") is unlikely to make them think of travel and adventure, the discovery of exotic lands suggested by the allusion to the Golden Fleece.

Students further need to be told that the use of *toison* for hair was not unusual in the nineteenth century. The instructor also needs to explain that *moutonnant* ("billowing"), which is linked to *mouton* in French, is frequently used to describe cloud formations.

In working with vocabulary, the instructor will want to stress the importance of connotation for the interpretation of a poem. Any definition of a word carries its own associations, and these should be brought out in class, discussed, and at times redirected. For example, the idea that *toison* "really applies to animals," as stated by student A in the above dialogue, especially if strengthened by one of the meanings of *encolure*, "neck" (of horse or person), and by the relation of *moutonnant* to *mouton*, might cause students to conclude that Baudelaire is portraying women like animals, a conclusion arguably supported by his purported attitude toward women, what with his mistresses, and so on. This idea could lead to a reductive reading, closing students' minds to the richness and variety of the imagery and to the poem's complex sensuality.

For a fairly sophisticated class, the changing meaning and associations of a word like *toison* may introduce a discussion about how artists' historical context determines their choice of words and how, in turn, the readers' understanding of these words—which is determined by the readers' historical and linguistic context—necessarily influences the response to the poem. While nineteenth-century readers would have come across texts where *toison* referred to hair, they would also have been familiar with the myth of the *toison d'or*. We may assume that such knowledge informed their understanding of "La Chevelure." It would seem desirable to re-create their—and Baudelaire's—understanding of this particular word in our reading of the poem. But it can be a subject of discussion in class, as it is among critics, whether such a re-creation is necessary for every poem or work of art. I return to this question in discussing "Le Cygne" (172–76; "The Swan").

We must start with words to understand a poem. Words, however, do not mean in isolation. As Stéphane Mallarmé stated in *Crise de vers*, they "s'allument de reflets réciproques" (366) ("their reciprocal reflections illuminate them"). After a basic meaning has been established, the next step must be to examine the way the words are used, the context they are given.

This method is particularly rewarding in a poem like "La Chevelure," with its highly original juxtaposition of words. To help students to perceive this originality, to really re-create in their minds what they first see only as black marks on the page, I like to suggest that they make a list of words or word combinations that seem odd or unusual in the poem they are reading. The results of this exercise keep surprising me: their lists are quite short. But when we read the poem from a contextual point of view in class, we agree that there is something striking in almost every line.

This exercise leads us to uncover some of the basic metaphors of the poem. It also makes it apparent how the images shift. Students can be asked to read "L'Albatros" ("The Albatross") and "La Musique" ("Music"), poems with sustained similes whose meaning is clearly stated in lines such as, respectively, "Le Poëte est semblable au prince des nuées" (16) ("The poet resembles the prince of clouds" [trans. mine]) and "La musique souvent me prend comme une mer!" (138) ("Music will often take me like the sea!" [139]). This reading should lead students to appreciate the complexity of the figures we encounter in "La Chevelure," where Baudelaire is not content with one simile: the *toison*-hair becomes a "mouchoir" (line 5) ("kerchief"), "forêt" (8) ("forest"), "houle" (13) ("swell" [trans. mine]), "mer d'ébène" (14) ("sea of ebony"), "noir océan" (22) ("black ocean"), "cheveux bleus" (26) ("blue head of hair"), "pavillon" (26) ("tent"), "crinière" (31) ("mane"), "oasis" (34), and "gourde" (34) ("drinking-gourd"). The hair is complemented by perfume, with which it is associated from line 2 on; both hair and perfume carry the "I" toward the world of dreams and the past.

Once the students have started to focus on words in context, their lists of strange word combinations grow longer, and we can then discuss another basic characteristic of Baudelaire's poetry. Since most students will have read "Correspondances" ("Correspondences"), they will pick up echoes, in "La Chevelure," of the famous pronouncement "Les parfums, les couleurs et les sons se répondent" (18) ("So perfumes, colours, sounds may correspond" [19]). It may require several readings before students realize the strangeness and suggestive richness of the hair being likened to a "mer d'ébène" sheltering "Un port retentissant où mon âme peut boire / A grands flots le parfum, le son et la couleur" (lines 16–17; "A sounding harbor where my soul can drink / From great floods subtle tones, perfumes and hues"). To perceive such richness requires that the students let words create images in their minds, images that at first seem incompatible but then merge to create a world of their own, the world of Baudelaire's poem.

If we can teach students to do that, it will be easier for them to discover that such unexpected juxtapositions of words lead, in "La Chevelure," not only to the fusion of all senses as predicated by "Correspondances" but also, in a way fundamental to Baudelaire's aesthetics, to a sensualization of the spiritual and a spiritualization of the sensual. It is the *âme*, the "soul," that drinks, that gulps the perfume, the sound, and the color, all contained in the ebony-colored sea, where ships, gliding through the gold and the moire, embrace the glory of a pure sky trembling with eternal heat (lines 18–20). There the poet is rocked infinitely in perfumed leisure. He seeks to abolish the passage of time by fusing past, present, and future, as he fuses all senses and his soul. This ebony sea quenches and should always quench his thirst; it is a "drinking-gourd," which allows him to smell/drink the wine of memory (lines 34–35). The memory that the poet sets out to rescue from extinction (4, 6) reaches back into a distant past, including the rocking motion, the "bercement" (24–25) that, in French, suggests cradling a child. The poet wills his memory into the future by his use of the future tense (11, 21, 24, 32), his energetic "je veux" ("I want" [trans. mine]) of the first stanza, and his expressed resolve in the last ("Longtemps! toujours! ma main dans ta crinière lourde / Sèmera le rubis, la perle et le saphir") ("For a long time! always! in your heavy mane / My hand will scatter ruby, pearl, and sapphire" [trans. mine]).

In "Hymne à la Beauté" ("Hymn to Beauty") Baudelaire proclaimed that the three elements of beauty are "[r]ythme, parfum, lueur" (44) ("rhythm, perfume, light" [trans. mine]). Their combination characterizes what I have called (*Poétiques*, ch. 3) the "poèmes de la plénitude" ("poems of fulfillment"), such as "Harmonie du soir" (96; "The Harmony of Evening"), "Le Balcon" (72–74; "The Balcony"), "Parfum exotique" (48; "Exotic Perfume"), "L'Invitation au voyage" (108–10; "Invitation to the Voyage"), and "*Mœsta et errabunda*" (128–30; Lat., "Sorrowful and wandering" [365]). An instructor might wish to introduce some of these poems to complement the discoveries made in reading "La Chevelure." All three elements of beauty can be found in "La Chevelure": the rhythm of the poem, of the waves, of the rocking motion; the perfume of the hair; and the light that penetrates all. "L'Albatros" and "La Musique," where the preferred trope is the simile, do not present such fusions, nor do the late poems.

Let us now turn to one of these late poems, the much-explicated "Le Cygne" ("The Swan") from the "Tableaux parisiens" ("Parisian Scenes") and start our reading again by examining what problems its vocabulary may present for the students. The problems differ radically from those encountered in "La Chevelure." To define them is to become aware that, at this time, Baudelaire had developed a new approach to poetry, an approach that the students might now be equipped to recognize. The juxtaposition of these two different aesthetics might enable them to understand something about the evolution of Baudelaire's art.

In "Le Cygne" (172–76), starting with words mostly means starting with names. The story of Andromache; "l'homme d'Ovide" (line 25) ("the man in Ovid's book"); the geography of Paris; and, to some extent, the architectural history of the city ("le nouveau Carrousel" [6]) ("the modern Carrousel") and "Le vieux Paris n'est plus" (7) ("the old Paris is gone") have to be explained before some poetic order can emerge from the "bric-à-brac confus" (12) ("the jumbled bric-à-brac") Baudelaire introduces. The instructor can find most of the needed explanations in the footnotes to any critical edition of *Les Fleurs du Mal* (or in Terdiman, this volume). Once more, the instructor has the opportunity, in presenting these explanations, to start from the meaning of words and then to introduce questions about poetry and art in general.

It is worth pointing out that, more explicitly even than the allusion to the Golden Fleece in "La Chevelure," the persistence of the Greco-Roman mythology in "Le Cygne" illustrates the reliance of the poet on the literary tradition of his time to nourish his creative impulse.

The class may then be led to discuss the importance of the cultural context to our understanding of a work of art. "Le Cygne" is, in some ways, a comment on the fleeting nature of this cultural context. For the instructor who shows the students a modern map of Paris with the Louvre and the Carrousel and, if possible, an old engraving of pre-Haussmann Paris, the opportunity presents itself to discuss the question whether an appreciation of a work of art depends on the readers' knowledge of what it meant to the artist's contemporaries and, further, whether this dependency applies to all works of art or only to some.

"Le Cygne" could also be used to introduce another set of questions debated by literary critics, that of the relevance of an artist's biography. Critics have commented on the factual presuppositions—Baudelaire's trip to exotic islands, the existence of the beautiful Dorothy remembered in "Bien loin d'ici" (342; "Very Far from France") or of the dedicatee of "A une Malabaraise" (318–20; "To a Girl of Malabar")—and have used elements of Baudelaire's biography for a psychoanalytic reading: for example, does the widow Andromache haunt his imagination because she stands for his widowed mother? However, I would be most hesitant to raise these questions with college students, who tend to treat artists of the past like modern movie stars and are all too eager to discover the secrets of their lives. If they read the poems in the light of the author's life instead of in terms of the words he uses, any effort to make them see poems as different from tabloid accounts will be futile.

More to the point, and less dangerously, the instructor might introduce the question of the role of the poet's persona, the *je*, the I, present in these poems. If, when the students first start to read "Le Cygne," they are encouraged once more to look at the juxtaposition of words, they may be shown how in the first line, "Andromaque, je pense à vous!" ("Andromache, I think of you"), the poet puts Andromache and the I side by side but also separates them: "je pense **à** vous" ("I think **of** you"). Instead of melting into the past as he did in "La Chevelure," resurrecting it to relive it and project it into the future, the I of "Le Cygne" looks with his mind's eye at a fixed and unchanging past: "Et mes chers souvenirs sont plus lourds que des rocs" (line 32) ("And my dear memories are heavier than stone").

The poem consists of a series of self-contained descriptions rather than images dissolving into one another. The I, who in "La Chevelure" plunged into the black sea of the woman's hair to let himself be rocked by sensual memories, here distances himself from what he evokes in the poem.

The I of "Le Cygne" sees and judges the past from the distance of the present. He expresses feelings *about* the past. The strangely disparate memories summoned in the poem are linked by these feelings, feelings of loss, of commiseration. The reader may sense that here, as in "La Chevelure," there is a very personal source to the sequence of images Baudelaire chooses. But, more important, one is struck by the fact that the images lack the fluidity of a personal world of dreams so characteristic of the former poem.

Words are the stuff of poetry. This statement is so obvious that most of us never consider its meaning. We may, however, find it worthwhile to repeat it to our students. They live in a world of flickering images—TV, video, film—and of sound, which are a constant background noise to their lives. Many students express a fear of poetry, perhaps because words, difficult, precise, carefully chosen words, are not part of their daily environment and seem hard to access. Yet words can be called up in times of need and in times of joy to help us recognize our feelings and our perceptions. They are much more permanent than images on a screen, and they are always available.

But, of course, be they in English or in French, words must first of all be understood. This understanding in itself requires an effort. When a poet of Baudelaire's stature has crafted them into a poem, they can be repeated again and again, each time revealing another shade of meaning. The condensation that is the basic law of poetry makes words similar to Mallarmé's fan, which can be unfolded to display its hidden message.

I have tried to show how starting with words can be a fruitful approach in teaching poetry. More than just a means of understanding a poem, it can also serve to raise basic questions about all poetry. Specifically, it can help us appreciate the evolution of Baudelaire's art, thus opening our eyes to the diversity of his œuvre.

Using Translation in Explicating
Les Fleurs du Mal: "La Cloche fêlée"

Judd Hubert

In upper-division and graduate courses, teachers can use translations to help students acquire a better understanding of the original poems. A translation of a French poem creates a new English poem capable of standing on its own while providing, through paraphrase, a critical interpretation of the original text. For this reason, several different renditions of the same poem, by proposing different paraphrases and hence divergent readings, can lead to valuable semantic discussions centering, of course, on the original. Paradoxically, a mistranslation may lead to a better explication than a felicitous rendition. Moreover, in pointing out deficiencies in a translation, the teacher can introduce valuable remarks concerning grammar and vocabulary.

Translators can trot out literal or word-for-word translations with the sole purpose of acquainting their readers with the surface meaning of the text, or they can compose a major poem inspired by the original, or they can strike some sort of balance between these two opposite approaches. Naturally, a translator would love to produce a poetic masterpiece faithful in every respect to the original. But such triumphs seldom if ever occur. James McGowan has in all probability provided felicitous English equivalents of *Les Fleurs du Mal* with greater frequency than any other translator. Wisely, he follows Baudelaire's rhyme schemes only when he finds it suitable to his purpose. Indeed, rhyming very often forces the translator to twist and turn to such an extent that meanings get lost in the shuffle. Most frequently, McGowan resorts to blank verse interspersed with occasional rhymes and assonances. In translating "La Cloche fêlée" (144; "The Cracked Bell"), a quatorzain rather than a proper sonnet, McGowan gradually moves from assonance to rhyme, an approach consistent with Baudelaire's unusual "rime normande" ("visual rhyme") *hiver-s'élever*, a deliberate phonetic break in the rhyming scheme that not only concretizes the crack in the bell but also somehow puts poetic composition and chimes on the same track.

> Il est amer et doux, pendant les nuits d'hiver,
> D'écouter, près du feu qui palpite et qui fume,
> Les souvenirs lointains lentement s'élever
> Au bruit des carillons qui chantent dans la brume.
>
> Bienheureuse la cloche au gosier vigoureux
> Qui, malgré sa vieillesse, alerte et bien portante,
> Jette fidèlement son cri religieux,
> Ainsi qu'un vieux soldat qui veille sous la tente!

Moi, mon âme est fêlée, et lorsqu'en ses ennuis
Elle veut de ses chants peupler l'air froid des nuits,
Il arrive souvent que sa voix affaiblie

Semble le râle épais d'un blessé qu'on oublie
Au bord d'un lac de sang, sous un grand tas de morts,
Et qui meurt, sans bouger, dans d'immenses efforts.

How bittersweet it is on winter nights
To hear old recollections raise themselves
Around the flickering fire's wisps of light
And through the mist, in voices of the bells.

Blessed is the bell of clear and virile throat
Alert and dignified despite his rust,
Who faithfully repeats religion's notes
As an old soldier keeps a watchman's trust.

My spirit, though, is cracked; when as she can
She chants to fill the cold night's emptiness,
Too often can her weakening voice be said

To sound the rattle of a wounded man
Beside a bloody pool, stacked with the dead,
Who cannot budge, and dies in fierce distress!   (145)

Looking for differences between original and translation in the first four lines of the poem, I find that duality in syntax, though not necessarily in concepts, has given way to, so to speak, a blending or collapsing of terms: "amer et doux" has become "bittersweet," an exact equivalent in meaning, while the felicitous "Around the flickering fire's wisps of light" provides a synesthetic rendition of "près du feu qui palpite et qui fume." In contriving this highly imaginative and nonetheless faithful translation, McGowan has had to sacrifice a duality essential to a bell, which inevitably consists of two distinct parts: the bell proper, whose vibrations provide the sound, and the indispensable clapper. It so happens that this duality recurs in various guises throughout the quatorzain. I hardly consider *flickering* a suitable equivalent of *palpite* even though it does come very close in the description of a fireplace. But the English word applies to fire and light. Moreover, *flickering* as a metaphor probably carries with it a foreboding of death, featured in the final line of the poem. Although *palpite* expresses no less than *flickering* the wavering movement of fire, in French it accomplishes this task metaphorically, for usually it conveys, rather than a visible motion, an organic tremor such as an accelerated heartbeat. In other words, *palpite* tends to personify the fire, in keeping with the humanization of the bell later in the poem. In fact, the fireplace itself, with its palpitating fire, displays the characteristics of a personified bell while referring to the poet himself. The same sort of personification enriches McGowan's poem: "in voices of the bells" corresponds to "carillons qui chantent." But here too I notice a difference, for while Baudelaire's line expresses expansiveness, McGowan subtly suggests intimacy. Indeed, the translator personifies the bells even more pointedly than Baudelaire. While maintaining a plurality of bells, McGowan has omitted a potentially ironic connotation of *carillons*, often associated with loud and joyous music in public festivities or even a concert. And what about "old recollections"? Of course, "souvenirs lointains," coming from a remote moment in time, can hardly avoid a reference to age. Nonetheless, Baudelaire has made metaphorical use of a spatial term in thus alluding to time. And by reason of its etymology, the English *recollections* conveys far more than the French *souvenirs* the idea of an accomplished act or fact—a sort of regurgitation of the past, closer perhaps to Proust or Beckett than to Baudelaire. McGowan by this device has actually personified the memories themselves, made still more intimate, as I have already suggested, by "in voices of the bells." Now, it so happens that spatialization plays a more important part in French literature, and in Baudelaire's writings in particular, than it does in English literature, always concerned with expressing self-contained and internalized sensations. Baudelaire, when translating Edgar Allan Poe, systematically substituted spatial distance for blunt sensation. He tended to transform the oppressive atmosphere of "The Fall of the House of Usher" into a rapier duel between the narrator and the Usher's haunted surroundings.

Differences of another and perhaps less poetic sort make their presence felt in the second quatrain. Students will immediately notice how cleverly the translator has followed Baudelaire's example in the jointly military and religious personification of a bell. Interestingly enough, the term *virile*, fully justified at the time by Baudelaire's comparison between the bell and an old soldier on guard duty, does not appear in "La Cloche fêlée." McGowan insists on the bell's clarity rather than on the bell's vigor, thereby compromising to a certain extent the comparison of the bell with the scream, no doubt piercing, of an old soldier. And what church warden would let a precious old bell gather rust? Actually, church bells may even improve their sound with age, provided the bell ringer treats them with the care they deserve. Cracked, the Liberty Bell still produces a pleasant sound. But in that second line, not only "rust" but also "dignified" can puzzle the reader, who might wonder to what extent *dignified* conveys the connotations of "bien portante" apart from pushing personification a step further. And who would dare question the dignity of this bell that functions in the dual capacity of brave soldier and religious person (a sort of church dignitary)? In short, *dignified* presents itself with spectacular and resounding credentials. The more precise term *healthy* would sound undignified if not trivial by comparison. But "bien portante" ("carrying afar") by means of a play on words, refers to a phenomenon of the utmost importance to a self-respecting bell. How far will its voice carry, or how far will the soldier's bullets travel toward their target? Later, we learn that the poet's voice has become too weak to reach an audience. Once again, space plays a not unimportant part. This subdued pun thus establishes relevant connections among the intimate hearth, the poet, the public church bells, and the battlefield featured in the second tercet. The line "Who faithfully repeats religion's notes" leaves out the vigorous spatial act of *jeter un cri*, untranslatable in English, which unfortunately does not allow its speakers to throw, cast, or even fling a shout or a scream. The idea of repetition appears in *religieux*,a term that carries with it a meaning not only appropriate to a church bell but also, because of the timed activities of monastic life, to a soldier. The "watchman's trust" ending the second quatrain arouses suspicions, but hardly because the reader can accuse the soldier of breaking his trust. Perhaps the translator's desire to find a word rhyming with *rust* led him to question the importance of *tente*, obviously a far more concrete aspect of soldiering than abstract *trust*. This substitution eliminates an image, that of a vigilant soldier in his tent at night: *veille* etymologically has close connections not only with vigilance but also with vigor. More important still, the soldier in his tent—the contained within the container—reiterates the relation between bell and clapper. The guard in his tent metamorphoses into a bell, as though in response to the bell's transformation into a soldier.

In the tercets, where the poet becomes a cracked bell unable to compose songs audible and appealing to an audience, the second line of the translation differs in some respects from the original. "She [*âme* ("spirit")] chants to fill the cold night's emptiness" somehow suggests that the poet sings to dissipate his solitude and, in addition, that he carries on the religious duties of the bell, for *chant* appears more appropriate to a devout monk than to a creative writer. But by evoking monotonous repetition, *chant* remains remarkably consonant with the poet's weakness and, hence, his lack of creativity. Baudelaire's persona, as opposed to McGowan's, seeks to deny this solitude and by dint of multiplying poems reaches out to an audience: "peupler l'air froid des nuits" ("to people the cold air of the nights"). Thus he tries in vain to imitate the *carillon*, a far more vigorous and successful performer.

In the first line of the second tercet, we search in vain for an equivalent of *oublie*, a term suitable not only to the forgotten soldier left to die but also to a forgotten poet whose songs nobody will ever hear and remember. By this omission, the translator has reduced, but in no way eliminated, the self-referentiality of "La Cloche fêlée," a text concerned mainly with poetic creation and sterility. The final line of the translation: "Who cannot budge, and dies in fierce distress!" applies far better to the moribund warrior than to the enfeebled poet or to the bell. The translator shows commendable empathy with the unfortunate war casualty and makes us share his distress. However, a term equivalent to *distress* appears nowhere in Baudelaire's text, though we can presume that the soldier abundantly suffers from his desperate state. Rather, the French poet creates a paradoxical spectacle by means of a surprising antithesis between "sans bouger" and "immenses efforts." I again see an analogy between the wounded warrior buried under a stack of bodies and a bell sounding its final note. Although the clapper has become motionless, the great bell continues to vibrate. The poem dies within the soul of the forgotten poet.

Selecting a complete translation of *Les Fleurs du Mal* by a single poet has its advantages; for one thing, it provides greater stylistic and tonal unity in English than one would have otherwise. Of course, a single translator can hardly do equal justice to every poem and may even nod at times. Making a selection of what one considers the best translations—as James Laver and Jackson Matthews, among others, have done—should reduce the risk of including a manifestly inferior translation. John Squire's "The Cracked Bell," included in Matthews's readily available edition as well as in Laver's, invites comparison with McGowan's. Paradoxically, Squire's and McGowan's translations differ from each other even more than from the original, although they both stick to it as closely as they can:

'Tis bitter-sweet when nights are long,
To watch, beside the flames which smoke and twist,
The distant memories which slowly throng,
Brought by the chime soft-singing through the mist.

Happy the sturdy, vigorous throated bell
Who, spite of age alert and confident,
Cries hourly, like some strong old sentinel
Flinging the ready challenge from his tent.

For me, my soul is cracked; when sick with care,
She strives with songs to people the cold air
It happens often that her feeble cries

Mock the harsh rattle of a man who lies
Wounded, forgotten, 'neath a mound of slain
And dies, pinned fast, writhing his limbs in vain.
                    (*Flowers* [Laver] 124)

Less modern perhaps than McGowan's version, Squire's rendition adds causal relations not present in the French. The *carillons* seem to have occasioned a recall of past events, whereas Baudelaire, followed in this respect by McGowan, has left the relation between the bell and the past in suspense. Because sound gives way to sight, space takes on greater importance in Squire's rendition than in McGowan's, though perhaps at the expense of inner depth. Moreover, Squire shows a propensity to make the various elements in the poem physically active, not to say athletic. But no more than McGowan does he retain, in the opening quatrain, a sense of duality.

In the second quatrain, we look in vain for the slightest trace of religiosity, so strong in McGowan's version and evident in the original. The bell has completely renounced its beatitude and even its blessedness in favor of a purely military career. The omission of the religious aspect allows the translator, in keeping with the original, to emphasize spatiality and find a place for the all-important tent. However, the reader may notice that the sentinel behaves somewhat mechanically, as soldiers so often do, by flinging his challenge regularly on the hour. By abstaining from any mention of the soldier's vigilance, Squire deprives him of subjectivity—of any kind of inner existence. And as the soldier does not specifically occupy a place "sous la tente" ("under or within the tent"), the analogy with a clapper and a bell disappears for all practical or poetic purposes.

In the tercets, the translator's spectacular approach in no way detracts from the analogy between the immobilized moribund warrior and a bell. But few readers will notice the connection, for hardly anything before that moment has prepared them to perceive it, unless they have closely read Squire's translation in conjunction with "La Cloche fêlée." Squire's direct and highly visible rendition lends itself less readily to semantic discussions of, and involvement with, the original text than does McGowan's more spiritual and thought-provoking translation.

By often favoring words with a plurality of meanings, poets increase the difficulties of translators who, attempting to remain as close as possible to the original, might have to use several words in the place of one and risk producing a prose paraphrase rather than poetry. By choosing one among a plurality of meanings, the translator can hardly avoid leaving out aspects of the original. By comparing this incomplete or curtailed translation with the original, the teacher can suddenly uncover a wealth of previously unsuspected meanings. Actually, the comparison between an original text and its translation may convey at first no more than a vague awareness of a reduction or, conversely, the feeling that the translator has somehow interpolated additional meanings. But such impressions, when analyzed, may eventually lead to the discovery of interesting and heretofore hidden aspects of the original.

From Metrics and Rhymes to Meanings

Peter Schofer

This essay assumes that literature classes in a foreign language are centered on question-and-answer class discussion, not on lectures. Although I seek to show how students can move from form to meaning, I do not propose any definitive readings or interpretations of Baudelaire's poems. To do so would deny the dialectic between professor and student. Guided discussion comes close to ensuring that multiple readings will come out of the class's work and the play between signifiers and content.

Approaching Baudelaire's poetry from the point of form is challenging yet rewarding, because it can show students dramatically how versification and rhyme are not simply ornaments added to the content of a text. To the contrary, students learn how form molds, generates, and creates meaning. Traditional explications de texte forced students to learn all the rules of versification (counting syllables, finding the caesura) and the difference between a *rime riche* and a *rime pauvre*, for example, but all too often the rules were applied in a mechanical way and students were seldom encouraged to relate the application of rules to content. More recently, content-driven criticism—such as some practices of the new historicism and even deconstruction—have overlooked the formal elements of poetry. Critical anthologies such as *Redrawing the Boundaries*, edited by Stephen Greenblatt and Giles Gunn, virtually ignore versification. Yet Baudelaire's poetry, with its rich variety and novelty of combinations, demands some attention to form.

The challenges and rewards of reading Baudelaire from the body (sound) up take on an urgency and a focus in the light of T. S. Eliot's declaration that Baudelaire's poems "have the external but not the internal form of classic art" ("Baudelaire" [1964] 372). While Eliot sought to qualify and to deprecate Baudelaire's work within the classical poetic tradition, the quotation can act as an excellent starting point for students by playing on tradition and novelty. To create an inner art, Baudelaire had recourse to external traditional forms, particularly sonnets, which make up nearly half the poems in the 1857 edition (44 of 100 poems). By modifying these conventional forms, he was able to create new effects. Of the forty-four sonnets, only four conform to the traditional rhyme scheme of *abba, abba, ccd, eed* (or *ede*).

To understand fully how Baudelaire reworked the sonnet form, students would do well to turn toward the beginnings of the sonnet tradition. Pierre de Ronsard would be appropriate as a contrast to Baudelaire, because his adherence to the rules permits students to review their knowledge of versification. In addition, the thematic resonances between Ronsard and Baudelaire add a semantic dimension to the comparisons. For illustration, I have selected Ronsard's "Quand vous serez bien vieille, au soir, à la chandelle" ("When you are old, in the evening, next to a candle") to establish guidelines (400).

Claire Kramsch advocates teaching poetry through dramatic readings, acting out the poem as it is recited in front of the class (141). Although some instructors might feel reluctant to dramatize poetry, there is no question that an initial reading, or readings, aloud in front of the class makes musicality a concrete reality and also attunes students to the subtleties of versification. The poem can be read once, the reader giving all words equal weight, and then a second time, with emphasis on key words and metrical peculiarities. The more we read poems to students in various ways, the more their ears become sensitive to phonetic nuances.

A visual reading (e.g., one supported by a highlighted text shown with an overhead projector) permits students to follow shifts in rhyme scheme, syntax, and pronoun use and the expressive effects of the very graphics of the text. Thus students encounter a vivid illustration of how formal shifts determine corresponding shifts in content. The turn at the beginning of Ronsard's ninth line, for example, is clearly marked: he shifts from *vous* (the woman in the future, when she will be old) to the *je* of the poet projecting his death: "Je serai sous la terre, et fantôme sans os" ("I'll be beneath the earth, a phantom without bones"). Students should be asked to play with the semantic differences at the rhyme. Jean Cohen argues convincingly that connotations arise from the coupling of rhymes (*Structure* 222). The most notable plays of difference occur in the pairs *filant-émerveillant*, *sommeillant-réveillant*, and *accroupie-vie*. Simply by being asked what the words mean, students can perceive patterns of boredom, sleep, and old age juxtaposed with wakefulness, wonder (hyperconsciousness), and vitality. In addition, two words that point toward a reading of the poem fall at the intersection between octave and sestet: *immortelle* at the end of line 8 and *sans os* at the end of line 9. By teasing out meaning from these associations at the rhyme, students have an initial entry into a reading of the poem.

Metrically, the poem is perfectly regular except for the first line, where commas create a 6-2-4 structure, emphasizing *au soir* and *à la chandelle*. In the rest of the poem, punctuation highlights the caesura and consequently emphasizes those words that fall at the sixth syllable. In the first quatrain alone, key words that are emphasized include *vieille*, *feu*, and *vers*. Without insisting on counting syllables in isolation or determining the richness of rhyme, we can observe how rhyme and rhythm establish semantic patterns.

The briefest examination of a Ronsard sonnet should give students the necessary prosodic background to Baudelaire. Specifically, they would be aware that:

> The constraints of the traditional sonnet (4-4-3-3) are also sources of connotations, with key words falling at strategic spots in the sonnet's grid.
> The play of sound in rhyming words points to meaning.
> Poetry is not music without meaning. To the contrary, the music generated by the regularity (and irregularity) of meter, coupled with punctuation, guides the reading in establishing semantic relations.
> Syntax and versification work hand in hand as the foundation for meaning.

I hope that this preface to Baudelaire has convinced my class that versification cannot be treated in splendid isolation. Of all the Romantic poets, Baudelaire needs most to be placed within a historical context, sketchy as it might be. His sonnets can also provide a context for his less conventional poems. By working with pairs of poems, a class can play off the inherent dialogue that Baudelaire's writing represents. Thus a class can see how Baudelaire builds on the past while reworking classical forms. Two pairs of poems can introduce students to the complexities of versification: "Parfum exotique" (48; "Exotic Perfume"), taught before *"Duellum"* (70–72; "The Duel" [360]); "Harmonie du soir" (96; "Evening Harmony" [trans. mine]) coupled with "L'Invitation au voyage" (108–10; "Invitation to the Voyage").

As one of the four regular sonnets by Baudelaire, "Parfum exotique" is almost a caricature of the traditional sonnet in its regularity and its insistence on form. Reading aloud can reveal to the class the near-monotonous regularity of the alexandrines. In addition, by emphasizing syntax, a reading shows how the clauses and sentences follow exactly the syllabic structure of 4-4-3-3. Here sentence structure linked to form contains and generates meaning. Students would need to look closely at the poem to trace the causal links in the octave.

The tercets continue the unification of syntax and verse structure, first in lines 9 to 11, which re-create the movement of quatrain 1 by returning to the motivating force of odor: "Guidé par ton odeur [. . .], je vois un port" ("Led by your fragrance [. . .] I see a bay"). Thus the turn at the beginning of the sestet goes full circle to the beginning of the poem rather than acts as a logical shift or change in direction, as in the Ronsard poem.

For students, syntax can be the key to discovering yet another shift, in the second tercet, where *pendant que* introduces a clause that dominates the final three lines and creates actions simultaneous to those in the first quatrain:

Pendant que le parfum des verts tamariniers,
Qui circule dans l'air et m'enfle la narine,
Se mêle dans mon âme au chant des mariniers.   (48)

While verdant tamarinds' enchanting scent,
Filling my nostrils, swirling to the brain,
Blends in my spirit with the boatmen's chant.   (49)

The rhyming words highlight the graphics of the sonnet. Students can be reminded that normally, rhymes demand dissonance or difference semantically, as in the Ronsard sonnet. Having been given the basic rules, students will discover that Baudelaire's rhymes are indeed rich here and that they often reinforce one another semantically—seeking harmony and similarity: *chaleureux-heureux, savoureux-vigoureux, tamariniers-mariniers* ("warm-happy," "savory-vigorous," "tamarinds-sailors" [trans. mine]). [Technically, to call the rhymes of the first two pairs rich is debatable, since despite the identity of the final three pronounced sounds within each pair, all four of the words are supposed also to rhyme with one another.—*LP*] All the words have positive connotations suggesting an ideal (warm) milieu of happiness and strength in exotic nature. The final word, *mariniers*, echoes the title by its suggestion of the voyage. Only two rhyming words might trouble students, as they point to the only notes of ambiguity and possible tension in the poem: *monotone* and *étonne*. Unless students are capable of a subtle reading, they will need to be coaxed into rethinking their accepted meaning for *monotone*; not as boring but as a positive force, as an even tone that reflects the musicality of the poem. The word *étonne* presents more of a problem for students. It occupies the strategic position of final word in the octave. But since it opens questions, it effects only an equivocal closure. Why should the women's gaze astonish? What kind of surprise is evoked? The answer is suggested when students find previous references to the gaze and to eyes. Just as the ninth line returns the reader to the beginning of the poem by its reference to the woman's odor, the final word of the octave recalls the man's closed eyes in the first line, closed eyes that blocked out the reality of Paris (and the mistress) and permitted the imaginary voyage. If students are puzzled by the contrast between the single woman in line 1 and the frankness of plural women in line 8, they might well expand their horizons to include other oppositions that can be related to the rhyme play: odor/perfume, here (Paris) / there (imaginary island), reality / imaginary paradise, real woman / ideal woman. This play of oppositions invites several possible readings, all spun from the single word *étonne*.

The study of the unifying role of versification in "Parfum exotique" can conclude with a glimpse at how lines begin in the octave, particularly the lines 2, 3, 6, and 7, where phonetic and grammatical repetition once again highlights the sonnet's phonetic and syntactic structure of similarity, repetition, and harmonious regularity:

Je respire [. . .]
Je vois [. . .]

Des arbres [. . .]
Des hommes [. . .]

The challenge for a class is to reconcile the overdetermination on the phonetic and syntactic levels with the oppositions (such as here/there) that arise from the rest of the poem. Baudelaire leads us from his celebrated musicality to his equally celebrated ambiguity.

With "*Duellum*," students learn how Baudelaire pushes the boundaries of the sonnet form and how violent dissonances replace monotonous harmony. The initial reading in class brings out the irregularity of the meter. If students have not yet learned to identify *rejet* and enjambment, "*Duellum*" offers a perfect starting point. The sonnet is given below, the cuts, extensions, and breaks in the poem italicized for emphasis:

> Deux guerriers ont couru l'un sur l'autre; *leurs armes*
> *Ont éclaboussé l'air* de lueurs et de sang.
> Ces jeux, ces cliquetis du fer sont *les vacarmes*
> *D'une jeunesse* en proie à l'amour vagissant.
>
> Les glaives sont brisés! comme notre jeunesse,
> *Ma chère!* Mais les dents, les ongles acérés,
> Vengent bientôt l'épée et la dague traîtresse.
> *— O fureur des cœurs mûrs par l'amour ulcérés!*
>
> Dans le ravin hanté des chats-pards et des onces
> *Nos héros*, s'étreignant méchamment, *ont roulé,*
> Et leur peau fleurira l'aridité des ronces.
>
> *— Ce gouffre, c'est l'enfer, de nos amis peuplé!*
> Roulons-y sans remords, amazone inhumaine,
> Afin d'éterniser l'ardeur de notre haine.

> Two warriors have grappled, and their arms
> Have flecked the air with blood and flashing steel.
> These frolics, this mad clanking, these alarms
> Proceed from childish love's frantic appeal.
>
> The swords are broken! like our youthful life
> My dear! But tooth and nail, avid and sharp,
> Soon fill the place of rapier and knife.
> —O bitter heat of love, o cankered hearts!
>
> In a ravine haunted by catlike forms
> These two have tumbled, struggling to the end;
> Shreds of their skin will bloom on arid thorns.
>
> —This pit is Hell, its denizens our friends!
> Amazon, let us roll there guiltlessly
> In spiteful fervour, for eternity!   (71–73)

Through an oral reading, a student with a sharp ear will perceive that the sonnet has a rough rhythm and does not follow, as "Parfum exotique" does, a traditional rhyme scheme. In fact it ends with a rhymed couplet, in the Shakespearean tradition. Taking into account the irregular rhyme (*abab, cdcd, efef, gg*) and the breaks in syntax and meter, students can mark the text as I just did and start creating a reading of the poem based on formal conflict.

But if treating the poem as a whole is a daunting chore for students, their attention can be focused on the rhyming words, on the same starting point as in "Parfum exotique." Although the poem describes amorous conflict, the rhyming words at first complement each other. By examining the meaning of the rhyming words, students can establish traces that lead to the final couplet. The following words all evoke violence, suffering, or inhumanity: *armes-vacarmes-acérés-ulcérés, onces-ronces-inhumaine-haine* ("arms"-"racket"-"sharp"-"ulcerated," "snow leopards"-"brambles"-"inhuman"-"hate"). Phonetically the weakest rhyme—*roulé-peuplé*—is also the weakest semantically. It makes sense only when integrated into the rest of the sestet, where the ironic notion of heroes rolling in an abyss takes on more impact when it is associated with the "friends" who people the special hell. Likewise, the remaining rhyming chains do not present neat patterns of clear similarity or difference: students will have to think in terms of dissonance and irony to understand them. As in the couple *roulé-peuplé*, the irony can be perceived only within the context of the entire poem. Thus *sang* and *vagissant* take on meaning when associated with the bloody battles of young love. In a similar vein, *jeunesse*, traditionally associated with innocence or purity, is undermined and devalued by its match with *traîtresse*.

This introduction to dissonance and irony provides solid preparation for other Baudelaire poems that follow similar strategies: "Au Lecteur" (4–6; "To the Reader"), with the wordplay of religious, moral, bestial, and culinary terms at the rhyme; the second "Spleen" poem (146); "Une Charogne" (58–62; "A Carcass"), with its ironic use of Renaissance diction at the rhyme; and parts of "Le Voyage" (282–92; "Voyaging"). When two contrasting poems rather than two contrasting rhyming words are juxtaposed, Baudelaire's irony emerges even more forcefully. By coupling the love poems "Parfum exotique" and *"Duellum,"* for example, students realize that there is no easy recipe to follow in reading Baudelaire.

Before leaving *"Duellum,"* students should note the extraordinary unification of metrics and sound patterns, particularly in line 8, where the sounds \y\, \R\, and \œR\ are distributed along the line: "— O fureur des cœurs mûrs par l'amour ulcérés!" ("—O bitter heat of love, o cankered hearts!"). To tell students that the sound patterns are exquisite, even beautiful, really says little; it is like saying that a sunset is beautiful. Moreover, to try to assign symbolic meanings to the individual sounds, as Maurice Grammont and others have done, falsifies the line and imposes an erroneous meaning. (See Gérard Genette, *Mimologiques*, for a thorough examination and history of sound symbolism.) Rather, the line shows how sound and meaning mutually influence and contaminate each other and how the word *amour* ("love"), surrounded by harsh sounds and meanings, takes on the meaning of *haine* ("hate"), the last word of the sonnet. The rich sound pattern suggests that students should seek those sound traces in the rest of the poem and discover the semantic links made by the sounds. (For example, the occurrence of \u\ is relatively rare but nonetheless revealing: *amour, roulé, gouffre, roulons-y*).

With "Harmonie du soir," we return to a traditional, even ancient, poetic form, the pantoum. As Henri Morier points out, it is an exotic Sumatran form, renewed by the Romantics and changed by Baudelaire, who did not repeat the first line at the very end and who used *rimes embrassées* ("enclosing") instead of *croisées* ("alternating"; 293–94). In addition he limited himself to only two rhymes. For Morier, the effect is of a "gripping obsession" and "a swirling style" (294).

Starting with the obvious, the repetition of lines and the extreme regularity of the meter, students can be led to see how the musicality of the form is reinforced by the musicality of meaning, with such words as *valse*, *vertige*, and, of course, *harmonie* in the title. Beyond this initial approach the most economical way to show how form and meaning are united resides in the exceptional construction of rhyme. Asking students to go from the richest rhyme to the weakest permits them to uncover the major topics of the poem: religion, nature, human suffering, a movement toward stasis (*se figer*) even as the poem suggests dance.

> religion: *encensoir, reposoir, ostensoir* ("censer," "altar," "monstrance")
> nature: *tige, soir, noir* ("stalk," "evening," "black")
> human feeling: *vertige, afflige, (se fige), vestige* ("vertigo," "afflicted," "congeal," "remnant")

Several of these rhymes overlap, like *se fige*, which both refers to the personified sun and recalls a dying person. Likewise, while referring to the night, the word *noir* resonates with the foreboding of death. From these suggestions of the rhyming words, an initial reading of the poem can be made, and students can better understand that the intertwining of sounds and verses accompanies the intertwining of multiple meanings that are brought together in the final line. Just as sounds in the title, particularly the \i\ and the \waR\, can be seen as generators for the poem, the final line, by creating surprise, forces the reader back to the rest of the poem. What better way to seek out patterns than through the prominent sounds in the line?

> *Ton souvenir* en *moi luit* comme un *ostensoir!*   (96)

> In me your memory, as in a monstrance, shines!   (97)

Different sounds lead to different meanings, just as the empty signifier of *ton* asks to be given meaning: as a real person, a woman, compared to nature or to religion; as a religious poem; as a poem on man and nature in which nature is personified.

The last poem to be touched on, "L'Invitation au voyage," renews the shock of the unexpected and raises very different questions for students, because it is written mostly in *vers impairs* ("uneven number of syllables"). Verlaine's famous declaration that true music comes from *le vers impair* rings in the heads of many professors:

> De la musique avant toute chose,
> Et pour cela préfère l'Impair
> Plus vague et plus soluble dans l'air
> Sans rien en lui qui pèse ou qui pose.   (326)

> Music before everything,
> And to that end prefer the odd [number of syllables per line]
> Vaguer and more soluble
> With nothing to stay or weigh down.

Standard manuals reiterate the lightness, vagueness, and musicality of the *vers impair*, but even if an odd-numbered group of syllables really has these inherent features, such generalizations do little to help students when they must deal with a real poem and decipher it. Baudelaire, of course, complicates the situation, by varying the length of the lines and introducing a refrain of seven syllables: 5-5-7-5-5-7-5-5-7-5-5-7 7-7. Verlaine's poem is indeed written in *vers impairs* but in regular lines of nine syllables that tend to stand by themselves and defy being combined to create *vers pairs* ("even number of syllables"), such as an eighteen-syllable line. Perverse mathematician that he was, Baudelaire conjured up lines that easily convert to *vers pairs* and even alexandrines: 5+5=10, 5+7=12. The only line to remain a pure *vers impair* is the last one falling before each refrain. The refrain brings the thrust of the *vers impairs* to a stop, but it also continues the play of odd and even by overflowing the boundaries of the alexandrine implicit in the other verses. This fullness is countered by the isolation of individual words and the resulting slow rhythm of the couplet that serves as a refrain in "L'Invitation au voyage":

> Là,/ tout/ n'est/ qu'or/ dre et/ beau/ té,
> Lu/ xe,/ cal/ me et/ vo/lup/ té.   (110)

> There, all is order and leisure,
> Luxury, beauty, and pleasure.   (111)

Two different oral readings of the poem can bring into play the imbalance and balance of the meter. The readings will underline the role of syntax, which at first follows the same patterns as the rhyme and then accelerates in the second half of each stanza before the pauses in the refrain: 557/557/557557/77.

What can students draw from such a mathematical approach to musicality? They are capable of inferring a number of oppositions: imbalance/equilibrium, asymmetry/symmetry, movement/stops, overflowing/constraint, openness/closure. They can relate the meter to a voyage, the sea, waves, and arrival at a destination. These pairs can then be the basis for reading around life and death, loving and repose, openness and closure.

The poems just discussed are perhaps exceptional in their treatment of form. Not all of Baudelaire's poems lend themselves to such neat readings. Versification and rhyme in some say little more than "This is a poem." But taken as a whole, Baudelaire's poetry teaches us to be alert to new situations and new approaches. While Baudelaire continually reminds us of the poetic tradition that nourished him, he then twists, turns, and rewrites the rules to generate new shocks and new meanings. Such should be the experience for students.

Narrativity in *Les Fleurs du Mal*

Timothy Unwin

As an undergraduate coming to Baudelaire for the first time, I became fascinated by one outstanding feature of the collection of poems that make up *Les Fleurs du Mal*. In addition to their thematic and symbolic cohesion—that "architecture" that has so often been spoken of (e.g., Mossop 115; Culler, Introduction xvii–xviii)—these poems seemed to fit together in another way. Quite simply, they told a story, even as each individual poem remained separate and distinct from the rest. Since making that simple discovery myself some twenty-five years ago, I have often seen relief in the eyes of mystified students of poetry when they encounter this narrative element in Baudelaire's collection. Consequently, I have found that attention to it provides an excellent preparation for studying the more formal aspects of the poetry, partly because the narrative approach requires that we establish the limits of its usefulness.

In this essay, I first outline more fully how I understand the term *narrativity* in *Les Fleurs du Mal*. I apply the concept to "L'Albatros" (14–16; "The Albatross"), "Spleen (4)" (148–50), and "Le Voyage" (282–92; "Voyaging"). Throughout, I stress what I hope becomes self-evident: that the concept of narrativity, far from allowing an easy divide between the poetic and the fictional, or perhaps between the metaphoric and the metonymic, leads to a refinement of the way the student approaches these constructs. By questioning the concept of narrative in its application to *Les Fleurs du Mal*, I try to show not only that students might become more aware of stylistic issues leading out of a narratological approach (time, sequence, tense, mode, repetition, etc.) in the context of poetry but also that they are in a position to develop a more sophisticated notion of narrative in its original fictional context. My approach thus provides students (when it is successful) with some tools for analyzing both poetry and fiction. There is something of a pedagogical economy in this.

First, though, what is this sequence of events, or progression of states, that I (and others) claim it is possible to detect in *Les Fleurs du Mal*? Do we sense that there are— applying an unashamedly old-fashioned framework—a beginning, a middle, and an end? Do we find a narrator and a participant? Certainly, students can readily see that the collection in some way recounts the poet's spiritual odyssey, outlining its different moods and phases, its difficulties and problems, even if there are relatively few precise focal points or dramatic twists in the "plot." The central figure of the collection is indeed, to use D. J. Mossop's term, a "tragic hero." We are clearly presented at the start with the artist's sense of a lost paradise (e.g., in "Bénédiction" [10–14; "Benediction"]) and his mission to re-create it aesthetically (as in the allegorical "Le Mauvais Moine" [26–28; "The Wretched Monk"]). To this sense of the ideal (so powerfully expressed, for example, in "Elévation" [16; "Elevation"]) corresponds the fall from grace into the misery of spleen and the oppressive awareness the artist has of his own mortality and sinfulness. In the section "Tableaux parisiens" ("Parisian Scenes") he provides his response in the context of the city, whose sights and sounds he wishes to convert into the timeless beauty of the poem. The section "Le Vin" ("Wine") evokes the sense of failure and escape into the false paradise of wine, the section "Fleurs du Mal" the rude reawakening to the curse of his own condition, the section "Révolte" ("Revolt") the desperate act of rebellion against the conditions of mortality, the section "La Mort" ("Death") the final acceptance of his condition. The outline organization of the collection thus confirms its progressive and sequential structure. Although to read *Les Fleurs du Mal* on this level alone would be a distortion (a point essential to underline at the outset), such a reading nonetheless obliges us to look for the components that make up this narrative sequence. Where, indeed, are they situated? What role do the individual poems play in furthering the action? If some are more important, can we therefore conclude that others are superfluous?

I have always stressed to students of *Les Fleurs du Mal* that if we look at the collection as forming some kind of story, then we must accept that virtually any single poem might be disregarded without significant alteration to the narrative outline. Such fluidity usually does not exist in prose narrative: removing episodes from a novel is almost always to weaken the plot, and removing sections of a story might make its progression incomprehensible. In *Les Fleurs du Mal*, the dominant themes in the various sequences of poems have a mutually reinforcing effect, and the orchestration of different elements relies on repeated evocations of the central experiences and on dense metaphoric overlay. Thus almost no poem is absolutely essential to an understanding of the story, which is distributed and reechoed through all of them. Now by a happy coincidence this coexistence of two opposed principles—fragmentation and totality, contingency and necessity—affords the teacher an opportunity to draw a parallel between the organization of *Les Fleurs du Mal* and that of the later *Spleen de Paris*. In the famous prefatory letter to Arsène Houssaye (*Œuvres* [Ruff] 146), Baudelaire stressed precisely the effect of unity within fragmentation that he hoped he had achieved. There was, he said, neither head nor tail, for everything was head and tail at once. The different fragments would always join, and the poems could be approached in any order, from any angle, and left at any point. This interconnectedness had the advantage of accommodating many different uses of, or routes through, the text. Everything was at the circumference, and yet by dint of that absence of hierarchy everything was also central.

Something of this perpetual displacement—from center to circumference and back to center—seems to have been anticipated in *Les Fleurs du Mal*, for in terms of the narrative sequence every poem is contingent while at the same time being an essential contributory element. Yet, notwithstanding this displacement, there remains in the volume a sense of overall progression, a necessary order, which is not apparent in *Le Spleen de Paris*. There is also the suggestion of key moments in the story. Many poems illustrate the pattern of recognitions and reversals (anagnorisis and peripeteia) that Aristotle in the *Poetics* saw as central constituents of the tragic plot. How, then, is such movement integrated into the overall framework despite its fragmentary character? And where does the narrative element of *Les Fleurs du Mal* differ from (and thus help to define) what we conventionally understand as narrative?

We should bear in mind that Baudelaire does not rely on past tenses—still less on the past historic (*le passé simple*)—to further the "story" of *Les Fleurs du Mal*. The sequence of events is a matter of textual ordering rather than of temporal progression, consecution rather than consequence. The different phases of the poet's spiritual drama coexist, interlocking with and reflecting one another in this timeless hall of mirrors. And yet at the same time we must ask ourselves what makes us understand the poems as an implied chronology. That they have been set out and ordered into a sequence creates a movement that we are obliged at least to acknowledge in the text. While each poem functions paradigmatically (its echoes and reverberations can be followed at will almost throughout the collection), it also has a specific function within the textual distribution. Each poem can therefore be understood as determined and yet gratuitous: determined as a contributory element in the overall symbolism of the work and gratuitous in its individuality. The poem escapes from the constrictions placed on it by the symbolic network within which it operates. Is it, perhaps, this gratuitousness that accounts in part for our sense of progression and movement? Instead of finally merging into the collection by way of analogy, the poem asserts its difference, standing apart as a separate and distinct allegory, and thus it suggests the possibility of temporality. Paul de Man's essay "The Rhetoric of Temporality" develops the theoretical aspect of the relation between allegory and temporality and is clearly a useful point of reference for discussing with students this aspect of *Les Fleurs du Mal*.

I now briefly discuss some examples from the collection and look at them in terms of the duality that I have termed the poetic/fictional or the metaphoric/metonymic—a binary divide that of course serves the commendable purpose of ultimately proving itself inadequate. I discuss three poems here, although in view of the aesthetic of gratuitousness outlined above, it should be stressed that any poem in the collection is amenable to an analysis along these lines (and correspondingly that no poem requires it exclusively). For the sake of symmetry, I select one poem from the beginning of the collection, one from the middle, and one from the end. The concluding poem, "Le Voyage," naturally raises additional, vital questions on the issue of narrativity. Is this conclusion a mere summing up, a ritualistic repetition, or does it add some new element to the story? And to what extent is the ending anticipated—as it frequently is in fictional narrative—by earlier "events"? But these questions beg our first and most urgent question. Precisely where, if anywhere, are the events of *Les Fleurs du Mal*, and what will we find out about them in the chosen poems?

"L'Albatros" confronts us with a single striking image, albeit allegorical, to illustrate the fall of the poet from his status as celestial being to his condition as terrestrial pariah. At first glance, the poem seems to provide an ideal close-up on the essential humiliating event that provides the impetus to the whole collection. The allegory of "L'Albatros" is indeed so clear and so simple in outline that it reinforces the singularity or uniqueness of this event. Yet the double reference of allegory immediately raises complications, and these are not easy to ignore. For the poet's own story, or situation, is of course described in terms of another event, which serves to illustrate and explain his current predicament. On closer examination, it turns out that the decking of the albatross is not even a single incident. Rather, it is a series of similar events, as suggested by the iterative "Souvent" (14) ("Often" [15]) with which the poem opens. So what had had the appearance of a story seems, on reflection, to be at a remove from whatever real event supposedly took place. We are soon left feeling that the event we seek is elusive. In a sense, there is no story, despite the illusion of one that has been created. But this discovery provides a further pedagogical opportunity: it allows the teacher to underline the simple point that even in fictional narrative there is rarely such a thing as a clear, unambiguous, and uncomplicated event, and that single or key occurrences are often embedded in narrative so that the metaphoric and the metonymic collude and overlap, as Gérard Genette pointed out in his discussion of Marcel Proust (*Figures III* 41–63).

To study the event in "L'Albatros" thus shows that it is almost impossible for us to read the poem without at some point shifting our attention away from its particular position in the text (the distributional or horizontal axis) and toward the vertical axis containing the paradigm of the artist's fall from grace. Although it might seem that "L'Albatros" constitutes, both through its position in the text and the clarity of its reference, the first turning point in the story of the poet's humiliation, the poem's allegorical status inevitably invites us to consider the situation of the artist in a wider context. The poem could indeed be seen, despite its key position in the text, as no more than a variation on a theme stated in many other poems. And, like them, it could perhaps be excised without significant loss to our understanding of the story. It needs to be stressed that this stance is not a judgment on the aesthetic quality of "L'Albatros." Rather, it recognizes the limits of the poem's purely narrative function and the strength of the metaphoric, associative dimension that binds the poems together as a collection. Not uncommonly in fictional narrative, an event may also be either allegorical or recounted many times, at various stages and in different forms. Genette's distinction between the singulative and the iterative (*Figures III* 145–56) can usefully enter the discussion here, and one might add that a truly single event is virtually an impossibility in narrative. The issue here is one not of extremes but of degree, and with a poetic collection like *Les Fleurs du Mal* the associative and metaphoric dimension is clearly stronger than the progressive, metonymic one. The story of the poet's fall from grace exists, then, in outline alone. It begins to dissolve as we seek to locate it more closely. Our concentration on narrativity uncovers the elusive complexity of the organization of the text, precisely where narrativity itself begins to be surpassed as a concept.

The discovery that the event located in the poem is perhaps as much a question of textual distribution as of dramatic focus is reinforced by study of "Spleen (4)" (148–50). This poem also corresponds to a particular moment or event in the poet's story—here, the feeling of intense depression, isolation, and defeat—yet its inclusion in a series of four poems all bearing the same title already indicates the important functions of relay and reduplication in the binding together of the different poems of the collection. Such reduplication reappears in the poem itself: although the poet appears to be giving us a sharply focused account of a particular stage of his spiritual journey, an associative progression generates the series of miniature pseudoevents that constitute the poem (the jangling of bells, the procession of corteges, Anguish planting her black flag in the poet's skull). All these elaborate the master image of enclosure and imprisonment by the low, heavy sky. There is, indeed, an effective conflict in this poem between the enumeration of apparently separate occurrences, on the one hand, and the sameness, inaction, and mental paralysis that these miniature events express, on the other. The increasingly dramatic verbs, *défilent, pleure, plante* (150) ("Deploy," "moans," "fixed" [151]); the sharp distinctions between moods and moments; the fragmented rhythms; and the vivid personifications—all stand in opposition to the undifferentiated, unchanging inner state that they describe and, most important, of which they are a metaphoric extension. Though having the appearance of events, they dissolve into an absence of event and a sense of associative unity.

In a paradoxical sense this absence of event or drama is itself the central drama of the poet's experience. But in terms of the syntactic structure of the poem, clearly any sense of narrative is also a carefully contrived illusion. Not until line 13, after three stanzas of subordinate clauses, do we happen on the main verb of that sentence:"Des cloches tout à coup sautent avec furie" (150) ("Bells all at once jump out with all their force" [151]). Yet by this point, any event that the verb indicates has been displaced and dismissed. The jangling bells become part of the state that the earlier stanzas have evoked rather than an autonomous occurrence. They are no more than a new image of the despair already evoked. In a fascinating inversion, what was syntactically subordinate (the first three stanzas) seems then to assume metaphoric superiority. The event itself dissolves amid a rich poetic structure, and the concept of narrativity leads us once again to recognize its limits, precisely as it guides us into the elaborate construction of this poem.

The final poem of the collection, "Le Voyage," fittingly evokes departure and, at the end, imminent death. It is a moving conclusion, so effective that it is easy to forget that it did not even figure in the first edition of *Les Fleurs du Mal*. To argue that the collection could not stand without this conclusion would, then, be an absurdity; yet in narrative terms the poem does seem to be a particularly appropriate ending. It carries the poet's story to the fictional present, or to what Genette in another context termed the "instance narrative" (*Figures III* 71–76). Indeed, the final lines of this final poem introduce a new, dramatic note. The impact of the conclusion is sharpened by the revelation of how the poet now arms himself for death. The resoundingly defiant rallying call of "Plonger au fond du gouffre, Enfer ou Ciel, qu'importe? / Au fond de l'Inconnu pour trouver du *nouveau!*" (292) ("And plunge to depths of Heaven or of Hell, / To fathom the Unknown, and find the *new!*" [293]) has all the appearance of a decision. It is of course a decision consequential to earlier poems, yet paradoxically it stands apart and asserts a severance with the past. Like all good conclusions, this final moment of *Les Fleurs du Mal* both sums up the past and urges toward the future. Janus-like, the writer seems temporally to glance in both directions. In symbols and imagery, the reemergence of the past is obvious in "Le Voyage," which for many readers blends almost perfectly into the symbolic unity of the collection as a whole. Thematically, too, the journey described here traces the entire movement of the collection, following the collection's various phases of hope and disillusionment. It is a perfect *mise en abyme*, which brings us, in its final lines, back to the final section of the collection, "La Mort." As an event, therefore, "Le Voyage" can hardly be said to offer a clear and unambiguous imitation of an action. Representationally, its field of reference seems more the collection of poems where it is situated than the real world (whatever that might be). Yet it is precisely this self-reflexiveness that constitutes progression in the narrative sense. "Le Voyage" thus effectively illustrates that narrative, far from representing supposedly real events in a world beyond the text, frequently derives its impetus from its own textual status.

The benefit of this approach to *Les Fleurs du Mal* in the classroom is that it provides us with the means both to bring students to a greater awareness of narratological issues and to show that these issues have a surprising presence in the poetic context. The approach provides us, more specifically, with the means to discuss such issues as metaphor and metonymy, the vertical and the horizontal axes, and unity and fragmentation. Though focusing on *Les Fleurs du Mal*, it requires us to range more widely. However, it would be foolish to see nothing but narrativity in this volume. It is precisely where narrativity reveals its limits that the complex metaphoric functions of the poems begin to emerge. The approach is, precisely, no more than an approach. Thereafter the real work must begin.

Unfamiliarity and Defamiliarization: Teaching *Les Fleurs du Mal* with the *Petits poèmes en prose*

Sonya Stephens

> Paresse, désespoir, accidents du langage, regards
> singuliers—tout ce que perd, rejette, ignore, élimine,
> oublie l'homme le plus *pratique*, le poète le cueille, et
> par son art lui donne quelque valeur.
>
> —Paul Valéry

> Laziness, despair, accidents of language, extraordinary
> glances—all that the most *practical* of men loses, rejects,
> eliminates, or does not notice is selected by the poet
> who, through his art, gives some value to it.

The marked preference of most students for prose fiction is making the teaching of poetry increasingly difficult, not just because of the built-in resistance of those who would rather read a stack of long nineteenth-century novels than the relatively small number of poems by Baudelaire but also because even when such students can be persuaded to take a poetry course (or read some poetry as part of a course), they come with an ever-diminishing experience of the genre. This unfamiliarity is most often the root of their reticence and is, needless to say, made more acute by the foreignness (in every sense) of the language. The complexities of the genre's syntax, the rarefied (even obscure) vocabulary, and the connotations and allusions of poetic discourse all contribute to the student's sense that poetry is inaccessible and inscrutable. This unfamiliarity with the language and conventions of poetry engenders an uneasiness that yields to panic when the student becomes aware not only that everything signifies but also that it is the reader's task to make everything signify.

Unfamiliarity is our starting point, then, because the difficulties of mastering the detailed linguistic environment of French poetry, here Baudelairean verse, are compounded by the poet's enterprise to defamiliarize, to be innovative in the manipulation of that language by transforming, in special and technical ways, the linguistic landscape. The process of understanding the text therefore requires more than the grasp of French grammar one might reasonably expect of an undergraduate student; it also requires experience and understanding of what Michael Riffaterre has called poetry's "semantic indirection," "ungrammaticality," and "nonsense" (*Semiotics* 2). Unfamiliarity begs the question of how to read poetry. Riffaterre identifies two stages of reading, the first heuristic, the second retroactive, with different levels of interpretation operating at both stages. Initially, the foreign-language student apprehends meaning at two levels. First, there is a straightforward decoding of words, a process that assumes that language is referential, that words relate to things. Depending on the linguistic competence and the literary experience and expertise of the student, this stage also includes a second level, the recognition that some words and phrases do not make literal sense and cannot be made to make literal sense without the reader's performing a semantic transfer and seeing this ungrammaticality as a poetic device.[1]

The retroactive rereading of the text is the place where interpretation comes into play, where disciplined attention to the intricacies of the whole can begin to modify and clarify earlier apprehensions and where these intricacies can be worked, through comparative and sense-making processes, into a structural unity that is the significance of the poem.

Given how often students are unfamiliar not only with Baudelaire but also with French poetry (since the study of French poetry frequently begins with Baudelaire), their familiarity with poetry's descriptive systems and themes is also necessarily limited, as may be their knowledge of French sociocultural norms, which poetic language often evokes. There are few ways of tackling this difficulty; all ways, in the long run, depend on students' will to read more and to gain the experience that will enable them to "fill in according to the hypogrammatic model" (Riffaterre, *Semiotics* 5; for a definition of this complicated concept, see 168–69n16). But as Christopher Prendergast notes, Riffaterre's model is "forbidding" for the average, uninitiated undergraduate (5). How the teacher approaches the reading of Baudelaire in such a context is therefore problematic. Should initiation take place by exposure to *Les Fleurs du Mal* without prior discussion of the kinds of poetic devices in operation there? Is showing and telling in the instance of a poem or two, or even with a specially selected combination of lines, enough to provide the student reader with the confidence to seek the devices in other poems? Most students' response to this method is to say, "I can see it now, but would never have come up with that reading on my own."

A fruitful way of combating unfamiliarity with Baudelaire, as well as with poetic context and technique more generally, is to present students with Baudelaire's doublets as a comparative and contrastive exercise. Verse and prose versions of the same poem provide a ready-made translation, which is itself poetic, though in the more familiar language of prose. They circumscribe the verse corpus, allowing the teacher to demonstrate a number of principles, and they also broaden the discussion to include questions of context, self-reference, and intertextuality. The notions presented in this introduction can be developed further by using other poetry-prose pairs. This method provides an equally circumscribed body of critical writing, appropriately focused and difficult, to engage the student's attention well beyond the classroom. "La Chevelure" ("Head of Hair") and "Un Hémisphère dans une chevelure" (B. Johnson, *Défigurations* 31–55), the two versions of "L'Invitation au voyage" ("Invitation to the Voyage"; Johnson 103–60), and "Le Crépuscule du soir" ("Dusk"; Chesters 145–70) prepare the study of Baudelaire's poetic discourse and of how that discourse generates meaning from within and beyond the poem.

We begin with a study of two poems from *Les Fleurs du Mal*, "L'Examen de minuit" (334–36; "Soul-Searching at Midnight" [trans. mine]) and "La Fin de la journée" (278–80"; "Day's End"), which are set in comparison and contrast to the prose poem "A une heure du matin" (152–54; "One in the Morning"). Other poems are referred to, as are statements formulated elsewhere in Baudelaire's prose. The choice of two poems taken from different sections of *Les Fleurs du Mal* brings out the recurrence of themes in the work and affords an opportunity to examine similarities and differences in poetic treatment. Questions of unity can be addressed first in terms of an initial heuristic reading: getting a sense of what the poems are "about." Then retroactive readings place this sense in the context of the whole work, making reference to other, similar poems and recovering additional points of comparison and contrast.

"L'Examen de minuit," as its title suggests, is a poem of self-examination and introspection. As in "La Fin de la journée," this examination occurs at a particular moment of the day: "La pendule, sonnant minuit" (334) ("The clock chimes the midnight in" [335]) and, in "La Fin de la journée," "La nuit voluptueuse monte" (278) ("The night has risen, charming, vast" [279]). The second version is less concrete, and students will readily say that they have a clearer understanding of time in "L'Examen de minuit" and "A une heure du matin" than they do in "La Fin de la journée." Their reaction is not surprising, since in the first two poems there is a clear-cut relation between words and the things they denote, as clear, say, as the conventions governing the way hands on a clock (and chimes) denote the measurement of minutes and hours; the way calendars denote the measurement of days, weeks, and years.

The space of these *examens de conscience* (soul-searchings) is also important. The clock of "L'Examen de minuit" suggests an interior, as does the lamp at the end of the poem. These interiors are themselves concrete objects. In "A une heure du matin," where the poet locks the door on the outside world, interiority is clearer still: "D'abord un double tour à la serrure. Il me semble que cette tour de clef augmentera ma solitude et fortifiera les barricades qui me séparent actuellement du monde" (*Œuvres* [Ruff] 152) ("First, double-lock the door. It seems to me that the double turn of the key will increase my solitude and strengthen the barricades that separate me from the world" [*Prose Poems* 41]). In "La Fin de la journée," however, the only word that might be said to denote an object belonging to the domestic interior—to any space or time, indeed—is *rideaux* ("curtains"). These curtains are themselves double, suggesting both the drapes of the domestic interior (pulled shut at night) and the landscape of darkness, "rafraîchissantes ténèbres" (280) ("Consoling comforters of black" [281]). In other words, despite the similar time and space represented in the three poems, each poem provides an entirely different experience. In the first two examples, the heuristic reading offers referentiality; in the last example, it produces an ungrammaticality. The reader cannot entertain the notion that the poet will really roll up in the drapes. The incompatibility of the word with the situation indicates a trope or figure, which is recovered into meaning, on retroactive reading, by the readers' surmounting the "mimesis hurdle" (Riffaterre, *Semiotics* 6). What soon becomes clear to the readers is that the prose poem too relies on tropes and figures, but its familiar syntax and the greater referentiality of its language reassure the novice. Students are able to discover similar forms of expression, recovering from each poem in turn the use of *ténèbres*. They discuss the word itself before examining the different syntagmatic units where it occurs.

What the prose poem does best for students is regulate the credit and debit of information across the texts, bringing into greater relief the conditions of reading poetry. In this instance, the prose poem focuses attention on the central self-examination of the text. In "La Fin de la journée," for example, self-examination is concentrated into a kernel of absurdity and despair: "Court, danse et se tord sans raison / La Vie, impudente et criarde" (278) ("She twists and dances mindlessly— / Life, in her brash effrontery" [279]). In "L'Examen de minuit" the ironic clock reminds the poet to reflect on the use he has made of the day now past. Here the catalog of events is more developed than in "La Fin de la journée," but it does not reassure the poet. The unfamiliarity of the terms that name these events makes the poem no more reassuring for the average undergraduate. Who or what are "Crésus," "La Bêtise au front de taureau," and "la stupide Matière" (334–36) ("profligate," "Folly with brow of a bull," and "mindless Matter" [335–37])? What do they mean in this context, and how do they relate to the absurd actions described: blaspheming "the most / Incontestable of all Gods," afflicting "The weak, who are wrongly despised," bowing to Folly, honoring "mindless Matter" and putrefaction? Unfamiliarity with the terms and with the social and literary mythologies to which they refer limits the student's understanding and appreciation. The catalog of events in "A une heure du matin" amplifies the meaning of this absurdity and brings it back from the realm of allusive mythologies into the everyday, the familiarity of handshakes and meaningless exchanges, which are the antithesis of lyricism.

These *examens de conscience* raise important questions relating to lyricism and its forms. First, the interior space is the space of lyricism, and the fear of the outside world is nothing more, as Emmanuel Adatte has argued, than "the reflexion of a more generalized anguish in the face of life, capable of terrorizing the poet through its absurd barrenness" (46). Second, the *examen de conscience* as an act, both of self-contemplation and composition, has a social and literary history linked to the Catholic tradition of Saint Ignatius and to the lyrical confessions of the Romantic poets. Baudelaire's poems are an example of the "examen particulier" (Prévost 170–79) ("examination of a particular sin"), which focuses on a single spiritual failing and rehearses a resolve not to fall prey to this failing in the future. The failing is one with which more than a few students can identify, a self-perpetuating sloth: sluggishness in working and lack of regular work habits culminating in resignation and self-reproach for having achieved nothing in the course of the day. The loss or wasting of time is a central anxiety in *Les Fleurs du Mal* and can be further explored with an examination of poems 7 to 11 (24-31).

Combining the example of the confessional with that of the private journal brings to the fore the nature of this anguish and enables students to grasp the dynamic both of these particular poems and of the poet's more generalized struggle with artistic creation and with Catholicism. The exclamation mark after the statement in "L'Examen de minuit" that even the most incontestable of gods, Jesus, has been blasphemed is part ironic, part pained confession. In "A une heure du matin," this confessional dynamic is laid bare as Baudelaire borrows the self-deprecating rhetoric of the petitionary prayer, which usually asks divine favors for others as well as for oneself, only to vitiate his plea with a proud assertion that rejects humility.

Prayer is here a useful model: it creates a *mise en abyme* of Baudelaire's "art poétique" and shows the students that generic questions are also at stake. For the poet, the prayer represents formulaic discourse capable of engendering spiritual and linguistic magic: "Il y a dans la prière une opération magique. La prière est une des grandes forces de la dynamique intellectuelle. Il y a là comme une récurrence électrique" (*Œuvres* [Ruff] 627; "Mon cœur mis à nu") ("Prayer involves a magical operation. Prayer is one of the great forces of the intellectual dynamic. There is in it something like an electrical induction"). Students recognize this prose poem as a prayer precisely because they are familiar with such forms of discourse. That prayer, so subject to standard repetitions, should have a powerful intellectual dynamic reminds us of its infinite individuality despite the recognizable forms of its discourse. The interest of such discourse lies precisely in the original expressive depths that become obscured by familiarity. As Baudelaire says in "Mon cœur mis à nu," there is a "profondeur immense de pensée dans les locutions vulgaires, trous creusés par des générations de fourmis" (623) ("an immense depth of thought in commonplace expressions, holes dug by generations of ants"). The prayer at the end of this prose poem is, in its conscious use of discursive models and in its subversion of more than linguistic convention, a microcosm of the question at the heart of many of the poems in *Les Fleurs du Mal*: Does art have the power to redeem? In the final lines of "A une heure du matin," the poem's prosaism finally is overthrown by lyricism. Incantation brings relief, and the prayer makes poetry come in form and in fact.

This return of poetry brings us back to those unfamiliar terms in the second and third stanzas of "L'Examen de minuit," the catalog of absurdities causing the poet to waste his substance. The morally and spiritually impoverished poet feeds parasitically at the table of wealth ("Crésus" = wealth, by association with the mythological figure Croesus and the popular expression, in French as in English, "as rich as Croesus"). Corrupted by such satiating wealth and abundance, as the end of the poem declares, "Bu sans soif et mangé sans faim" (336) ("[having] Eaten and drunk like a swine!" [337]), the poet is led to betray all that he holds most dear. More particularly, he betrays his artistic creed by bowing to

"Bêtise," a Minotaur in reverse, having the body of a man and the head of a beast, and by swearing devotion to "la stupide Matière"—a sardonic reference to poetic beauty, because, as Yves Bonnefoy puts it, "Beauty should cure humanity of matter" (80). Although "L'Examen de minuit" seems to end in defeat, in the "vaporization" of the poet's will, what triumphs is not sloth but form, for out of self-reproach comes such form, just as prayer releases poetry. "La Bêtise" and "la stupide Matière" are represented by the clamor of the prose poem; by the different voices in direct and indirect speech; by the parentheses, asides, and the italicized inclusion of another's mispronunciation; by insincerity; and by ignorance of every kind. The prayer brings redemption in a value system that has no real belief in or need for God: the paradox of this liturgy is resolved in form by the "prêtre orgueilleux de la Lyre" (336) ("proud priest of the Lyre" [337]).

Using the prose poem as a foil counters the unfamiliarity of poetic language in *Les Fleurs du Mal* with an apparently reassuring prose that, in its turn, shows how the magic of poetry can work. Like the rhetoric of prayer, the act of writing is one of our "opérations magiques" and a "sorcellerie évocatoire" (*Œuvres* [Ruff] 626; "Mon cœur mis à nu") ("evocative witchcraft"). Poetry operates, in other words, precisely by defamiliarizing: it works at a remove from referentiality and from the prosaic norms of everyday exchange. Its ungrammaticality invites the reader into uncharted linguistic territory, so that the hypogrammatical model can be filled only by experience, knowledge of cultural norms, and imagination. The foil of prose poetry then becomes more instructive still, for it defamiliarizes the text for the seasoned reader of poetry by replacing poetic conventions with prosaism. In this light, a close reading of *Les Fleurs du Mal* reveals, as Carol de Dobay Rifelj suggests, that "familiar language itself can become a kind of figure, in Genette's sense—a figurative sense—of the gap between the expression used and that which would be felt to be 'normal' in its context" (99). In other words, by refamiliarizing the poetic text through the insertion of phrases of ordinary prose, the poet paradoxically gratifies the readers' quest for defamiliarization while contesting the very nature of poetic discourse. Because readers expect a poem to be exotic, ordinary language within it surprises them.

Such contesting is, of course, at the heart of poetry if one subscribes to the view that poetry is the site of a permanent dialogue between tradition and innovation. As Baudelaire puts it so eloquently in "Le Voyage," "Plonger au fond du gouffre, Enfer ou Ciel, qu'importe? / Au fond de l'Inconnu pour trouver du *nouveau!*" (292) ("And plunge to depths of Heaven or of Hell, / To fathom the Unknown, and find the *new!*" [293]). "La Fin de la journée" maps this same space, which is not death itself but a "cœur plein de songes funèbres" ("heart so full of mournful dreams"), a liberation, a release into the world of the unknown, as in "La Mort des pauvres" ("The Death of the Poor"), where there is a "portique ouvert sur les Cieux inconnus" (278) ("the porch looking out on mysterious skies" [279]). The quest for the new and unknown implies a known tradition, and while it may not always be possible to explore fully the ramifications of such traditions with students unfamiliar with them, once again the foil of the prose poem allows one to introduce notions of self-reference and intertextuality in poetry.

The prayer at the end of "A une heure du matin" specifically asks for "quelques beaux vers" (154) ("the inspiration for some beautiful lines of poetry"), which will affirm the poet's self-worth and set him apart from those he despises. The exasperation of *enfin* ("finally") found in all the three poems examined here in fact precedes, in "L'Examen de minuit," the same plea for inspiration. The students have already made the connection between the prayer and formulaic discourse. It is not difficult for them to see such formulas as existing outside the realm of poetry, that is to say, in another genre. Intertextuality is not difficult to understand in these terms, and it is a small leap from here to consider how other voices might be appropriated (as indeed they are in the citation of encounters in the prose poem). Students can understand, too, how the *examen de conscience* makes reference to both a Christian and a Romantic tradition. The self-rewriting that such a doublet implies is also self-evident, since the casting of similar ideas in different forms appears clearly to students in this circumscribed corpus of texts.

This is the point where telling becomes necessary not just for students but for scholars too. The experience of other readers can thus be assimilated and contribute to one's own experience. A practical lesson in intertextuality, in other words, makes available to the student an understanding of an otherwise hidden secret. The rhyme *Lyre-délire* in "L'Examen de minuit" (336) is a cliché, this "saint délire" is caused less by lyricism than by the excesses of eating and drinking (a clue to the irony hidden in the rhyme), and Baudelaire plays on its exhaustion to transform banality into a poetic virtue (Robb 301). In this way, poems can be seen to talk not only about themselves but also about other poems (and also to other poets). The prose poem foil here comes into its own again, for it makes manifest, in its familiarization and defamiliarization of poetic language, what Prendergast calls the "more restless, combative and dynamic role for a poem in its transactions with its predecessors" (23) and opens a broader discussion on and analysis of the innovative poetics of *Les Fleurs du Mal* and the work's role in the shaping of modernity.

NOTE

[1]Riffaterre defines *ungrammaticality* as a contradiction or spuriousness in the mimesis of language, in its referentiality. The term is used to describe the way in which poetic language signifies on what students may call a second level or on what Riffaterre describes as "a different network of relationships" and "a higher level of text" (*Semiotics* 4–5).

Baudelaire and the Poetry of Memory

J. A. Hiddleston

The greatest problem for many students is to acquire a sense of the coherence of *Les Fleurs du Mal*. Approaches that overemphasize the "secret architecture" of the collection and invite students to read it like a novel are to be avoided for doing violence to the text and conveying a false impression of poetic creation. Poetry, the most demanding of literary genres, requires much concentration on individual texts, with the result that readers, especially of a work in a foreign language, are often left with a distressing sense of fragmentation, with little grasp of the work as a whole or of the vision that informs it. To counteract this problem, I have found it helpful to organize discussion around the notions of time and memory, which, when sustained, can lead to a sense of synthesis, enabling students to enter more fully into Baudelaire's mental universe.

One can start by stressing the importance Baudelaire gives to memory in the art of his time. According to Baudelaire, the great merit of Eugène Delacroix is not just that his paintings have all the ingredients of Romantic art—intimacy, spirituality, color, aspiration toward the infinite (*Œuvres* [Ruff] 230; "Salon de 1846")—but also that in giving more importance to color than to outline, in painting rapidly and from memory, he endows his paintings with a universality and suggestive depth capable of arousing the memory of the spectator. His paintings not only proceed from memory, they speak to memory, so that the spectator is made to participate in the creative élan of the artist and at the same time to deepen his own reverie and self-knowledge. The result is that the creation and appreciation of a picture are phenomena that depend for their effect on the mobilization and orchestration of the power of memory.

It is a critical commonplace to emphasize the close relation between poetry and painting in the nineteenth century. Many poets of the time were critics of art or practitioners—Victor Hugo, Théophile Gautier, Stéphane Mallarmé, and of course Baudelaire himself. In a sense nothing could be more natural, since Romantic poetry had tended increasingly to replace the abstractions of previous generations with concrete, physical notations. As the spiritual and emotional turmoil of the canvases of Delacroix is expressed by the agitation of forms and the interplay and clash of color, so also poetry, having set aside the Romantic rhetoric of the spontaneous overflow of powerful emotion in favor of an art concerned with sensations and the objects that arouse them, develops a greater suggestive power. In appealing to the affective memory of the readers, it allows them, as Delacroix's paintings do, to participate in the creative process and at the same time to recognize themselves. The color-less figures of an outmoded neoclassicism can be contrasted with what Jules Laforgue was later to call Baudelaire's "enormous," "Yankee" similes reminis-cent of the Song of Solomon: "Thy teeth are like a flock of sheep that are even shorn, which came up from the washing," in which the distance between the terms of the comparison has the power to disconcert and invigorate at the same time (see Hiddleston 97–98 and 106–07). Take the following examples: night thickening like a partition (74–75), a woman's bosom compared to a beautiful cupboard (106–07), eyes lit up like boutiques (52–53), a carcass with its legs in the air like a lecherous whore (58–59), an angel whipping the sun (284–85), or the flesh of lesbians flapping in the wind like an old flag (244–45). It is above all the juxtaposition of the sublime and the grotesque, the sudden and forced alignment of elevated preoccupations with the banal objects of everyday experience, that makes for the power and immediacy of Baudelaire's poetry. When he writes of clandestine pleasures that we press like an old orange (4–5), of a heart bruised like a peach (200–01), of kisses fresh as water melons (232–33), he exemplifies his famous "suggestive magic containing object and subject, the world external to the artist and the artist himself" (*Œuvres* [Ruff] 424; "L'Art philosophique"). The sublime and grotesque often unite to make a "mnemonics of the beautiful" (*Salon* 244), illustrating the fundamental truth that the poetic image, in Baudelaire's work as in Delacroix's painting, is essentially a phenomenon of memory. The reader experiences astonishment at the uniqueness of the poet's imagination but at the same time has a sense of déjà vu, recognizing a part of his own experience resuscitated by the operation of affective memory. The abstractions of an-guish, melancholy, or the pursuit of happiness have been made present through humble and concrete images, all the more powerfully as the discrep-ancy between the terms of the comparisons produces a shock strong enough to arouse and activate the deeper strata of memory. It may be difficult for us to identify with an unparticularized anguish or lost love, but we can all recog-nize the ambivalent sensations of appetite and disgust before an old orange or a bruised peach. The bizarreness of Baudelaire's poetry—he thought that the beautiful was always bizarre (*Œuvres* [Ruff] 362; "Exposition universelle 1855")—acts like a jolt in the mind. Divergent objects and sensations from opposite poles of experience upset our normal perceptions and open our mental space to a new supernatural world.

The second aspect of memory is metaphysical rather than aesthetic. It concerns an existential experience of time within a Christian or quasi-Christian context. The poet's attitude toward Christianity is far from orthodox, but one thing is clear, his adhesion to the doctrine of original sin, the "catholic idea" that Baudelaire claimed was the starting point for Les Fleurs du Mal (Correspondance 2: 141). This fundamental teaching of the Christian religion is unknown and incomprehensible to all but a few students, even those who claim to be practicing Christians; but it is essential to a proper understanding of the moral dimension of the collection. In the context of memory, one should stress the sense of an eternal present and the ignorance of good and evil in the Garden of Eden, as contrasted with the fallen state after the expulsion of Adam and Eve and humankind's subjection to time in the real world. Spleen and ennui can be readily understood as a pathological apprehension of time and imperfection, an apprehension not by the intellect but by the senses.

The effect of the happy memory in Baudelaire is the illusion of a reintegration into this lost paradise or the creation of an artificial one. Here, one can point to the golden age of "I love the thought . . ." (19) or the exotic paradise of "Exotic Perfume" (49) or "Invitation to the Voyage" (109), where paradise is projected into the future or a distant land. The best example is probably "Head of Hair" (51), the anthology piece most used to illustrate analogy and correspondence. But the poem also provides an excellent example of the poet's temporal imagination: for time undergoes a radical transformation as the reader is made to live, or relive, the poem as a journey of discovery, as a deliverance from the bonds of the present, as an unfolding of the past and all its memories, and above all as an opening to the future. Thanks to this "evocative witchcraft" (Œuvres [Ruff] 464), the poet seems installed within a time that is, so to speak, circular: the past is projected into a future both open to joy and closed to uncertainty; and the future is endowed with the reassuring certainty of the past while still issuing the future's summons to adventure and novelty.

Similarly, the intimate space of the alcove, the starting point of "Head of Hair," following the expansive reverie from languorous Asia to scorching Africa, takes on the dimensions of the infinite, without losing anything of its intimate and finite quality. Space, following the same impulsion and development as time and memory, also undergoes a transformation. No longer some bottomless abyss, it becomes a habitable milieu, reduced to human dimensions, without vertigo or restriction. The effect of the hair and the memories the hair contains is to make the azure of the sky "immense and round" (trans. mine) and this roundness of time and space is the very perfection the poet dreams of, in which past and future, alcove and abyss, claustrophobia and vertigo cease to be perceived as contradictory. These privileged moments are properly lyrical, what Baudelaire elsewhere calls "the soul in its fine hours" (Œuvres [Ruff] 404; "Salon de 1859"), in which the infinite is experienced in the finite, in moments when the poet drinks the wine of memory. They represent a summit in his reverie, but they are rare.

Many poems convey the sense of an obstacle, or of nostalgia for an elsewhere that constantly recedes; disquieting images or thoughts intrude into a promised harmony. Take for example the violin in "The Harmony of Evening" that trembles like an afflicted heart, or the sun drowning in its coagulating blood (97). No matter how great the creative explosion, there is often some element to trouble the confidence, some threat, fear, unease, or ambiguity to signify that dream and the ideal by definition cannot be made present in reality. There are also the bad days of the mind, in which spring has lost its perfume (152–53); in which "The Hope that shines at windows in the Inn / Is gone" (113); in which space deepens as with a happy dream or an opium trance, but only to give objects a spectral or nightmarish presence. Think of what is threatening in "The Seven Old Men," with its yellow, dirty fog and houses "rendered taller by the mist" (177). Similarly, there are moments when the onrush of memories, instead of transfiguring time, merely emphasizes what is irreparable and irreversible and when the resurrection of the past and of a happiness that is gone is replaced by the painful experience of disintegration. "Spleen (2)" and "The Swan" both leave an ill-assorted and random bric-a-brac of memories like the flotsam of some sentimental and cultural shipwreck. Instead of that expansion in concentric circles of "Head of Hair," the memories give no feeling of elevation, but "heavier than rocks" (174; trans. mine), they give the depressing feeling of a fall.

There are then moments when time does not open onto an eternity of joy or fulfillment but seems to have stopped, as with the "smoking log" and the "wheezing clock" of "Spleen (1)" (145). It is as if time were ill and about to die, arresting all movement and with it the life not just of the poet but also of the whole of reality, in a return to a primitive absence or chaos. The autumn poems ("Autumn Song," "Autumn Sonnet") can be read as prefiguring this state, as can those, such as "The Irremediable," which depict the sun imprisoned in a polar hell, once again denoting the stopping of time without hope of liberation or resurrection. So there is a hellish time, bringing a flood of meaningless memories, or a time that imprisons. But perhaps more disturbing is the sense of time as a vain repetition, as with the polyglot clock repeating "Remember!" in various languages and its inexorable ticking of seconds three thousand six hundred times an hour (163), like the autumnal unloading of firewood in courtyards, but more sinister because more insistent. In "The Seven Old Men" the emphasis passes from the ticking of time to time's content, the vision it contains. (Reviewing the various interpretations of this poem can lead to discussion of the relevance of suggested intertexts—*Macbeth*, for example—and of the way that Baudelaire's imagery is rarely elliptical, as in later poets, but presents to the reader both tenor and vehicle.) What the poem invites the reader to share is the experience of repetition itself, the nightmare of time as a baleful, absurd concatenation of identical moments, intimating evil, spite, and resentment. This frightening representation of time as a combination of movement and immobility can be contrasted with positive contexts in which a similar but opposite combination occurs, in the "[i]nfinite lulling, leisure steeped in balm" of "Head of Hair" (51) or the swaying movement in "The Dancing Serpent" like the rocking of ships at anchor (59); such contexts indicate an ideal, supernatural time. Similarly, time stopped has its positive counterpart in "To a Woman Passing By," which celebrates a unique moment that has no before or after, a moment of love at first and last sight that cannot be corrupted by repetition, since the shared love it evokes can never be put to the test. This vision has all the prestige of virtuality over reality; it is a privileged moment that seems to stand outside time, preserved and eternalized by memory.

These various contrasts are part of the system of opposites structuring the poet's mental world—spleen and ideal, God and Satan, heaven and hell, and so on. At this point, class discussion can widen to examine Baudelaire's binary vision; its function; the extent to which it can be thought stable, providing a framework for moral decisions (in the broadest sense); and the extent to which it is unstable, illusory, collapsing.

What one might call intratextual memory concerns echoes and resonances within the collection itself. As we read Les Fleurs du Mal, our minds are constantly brought back to previous poems, through repetitions or similarities of rhyme, rhythm, and, principally, image. There emerges a network of themes and images that as we read, appeals to our memory, widening and deepening our understanding of Baudelaire's mental world. Take, for example, eyes: the fearful, awe-inspiring eyes of "Beauty"; eyes lit up like boutiques and "blazing yews" (52; trans. mine; McGowan incorrectly has "blazing stanchions" [53]); sphinxlike eyes; eyes like steel, diamonds, metal, or agate; eyes covered with a veil like an autumn sun; eyes of the blind, whose spark has gone; and eyes that pass triumphantly before the poet, full of light. There are the images of the sea; various balconies as places of intimacy and meditation; high places, sad places, cruel places. More than anything else there are the spatial images: of the alcove, the azure blue of the sky "immense and round," the gouffre up or down, the tombs and cemeteries, the palaces of the soul, the underground altars, and so on. The discussion can eventually lead to the realization that there is a Baudelairean poetic universe, coherent and resembling no other. It may be that the collection finds a unity in its so-called secret architecture, but there is another sense in which the collection forms a whole, as an identifiable universe of objects, sensations, and obsessions stemming from the same temperament. It was Marcel Proust who most explicitly maintained that all great artists produce a peculiar world or country and that it is the duty of the critic to help the reader discover it. He writes of "the world of Baudelaire's thought, this country of his genius of which each poem is but a fragment" (Contre Sainte-Beuve 255; see A la recherche 3: 375, 377). This idea can be traced to Baudelaire himself, who states that criticism, instead of analyzing each work in detail, should seek to penetrate the temperament of the artist and the motives that cause the artist to act (*Œuvres* [Ruff] 364; "Exposition universelle 1855"). Discussion can broaden at this point to include the Geneva school of criticism, its virtues and shortcomings, and the extent to which it may be more relevant for the study of some writers than for others.

The analysis of intratextual memory can, if appropriate, be taken beyond *Les Fleurs du Mal* to *Le Spleen de Paris*. Such analysis would involve a comparison of the various doublets from the two collections and, crucially, the nature of prose and poetry. But if the prose poems are not included at this stage, the nature of poetry can be approached in the context of the overarching theme of memory, beginning with rhyme and moving on to meter, enjambment, and more intricate problems of prosody. This study in turn can lead to a consideration of the specificity of prose and poetry, focusing perhaps on Jean Cohen's *Structure du language poétique* and *Le Haut Langage* and on the sense of the lyrical as repetition, incantation, and a constant appeal to memory. From there the discussion can readily move to the expression in poetry of the grotesque, the caricatural, and the stridency of modern life.

Much of Baudelaire's production alludes to canonical works and figures of Western culture: the Bible, the ancient world, Dante, Tasso, Shakespeare, and Delacroix and other masters contemporary to Baudelaire. Such allusions appeal to the reader's field of reference and also place the spiritual drama of the collection in a continuing culture, no matter how fragmented it may be. The examples are endless, the most rewarding being the most expansive, as with "The Dancing Serpent," where the allusions extend from the Garden of Eden to the brazen serpent of Moses (Num. 21) to Hermes and his caduceus, surrounding the figure of the woman with intimations of temptation, healing, the penetration of the ultimate mysteries, and the triumph over time and death. Or one might take the last quatrain from "The Swan" where, in the forest to which the poet's mind is exiled, "Old Memory sings out a full note of the horn" (177). The line prolongs a reverie that starts in the dark forest reminiscent of the first stanza of Dante's *Inferno*; passes through the sounds of the horn in *La Chanson de Roland*, which are taken up in turn in Alfred de Vigny's "Le Cor"; and finally refers back intratextually to "The Beacons": "It is a beacon on a thousand citadels, / A cry of hunters lost within a mighty wood!" (25). The example shows how cultural associations can radiate out through *Les Fleurs du Mal* and beyond, in an expansion analogous to the sensations in "Head of Hair" that go from languorous Asia to scorching Africa.

The most rewarding allusions are often the most hidden, as in "The Love of Illusion": "I think, how lovely! and how oddly innocent! / Massive remembrance, that great tower raised above, / Crowns her" (201). The image of memory as a tower pleases by its majestic, surprising qualities, but also because it contains and prolongs all kinds of literary and cultural resonances. Memory stands out above a bland and featureless landscape, with overtones of elevation, permanence, solidity, and domination. Culturally, it contains a reference to Cybele, the mother goddess of earth and harvest who is represented in

Greek statues with a mural crown on her head. The allusion gives to the figure of the woman a noble, statuesque, and divine quality (significantly, a variant reading is "divine remembrance"). There is possibly a further allusion to the Song of Solomon, where it is said of the Sulamite, "Thy neck is like the tower of David builded for an armory" (4.4). And one might legitimately think also of the castles, palaces, and towers of the soul in Saint Teresa or John of the Cross, the broken tower of the tarot pack, or Gérard de Nerval's Prince of Aquitaine "with the abolished tower" (1: 693; "El Desdichado"). The cultural allusion is most appealing when indirect, veiled, and suggestive, like Baudelaire's imagery.

Finally, a form of what might be called negative intertextuality serves to upset our expectations as readers by making the poem into an ironic or subversive retort to a previous text, genre, or topos. The numerous examples of this device show it to be a fundamental part of the poet's aesthetic and a gauge of his originality. *"Duellum,"* for example, promises some kind of armed conflict, but it immediately pirouettes to treat the ambiguities of love and hatred. Similarly, with "I love you as I love . . . ," the reader expects effusive praise of the mysterious charms of the lady but is soon disoriented and disabused by the description of the poet's attacking her like "[a] choir of wormlets pressing towards a corpse" (53). "I give to you these verses . . ." seems set in the context of the gift of the poem, typical of Renaissance poets, but the tercets upset our expectations and proceed not to bless the poet's muse but to curse her. Nothing could be further from the Renaissance muses or even those of Romanticism—think of "L'Immortelle" of Alfred de Musset's "Night of May"—than Baudelaire's muse, whose hollow eyes, blue feet, shivering shoulders, madness, and anguish replace the health and innocence of the white muses of tradition. And to understand what was shocking about his interiors in the "Spleen" poems and "Parisian Scenes," one need only consider Hugo's "Regard jeté dans une mansarde" ("a glance into an attic window") in *Les Rayons et les ombres* (*Œuvres* 1037). Both poets appear as voyeurs, but while Hugo finds the chaste and limpid gaze of a poor and impeccably innocent young girl, Baudelaire sees what is sordid, impure, and unhealthy, uncovering the decadence and degeneration of the modern capital.

To read *Les Fleurs du Mal*, we must try to re-create it in ourselves and respond to the appeal it makes to our memory; but at the same time we must place it as much as possible in its historic and cultural context, to see it from a contemporary point of view. Only then shall we be able to form an idea of its originality and power to shock. Curiously, its ironic and critical intertextuality not only brings out the originality of the work but relativizes it at the same time. By emphasizing its literary character and appealing to the cultural memory of the reader, such intertextuality causes the reader to doubt the work's ability to come to grips with a reality other than literary. By a supreme irony, *Les Fleurs du Mal*, which was above all to record a spiritual adventure, celebrating the exalted mission of art, is among the first works to suggest, if not to proclaim, its self-referentiality. In *Le Spleen de Paris* the poet's pessimism and literary agnosticism deepen, and the ambiguities are less delicate and nuanced. But from our reading of *Les Fleurs du Mal*, in spite of the poet's protests of its seriousness and spiritual intensity, one gets a hint from time to time of a doubt concerning the efficacy of poetry itself, as if poetry were little more than a complicated interrelation of sounds and words. Such an ambiguity would in a sense be hardly astonishing in a poet whose mental world is built on the interplay of opposites; it would be but another proof of his many-sided modernity.

NOTE

An earlier version of this essay, less focused on teaching, was published in French, in *Baudelaire*, Les Fleurs du Mal: *l'intériorité de la forme* (Paris: SEDES, 1984) 321–39.

Baudelaire and the Poetics of Perversity
Deborah A. Harter

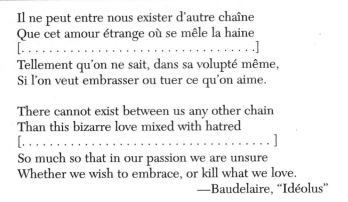

Il ne peut entre nous exister d'autre chaîne
Que cet amour étrange où se mêle la haine
[. . . . .]
Tellement qu'on ne sait, dans sa volupté même,
Si l'on veut embrasser ou tuer ce qu'on aime.

There cannot exist between us any other chain
Than this bizarre love mixed with hatred
[. . . . .]
So much so that in our passion we are unsure
Whether we wish to embrace, or kill what we love.
       —Baudelaire, "Idéolus"

The texts I most enjoy teaching are those that take my students by surprise—
that are not just rich in substance but also so subversive, or aesthetically stun-
ning, or psychologically unsettling, that their impact is irresistible. I value the
way such texts as these test our best interpretive strategies. And I value the way
they provoke, among my students and myself, dramatic exchanges that make a
difference to each of us—that change us, that compel us to new understand-
ing, that have little to do with our being in a classroom. To teach Baudelaire's
Fleurs du Mal in all its dimensions is to have just such an occasion. One finds
oneself teaching a poetry that is powerful for the radical boldness with which
it explores love and sexuality, life and death, in images stripped of their usual
romantic trappings. It is a poetry where sexuality is often allied to calculated
cruelty; where the contours of a modern consciousness, in all its hysteria, its
cynicism, its fragmentariness, are starkly sketched; where evil, alternately
embraced and resisted, alternately titillating and horrific, is made articulate;
where there is a certain pleasure in figuring those forces that lie on the side of
violence and violation. It is a poetry that widens the scope of our experience
even as it shocks our sensibilities: a poetry, I would suggest, in which what is
perverse (I use the term in its broadest sense) might well function to name the
abiding power at the heart of all that poetry's images.

 With its very title and with each successive poem, *Les Fleurs du Mal* irrev-
erently announces it will not be another pretty collection of pretty words about
pretty things. In what appears a gesture of both admiration and irony, Baude-
laire dedicates "ces fleurs maladives" (2) ("these sickly flowers" [3]) to
Théophile Gautier, "impeccable poet," whose own exquisitely wrought *Emaux
et Camées* (1852) would seem to stand in the sharpest possible contrast to these
wild offerings. Baudelaire's poetry, we quickly learn, will take the body, and
nature, and the city, and the human psyche itself and narrate the poet's varying

encounters with these, deploying all the force and beauty—but also all the violence—this might entail. Teeming larvae move and feast in rhythmic, erotic waves on a rotting corpse (60; "Une Charogne"); love sits on "the skull / of Humanity," gaily blowing bubbles with the brains and blood and flesh sucked up from the luminous globe beneath it (258–61; "L'Amour et le crâne"); ferocious birds perch on a hanged man, planting their beaks in every corner of his putrid flesh and emerging "gorgés de hideuses délices" (256; "Un Voyage à Cythère") ("gorged with hideous delights" [trans. mine]). The body, in Baudelaire, is a site of exquisite contemplation that is picked apart and punished for its passions; that is subjected to self-division and devouring; that inspires, in its feminine form, both luxurious memory ("N'es-tu pas l'oasis où je rêve, et la gourde / Où je hume à longs traits le vin du souvenir?") (52; "La Chevelure") ("Are you not the oasis where I dream, and the gourd / Where I savor in long draughts the wine of memory?" [trans. mine]) and reactive hatred ("Machine aveugle et sourde [. . .] buveur du sang du monde") (52; "Tu mettrais l'univers entier . . .") ("Blind and deaf machine [. . .] that drinks the whole world's blood" [trans. mine]).

Nature surprises us no less than the body in this poetry that finds in the natural world little of the idyllic bliss earlier poets had celebrated. If Alphonse de Lamartine's lyric self is consoled by an eternal nature that he feels might prolong the memory of his mistress, in *Les Fleurs du Mal* nature mocks the poet's shattered nerves and his dizzying steps across a psychological and emotional abyss. In the condemned piece "A celle qui est trop gaie," the poet feels the sun "comme une ironie" (88) ("like an irony" [89]) ripping at his chest and "humiliating" his heart so that in revenge he must punish, "on a flower," the "insolence" of Nature (88 [trans. mine]). In "Un Voyage à Cythère," an island of imagined enchantment and greenery proves to be a wilderness of rocks ("Un désert rocailleux" [256]). At moments, as in "Correspondances" (18), Baudelaire evokes nature as a silent, almost mystical presence whose beauties are at best partially glimpsed. More often the flowers and trees in *Les Fleurs du Mal* are, in Martin Turnell's words, "monstrous blooms that symbolize sex and death" (201). "Nature is ugly," Baudelaire would write, "and I prefer the monsters of my fantasy to positive triviality" (*Œuvres* [Ruff] 396; "Salon de 1859").

Enveloping the body and defying nature in these poems is the pulse of a modern urban city at once exhilarating and nightmarish. It is a place where "everything, even horror, turns to enchantment" (180 [trans. mine]; "Les Petites Vieilles"); where the flaneur bathes in rich anonymity; and where such startling visions as the fugitive beauty, in "A une passante," tantalize and rejuvenate the disillusioned poet as he sits in a café "crispé comme un extravagant" (188) ("wincing like a madman" [trans. mine]), seduced by those conscious shocks that render poignant the urban experience (see Benjamin, "On Some Motifs"). But this modern metropolis also inspires hysterical alarm. As the poet of "Les Sept Vieillards" wanders the avenues of Paris, picking his way through yellow fog along streets shaken by the rumbling of carts, his imaginative stroll leads him only to the insidious spectacle of a series of cracked, cruel old men (offspring perhaps of a cracked and cruel cityscape)—broken in body, more hostile than indifferent, crushing, humiliating, their gaze steeped in bitterness—from whose presence he finally flees in delirious apprehension, "horrified, sick, and trembling" (trans. mine) ("Exaspéré [. . .] / Malade et morfondu" [180]).

In all these domains *Les Fleurs du Mal* reflects a certain poetics of perversity both profound in its implications and critical to our teaching. Embracing the violent along with the banally mundane, it is a poetics that shocks not just in the murderousness of its sexual content (in "A une Madone" the poet constructs an altar to his "mortal Mary" [119], thrilling with sadistic pleasure at the thought of planting seven knives—one each for the seven deadly sins, one each for the seven sorrows of Mary in the Catholic tradition—in his mistress's panting and bleeding heart). It shocks in the license it takes in the selection of poetic matter (in "Les Aveugles" the poet writes of the blind of Paris, those peculiar sleepwalkers who roam the streets "Dardant on ne sait où leurs globes ténébreux" [186; "flashing—who knows where—their sightless orbs" (trans. mine)]). It shocks in the vocabulary that comes into play to envision a new urban order. Dominique Rincé has noted the stunning lexical effects in *Les Fleurs du Mal*, where such neologisms as *wagon* ("train car"), *quinquet* ("oil lamp"), *réverbère* ("streetlamp"), *bilan* ("statement of balance"), *voirie* ("city streets and waterways"), and *omnibus* ("local train") are allowed for the first time to enter "the sacred space of the poem" (79). It shocks, finally, in the power and surprise with which Baudelaire joins, with uncanny seamlessness, distinctly different, often discordant domains. Baudelaire compels us to see a thing because we can't resist either the strangeness or the rightness of these joinings—as in "La Cloche fêlée," where he glides remarkably from the image of a smoking fireplace to memories slowly rising in the fog, to church bells vigorously chiming their cries in the night, to the image of his own soul, cracked and weak: a cracked bell that wishes to fill the cold void of night with its song but produces only something like the thick death rattle of a wounded man forgotten by the side of a lake of blood, dying "without moving and with immense effort" (144 [trans. mine]) beneath a heap of other dying men.

But Baudelaire does more than simply bring into synchronic view images of discordant domains. He juxtaposes, as Eric Auerbach has noted, the lofty and the base, the grand and the grotesque, in a massive breach of stylistic decorum that was unprecedented and that must have "startled if not horrified" his contemporaries (203). In "Spleen (4)," Auerbach suggests, every traditional notion of the sublime is exploded when church bells leap with fury and fling their enraged howling (the image is almost surrealistic) at the sky (204). One thinks as well of "Une Charogne," where a rotting carcass shifts hazily in and out of view as vermin writhe upon and modify its shape, reminding the poet, suddenly, of the way a painting might shift and form in the memory and imagination of an artist as he or she begins to sketch. In "Une Martyre" a woman's garter, lying solitary near her decapitated torso, hurls its cold glance like a blazing eye ("ainsi qu'un œil [. . .] qui flambe" [230]). Her severed head, as though some elegant vase or sleeping child, "reposes" on the night table like a ranunculus, while flowers, nearby, expire in their "coffins" of glass (230, 228). Like "the museum of love" Baudelaire once imagined, where everything would have a place "from the tenderness of a Saint Teresa [. . .] to the wretched drawings that hang in harlots' bedrooms above cracked jugs and rickety console tables" (*Curiosités* 132–33), nothing for this poet—not the great, not the hideous, not the degraded—is excluded as possible subject matter for the loftiest expression.

With every poem they read I ask my students to locate the ways in which it shocks. How, at the levels of language and idea, does it provoke either their interest or their sensibilities? Where does it leave them behind? In what way is it nothing new? Is there a difference, in these poems or in their outlook, between the merely shocking and the perverse? (What, for example, is the difference between the shock of the image of the stumbling albatross that maladroitly—and spectacularly, for the reader—drags its wings at its sides like useless oars ["Comme des avirons" (14)] and the shock in "Une Martyre," so much more violent, where the murdered woman's nude torso displays its "secret splendors" with "complete abandon" and "without scruple" as it lies, headless, on bloody sheets [230 (trans. mine)]?) What connects perversity and pleasure in these poems? Whose perversity is it? Whose pleasure? (Is Baudelaire's pleasure in writing the same as or different from our pleasure in reading?) Are the aesthetic pleasures of reading these poems allied entirely with the psychic pleasures described? How do our responses to this poetry, as twentieth-century readers, differ from what must have been the responses of Baudelaire's contemporaries?

There are elements in Baudelaire that provoke in my students a resistance I welcome. They are outraged, for example, at the way the female body in this text provides an occasion either for reverence or revulsion—the way it is undulating and adored in "Le Serpent qui danse," while in the very next poem, "Une Charogne," it is aligned with a putrid mass that splays its legs in the air "comme une femme lubrique, / Brûlante et suant les poisons" (58) ("like a lustful harlot, / sweating out her poisons" [trans. mine]). We talk about how Baudelaire's poetry punishes women as much as it idealizes them, rendering poignantly the fundamentally fetishistic, misogynistic relation to the female body that Charles Bernheimer sees not just in this poet but among this century's male artists generally. A woman's body, Bernheimer suggests, is often distilled and reduced to the prostitute's body; it fascinates "to the degree that that fascination can produce structures to contain, sublimate, or metaphorize the contaminating decomposition of [its] sexual ferment" (2).

But my students also resist and misinterpret a whole level of representation in Baudelaire that is simply more radical in its implications than what they are accustomed to considering. They are so unaccustomed, indeed, to suspecting such poetical giants as Baudelaire of perversity that it is not Baudelaire's position that they first experience as perverse but mine—as I point to moments, underline certain images, that make them cringe in disbelief. It is not so much that they don't love to be disgusted: in "Une Charogne" they cheerfully take in the grim spectacle of larvae so thick they flow and writhe like a living liquid (60). But my students become uncomfortable when the narrating voice in "Je t'adore à l'égal . . ." announces it will "mount to the assault" of its mistress "Comme après un cadavre un chœur de vermisseaux" (52) ("like a chorus of worms assailing a corpse" [trans. mine]) or when that voice revels, in "L'Héautontimorouménos," in the excitement it will experience witnessing the suffering it inflicts on a body that is ultimately its own—when it thinks how its desire, "gonflé d'espérance" (156) ("great with hope" [trans. mine]), will soon be swimming in that other's salty tears. When we study "Le Vampire," my students come up with any number of interpretations for the concluding stanza other than the one whereby the poet is chastised for his inextricable bond with the inner afflictions from which he seeks relief. How do we read those lines, they ask, in which the poet is scolded that if his vampire were killed on his behalf, he would soon revive its corpse with his kisses (64)?

At moments of resistance I find it helpful to introduce critical perspectives that illuminate Baudelaire's modernity. Leo Bersani, for example, has written elegantly on the "Baudelairean discovery of psychic mobility [and] of unanchored identity" (2). *Les Fleurs du Mal* provides, in his view, a radical departure from both previous and contemporary notions of the self, notions that envisioned subjectivity and desire as essentially pastoral and essentially anchored. Here, instead, the poet's identity is starkly fragmented and utterly unstable, registering this instability in the very unfolding of poetic fantasy. Thus, in "La Chevelure," the poet floats freely between images of a woman's hair and images of his own body, as his poetic imagination savors, already, the memories it imagines her body will incite:

> Je plongerai ma tête amoureuse d'ivresse
> Dans ce noir océan où l'autre est enfermé;
> Et mon esprit subtil que le roulis caresse
> Saura vous retrouver, ô féconde paresse!   (50)

> I'll plunge my head, in love with drunkenness,
> In this dark sea where the other is held;
> And my cunning mind, rocked in its caress,
> Will find you there, O fertile indolence!   (trans. mine)

In the end the woman's body is all but lost in the heat of the poet's desiring imagination, as the erotic is shifted from its point of departure (in her) to the ecstatic experience of the movement of fantasy itself.

It is this very mobility of desire, Bersani suggests, and of the self shattered into multiple selves, that helps explain how in Baudelaire pleasure is linked to pain and, ultimately, to crime. The violent sadism of *"L'Héautonti-moroumếnos"* ("the self-torturer") runs tandem with a masochistic fantasy of pleasurable self-annihilation as the poet moves alternately between descriptions of cold cruelty to a woman and self-devouring. His exclamation, "Je suis le sinistre miroir / Où la mégère se regarde!" (156) ("I am the deadly mirror in which the shrew beholds herself" [trans. mine]), expresses the fullest possible union between the violence he would perpetrate ("Je te frapperai sans colère" [154] ["I will strike you without anger"]) and the masochistic self-destruction he simultaneously imagines ("Je suis de mon cœur le vampire" [156] ["I am, of my own heart, the vampire"]). When he cries out, "Je suis la plaie et le couteau! / [. . .] les membres et la roue, / Et la victime et le bourreau!" ("I am the wound and the knife! / [. . .] the limbs and the wrack! / the victim and the torturer!"), his words are charged with both pleasure and bitterness, with both ironic, self-conscious triumph and arid emptiness.

Baudelaire invents a modern poetry unshaken by the often anguished movements of his mind's eye. He gives us a work "of gruesome hopelessness," as Auerbach has suggested (226), but of hopelessness spoken (perversely, one might say) in good faith. At its most powerful his work offers to us not just such extraordinary and punishing poems as *"L'Héautontimoroumếnos"* and "A celle qui est trop gaie" but also "Recueillement," a poem that is neither punishing nor scandalous and yet that startles when the poet invites his Sorrow to "quiet" its despair (346; "Sois sage, ô ma Douleur, et tiens-toi plus tranquille"), to take his hand, and to come away from the furors of men who, "Lashed by their Lust," gather remorse "in servile holiday" (trans. mine). He imagines the years that have passed as a set of bemused figures in outdated gowns leaning down from celestial balconies ("Vois se pencher les défuntes Années, / Sur les balcons du ciel, en robes surannées"); he envisions abstract mood ("smiling Regret") as a strangely amphibious, strangely human shape rising from watery depths ("Vois [. . .] / Surgir du fond des eaux le Regret souriant"); then he asks his Sorrow to watch as the dying Sun ("le Soleil moribond") sleeps beneath the arch of the sky. With a supremely bittersweet gentleness, in images that render the scene both eerie and immensely intimate, in a city that in other poems has inspired every possible shade of anguish, hysteria, and ironic glee, the poet asks his Sorrow to listen (the verb gains its power, curiously, from the visual weight of the image that follows), as the night ambles forth "comme un long linceul traînant à l'Orient" (346; "like an endless shroud trailing to the Orient" [trans. mine]).

In a recent study of what he calls "the death of Satan" in American culture, Andrew Delbanco suggests that we have lost the power to articulate evil. "We have no language" any longer "to connect our inner lives with the horrors that pass before our eyes in the outer world" (3). This could certainly not be said of Baudelaire, whose poems forge into word and idea an inner life fascinated with and shattered by its own productions of violent fantasy and image. In "Mon cœur mis à nu" he would write, "When I have inspired universal horror and disgust, I shall have overcome solitude" (*Œuvres* [Ruff] 627). If, as Ross Chambers has so rightly noted, "it is from the experience of discovering how the apparently remote and alien proves, on reflection, to be unexpectedly germane to oneself [. . .] that important insights emerge" ("Relevance" 145), then Baudelaire's *Fleurs du Mal* must continue to speak to us for the power with which it challenges us to push it away—for the power with which the perversely violent and violating images it calls forth are also a paradigm for its undeniable share in beauty.

NOTE

I wish to thank Kenneth Berri for his helpful reading.

Searching for Swans: Baudelaire's "Le Cygne"

Richard Terdiman

What's the swan doing in Baudelaire's "Le Cygne" (172–76)? Let's say students decide to keep a journal as they read the poem. They record what they expect as they encounter each line and how the poem responds to that expectation. To begin with, they might think that a poem called "The Swan" would honor its title by getting us right to swans. But "Le Cygne" doesn't. Rather, it holds us up: no trace of a swan until the fifth stanza. So our expectation is first aroused, then frustrated. Not that nothing has been going on in the text. By the time we first meet a swan, we've encountered a considerable number of nonswan figures and situations: the Trojan princess Andromache, whom Baudelaire invokes in the first line, is mourning her husband, Hector, on the banks of the Simoïs River; we see the Carrousel quarter in Paris and beyond it the city of Paris itself, where the poet is walking on the day the poem refers to; we see a menagerie that used to exist in the Carrousel district. It's only at this moment, after a vertiginous shift from classical Troy to modern Paris, that we come upon the swan we suppose the poem is named for.

Baudelaire recalls him from years before. The bird has momentarily escaped from the little zoo where he was caged, and he is searching helplessly for water. But our students' journals might then note that, having introduced us to the swan at last, after a few lines the poem again leaves him. "Le Cygne" goes on to mention the Louvre palace, circles back briefly to the swan and to Andromache, evokes an unnamed black woman suffering from tuberculosis and dreaming of Africa, then some orphans, a forest, shipwrecked sailors, a group of prisoners, and a presumably different group of men who have lost some unnamed battle. Finally the poem trails off with an even vaguer evocation of "many others."

By this point, our students' heads might well be spinning. Their journals record a considerable amount of annoyance. What is going on here? Who are these people? How do they link up with swans? There's something almost irritating about the structure of "Le Cygne," which seems to skip from item to item with no explanation. To grasp the poem, we need to make sense of the connections among the strange collection of individuals, groups, situations, and places named. What, our students might ask, makes Parisian swans and Trojan princesses parts of the same textual world?

There are other things likely registered in our students' journals. The students probably noticed that as the cast of characters keeps shifting, time and place jump around abruptly. "Le Cygne" begins in the age of the Trojan War, around 1300 BC, but it doesn't stay there long. By the fifth line, the text snaps us thirty-two centuries ahead, from ancient Troy to Baudelaire's mid-nineteenth-century Paris. Just at the moment of this chronological and geographic leap from Asia Minor, where Andromache is mourning, to contemporary Paris, Baudelaire names the mechanism behind these strange connections: _memory_. The river on whose banks Andromache was mourning (an act of recollection) has suddenly stimulated his own recollection (line 5). For memory is capable of pulling the most surprising entities together; it can call up associations between just about any two things.

But students reading "Le Cygne" today face a problem: Baudelaire's associations are not necessarily ours. His world included a multitude of things about which we may know nearly nothing. His education was very different from the one people generally get now. For example, he was fluent in Latin, knowing much of Vergil by heart from an early age (it was in Vergil's _Aeneid_ that Baudelaire learned about Andromache). He knew his classical mythology cold. For our students the culture and history of the classics or of nineteenth-century France are available only as book learning. So to make sense of the associations in Baudelaire's swan poem, we need memories that we probably don't possess. Consequently, reading "Le Cygne" today requires what we might call an improvised recollection: a set of historical, political, cultural, and literary elements and associations that were familiar to Baudelaire and that he drew on for his construction of meaning in the poem (for a more extensive account of these historical and thematic associations, with considerable documentation, see Terdiman, "Le Cygne").

But there is one association that is available to us just by our knowing French. This is the play on words in the poem's title. In French the pronunciation of _le cygne_ is identical to that of _le signe_. So the swan in Baudelaire's poem is not there just in his own right; he is also a sign. The homonym suggests that we should be alert to anything in the poem that might refer not only to the ornithological realm of swans but also to the semiotic realm of signs. I return to this connection in the second part of this essay. But how should we begin our interpretation of the text itself?

Since, as we saw, "Le Cygne" so obviously plays with time, it makes sense to start with time and history in analyzing the relations of elements and characters within the poem. To begin with, Baudelaire wrote "Le Cygne" in 1859, during the French Second Empire. Louis-Napoléon Bonaparte (the nephew of Napoleon the Great) had declared himself Emperor Napoleon III in a coup d'état in 1852. His rule was contested by prestigious figures, including the poet Victor Hugo, to whom Baudelaire dedicated "Le Cygne." But they were not able to overturn it. Hugo went into exile to protest Napoleon's seizure of power, and from 1852 on he publicly attacked the emperor in a series of satirical texts. By 1859, despite such opposition, Napoleon had consolidated his regime, and he offered an amnesty to his opponents, including Hugo. This was big news that year.

Hugo contemptuously refused the emperor's offer, deciding to remain in exile. Baudelaire wrote him a letter to express admiration for his principled intransigence. But Hugo wasn't the only poet who found himself a victim of imperial power. In 1857, Baudelaire himself was hauled into court for what the state prosecutor claimed was the immorality of *Les Fleurs du Mal*. The state won, and Baudelaire was forced to remove six offending poems from the collection. "Le Cygne," written two years later for a revised edition, might be thought of as Baudelaire's response to this censorship—almost as an act of vengeance against the emperor and his regime. By dedicating "Le Cygne" to Hugo, Baudelaire was not just honoring the fraternity of poets; he was also making a forceful political statement, and just as forcefully mocking Napoleon III. This context suggests that we ought to be alert to elements in "Le Cygne" evoking relations between political authority and those who suffer the weight of it.

What elements of the text might readers connect with this concern? To begin with, Andromache is a traditional symbol for victims of power. She had suffered a painful exile. When the Trojans lost their war with the Greeks, her husband was killed, and she was brought as a slave to the Greek city of Buthrotum. There, still faithful to the past and to Hector's memory, she constructed a small-scale Troy by the banks of the Simoïs River and ritually mourned her husband, as Vergil narrates in the *Aeneid*, book 3, and as Baudelaire indirectly recalls in the first quatrain of "Le Cygne."

But the miniature Troy built by Andromache in her exile is not the only city under construction in the poem. In 1859 Paris was undergoing the most extensive reconstruction in its history, refashioned as ordered by the emperor and directed by Baron Haussmann. A favorite project of Napoleon was to modernize the capital, which he proceeded to do in one of the earliest systematic examples of what we have come to call urban renewal. While this work built many of the wide boulevards and spacious squares that make modern Paris so charming, it had a downside many forget. Haussmann's reconstructions involved the brutal expulsion from the city of thousands of poor citizens who lived in the districts that were suddenly razed and rebuilt.

The Carrousel neighborhood (mentioned in line 6 of "Le Cygne"), lying between the Louvre and the Tuileries palaces, was where the demolitions began. The project of transforming the Carrousel had been put in motion only a few days after Napoleon came to power. So in 1859, as Baudelaire recalls the *quartier* and the swan he once saw there, he is remembering things that no longer existed, in a place that had been abruptly destroyed in 1852. Now it becomes clearer why the entire population and situation of the poem appear refracted through memory and what kind of memory this is. Beginning with the Carrousel, everything evoked in "Le Cygne" exists only under the sign of the irretrievable. The first thing that brings these disparate people and places together in the poem is that they all are gone. Baudelaire evokes a world of dispossession, destruction, loss, and exile. Each of the poem's characters symbolizes some aspect of this theme: Andromache, who has lost her home and her husband; the black woman (lines 41–44)—perhaps the offspring of slaves transported against their will to Europe—who mourns her distant Africa; the shipwrecked sailors and defeated soldiers with whom the poem concludes. "Le Cygne" is a text, as Baudelaire resonantly says himself (lines 44–45), dedicated to everyone who has lost something that can never be recovered ("[Je pense] à quiconque a perdu ce qui ne se retrouve / Jamais, jamais!").

When do we need memory? Only to evoke what is gone—whether from the immediate field of our perception or, more radically, from our material and emotional world. This is true in any period, but it is particularly pertinent in a situation like the one in which Baudelaire found himself, surrounded by the mid-nineteenth-century demolitions that were remaking Paris. It must have seemed that nothing was stable, that everything was disappearing or mutating before Parisian eyes. In the face of such rapid change, the nostalgia of "Le Cygne" is an easily comprehensible reaction.

The poem's nostalgia focuses on the Carrousel district itself. Before 1852 the quarter was a modest area of low-rent apartments and marginal shops. We can see it in the recollected confusion of objects in the poem's third stanza. For Parisians the Carrousel had a distinctive flavor: the almost pastoral isolation of the area despite its location in the heart of the city, the remarkably diverse character of the local inhabitants and merchants. Because of its run-down charm, the area had become a hangout of the counterculture, of bohemia (*bohème*). We might imagine it a bit in the image of Haight-Ashbury in San Francisco in the late sixties, or New York's Greenwich Village. A group of dissident artists and intellectuals, including Baudelaire, frequented the quarter. The Carrousel was thus a place where disenchanted artists, who liked to represent themselves as figuratively homeless in Paris, felt at home. The demolition of the Carrousel quarter was, then, a powerful symbolic eviction.

Baudelaire describes his walk across the old Carrousel "one morning when the sky was cold and clear, / The hour when Labor wakes" (trans. mine, of lines 14–15). We might wonder what the poet was doing there at the crack of dawn. But against the background of the *bohème*, Baudelaire's relation to the waking city makes sense. Unlike the workers just bestirring themselves, the poet, we might imagine, has been up all night with his artistic friends and, as the conventional city begins its workaday routine, is himself on his way to bed.

In this simultaneous coincidence and distinction between workers and poets in "Le Cygne" we can read a story of social class. Class is an issue in many of Baudelaire's texts—from "La Mort des pauvres" (276–78; "The Death of the Poor") in *Les Fleurs du Mal* to "Assommons les pauvres!" (182–83; "Let's Beat Up the Poor!") in the *Petits poëmes en prose* (in *Œuvres* [Ruff]). After the failed revolution of 1848, Baudelaire had repeatedly returned in his writing to the poor, the disadvantaged, and the working class—those who in his prose poem "Les Veuves" he termed "les éclopés de la vie" (*Œuvres* [Ruff] 155–56) ("life's disabled veterans"). He identified with them as victims, like him, of wealth and power, and they became a symbol of his own personal alienation. Poets, he wrote in the same text, "are drawn irresistibly to everything weak, ruined, grief-stricken, orphaned" (155). His hostility to his class origins in the bourgeoisie made the working class look like an ally—but a very problematic ally, one with which the intellectually elitist Baudelaire would never consent to any simple fusion. This social contradiction left him uncomfortably adrift.

Napoleon III's transformations of the city had indeed been motivated in part by a desire to control the Paris workers and prevent any repeat of the proletarian insurrection of 1848. In the June Days of 1848 the workers turned against the revolutionary government they had helped establish in the February fighting that year. The government then crushed them. Ever since, each succeeding national administration followed a policy of limiting the population of workers in Paris. In his refashioning of the city, the emperor was putting into practice a pattern still familiar today: urban renewal meant working-class removal. Moreover, the propertied class was making fortunes by building on the newly cleared plots of land that Haussmann's demolitions created. So when a poor quarter like the Carrousel was razed, the poor and the poets lost their lodgings—but the speculators made out like bandits.

Now we can better understand the phrase "Paris change!" (174) ("Paris is changing! [trans. mine]) with which the second part of "Le Cygne" begins. It is as resonant an utterance as any in *Les Fleurs du Mal*. But it is far from celebrating a myth of social progress and urban improvement. Change here means *loss*. These perceptions of the new Paris help explain the uncanny sense of exile at home that preoccupied writers and artists during the period of the Second Empire—as if the city were a language that had mutated so rapidly that even its native speakers discovered they could no longer use it to communicate. The resources of memory and nostalgia came to stand in for what had disappeared or been transformed beyond recognition.

It was not only the urban topography that had changed. The modifications Baudelaire and his fellow Parisians were living through were transforming the familiar complex of signs in which the old Paris had embedded the city's inhabitants—disorienting those inhabitants; reshaping their activities and their movements; transforming the character of the districts where they lived, worked, and took their leisure.

Now we are in a position to unpack the significance of the swan-sign pun that we noted earlier in Baudelaire's title. Here the celebrated theory of the sign developed by Ferdinand de Saussure proves helpful (see Saussure). For Saussure a sign is any element that carries meaning. But Saussure observed that every sign can be understood as the coincidence of two parts. A signifier is what materially carries the message—the pattern of ink on a page when we write a word or the vibrations in the air that are produced when we speak it. A signified, conversely, is the conceptual content of the message carried. There is no necessary or predetermined relation between signifier and signified. Biological cows need not be represented by the word *cow*—since we know that other languages have quite different names for them. Moreover, because signifiers are arbitrary and conventional, their meaning can change; the signifieds they carry can mutate. These notions help us understand the reflection on meaning, change, and loss that Baudelaire made the heart of "Le Cygne."

How did the poet experience the forcible transformation of the urban and social signs that once meant Paris, that communicated, "This is where I live"? Much depended on a widespread perception by the opponents of Napoleon III's regime that the emperor's renovation of the capital was in fact a degrading commercial violation of the beauty, history, and character of the most extraordinary city in the world. They believed that Paris was being remade by men devoid of taste, was being sacrificed to the most naked greed. They saw the emperor's new constructions as cut-rate efforts at monumentalism, possessing none of the organic dignity of traditional Paris. A typical broadside described the newly constructed apartment buildings—presumably built for the regime's newly constructed rich—on the Rue de Rivoli: "This bronze is really tin, this gold is painted on. These mansions are like theater sets: it's best to see them from a distance" (Fournel, qtd. in Burton, *Context* 44). One centerpiece of the new imperial architecture, the expansion of the Louvre along the edge of the "renewed" Carrousel, was subjected to a similar critical lambasting. This new Napoleonic portion of the Louvre was inaugurated in 1857. Two years later Baudelaire contemptuously memorialized it in "Le Cygne," denying to what he saw as the emperor's tacky palace the authenticity even of a definite article, devalorizing the building as "ce Louvre" (line 33) ("*that* Louvre [trans. mine]).

As the familiar sign system of the city was displaced, the signifiers that came to compose its new and unfamiliar language were increasingly perceived as artificial, inauthentic, or counterfeit. The Paris refashioned by the emperor began to feel like a space of bogus signs. His opponents saw a city in which styles, forms, and functions were garbled and counterfeited. As this scornful rhetoric evolved, three linked metaphors came to dominate its imagery: merchandising, theater, and prostitution. These were figures drawn from the everyday reality of Second Empire Paris, available for representing a falsified world in which nothing genuine corresponded to its surface. And at the center of the new ersatz imperial reality stood Napoleon III himself, seen from the first moments of the empire in 1852 by a broad group of critics—ranging from the revolutionary Karl Marx to the aristocratic Alexis de Tocqueville—as a debased forgery, a knockoff imitation, of his illustrious revolutionary uncle. Louis-Napoléon appeared a plagiarism, and his empire seemed founded on a systematic politics of sham. The transformed (or debased) Haussmannian city then could serve as a figure for a deeper perception about Second Empire reality: the notion that such reality was itself slipping away under the pressure of appearance, image, and manipulated belief—a critique we might be sympathetic to ourselves, in our culture of image, spin, and sound bites.

But simultaneously this instability made possible the critical consciousness of the sign phenomenon itself, and it also made possible the wordplay of the title of "Le Cygne." What was new and urgent in the Paris of Napoleon III was an atmosphere of trouble around the sign. In such an unsettled situation, signs themselves no longer seemed natural. They precipitated out, becoming a problem with which the culture had to deal. In the face of the anxieties such a situation generated, we can easily understand nostalgia for the recovery of an unproblematic relation to the real—the retrospective, elegiac atmosphere that dominates "Le Cygne." If only one could forestall the fragmentation of the past, if only one could reliably stabilize the present . . . But under Napoleon III's regime, like urban geography itself, language declined to be stable, refused to settle down and serve as the docile carrier of unambiguous meanings. Second Empire culture had no unambiguous meanings for language to carry: its meaning was that meaning could mean anything. The pun in Baudelaire's title instantiates and profits from just this slippage.

Under such circumstances, language separates itself from its speakers and confronts them almost as an adversary. Writing becomes an intricate and risky sport:

> Je vais m'exercer seul à ma fantasque escrime,
> Flairant dans tous les coins les hasards de la rime,
> Trébuchant sur les mots comme sur les pavés, [. . .]
>   (168; "Le Soleil" lines 5–7)

> I go practicing solo my fantastic swordsmanship,
> Sniffing out the chances of rhyme at every street corner,
> Tripping on words like cobblestones.   (trans. mine)

Then exile and dispossession—the mood of "Le Cygne" and of so much cultural expression after mid-century—become comprehensible as effects of a newly perceived density and indocility of language.

"Le Cygne" thematizes these developments in the figure of memory. To remember is to be separated. For we don't need to recollect what lies before our eyes. Signs express a similar separation. In the poem that separation becomes the subject of a series of evocations of loss. The logic of signs, as it comes into focus in the period of the Second Empire, affirms that the signified is always alienated, or unavailable, or simply absent. What "Le Cygne" manifests is that the sign arises in a fundamental displacement, the distance that separates, that in effect exiles, all signifiers from their signifieds. Now we could call "Le Cygne" Baudelaire's sign poem.

We can get at this separation through one of the most striking effects in the poem, the memorable apostrophe to Andromache with which it begins. Baudelaire might have started his poem with anything. Yet for well over a century readers have found the beginning of "Le Cygne" astounding. "Andromaque, je pense à vous!" ("Andromache, I'm thinking about you!" [trans. mine]). Reading the line today, we may still wonder at the startling materialization of the Trojan princess Andromache in the heart of nineteenth-century Paris—and of Baudelaire's "Tableaux parisiens" ("Parisian Scenes"). What could she possibly be doing there?

A simple condition makes sense of her irruption into such an implausible setting. In a world of loss, everything is equally distant. What's gone is beyond degree, is simply gone. Like the object of a memory, the signified is always absent. In the mode defined by the instability of signs, the materialization of Andromache at dawn in the streets of central Paris one day in the early Second Empire is no less probable than anyone's appearance in language, anywhere, at any time. The paradox of "Le Cygne" is thus a disorienting coexistence, within the text, of the appropriate and the utterly incongruous. Such coexistence tests the arbitrariness of the semiotic. Like the mobile Andromache, the language fragments that materialize in "Le Cygne" might turn up anywhere. But for now, they turn up here.

They are all exiled, banished, or dispossessed: Hugo, who for the entire period of the Second Empire daily contemplated his exile from an island a few kilometers off the French coast; Andromache, who mourned Hector in Buthrotum after the fall of Troy; Ovid (line 25), whose conflict with the Roman emperor Augustus was as intense, and whose exile as painful, as Hugo's under Napoleon III; the swan held in a cage far from "son beau lac natal" (174) ("the beautiful lake where he was born" [trans. mine]); the black woman grieving for Africa; the shipwrecked sailors; and so on. In the common experience of the poem's heterogeneous cast of characters, the distance between home and exile is established as a powerful figure for the internally divided sign.

The drama of "Le Cygne" makes it clear that the painful relations of the historical and the social are what renders visible the contingency and instability of the sign. To those in positions of domination, signs may appear unproblematic. Reality dances when they tell it to. But for Baudelaire, suffering the sense of dispossession that he figures in his poem, the losses, the displacements that signs represent are comprehensible as a narrative of bereavement and banishment. In such a critical conjuncture, the sign seems disoriented and frantic out of its element, seems to struggle helplessly, like the forlorn swan whose story Baudelaire memorialized in "Le Cygne."

Baudelaire's Sepulchers

Susan L. Wolf

In my feminist approach to teaching Baudelaire's *Fleurs du Mal*, I seek to offer undergraduate students and their teachers ways of using contemporary theory to illuminate a text. More specifically, I present aspects of feminist philosophy that I hope will generate compelling readings of Baudelaire's poems, providing students direction for subsequent explorations of these original and haunting yet strangely predictable productions of what I call, after Luce Irigaray, the male imaginary. By the imaginary I wish to suggest a collective unconscious subtending cultural constructions of all types, including works of art. Since women and especially the mother, according to Irigaray, support the processes of this imaginary but are never represented in it as subjects, male cultural productions, however inventive, continue to exclude women except as mute objects of representation whose primary function is to mirror male desire.

Irigaray, whose ground-breaking essays in psychoanalysis and philosophy have made her, to quote a recent biographer, "a leading philosopher of the twentieth century" (Stephenson 230), repeatedly emphasizes two principles as vital to the development of a valid cultural critique, a critique that would challenge the primacy of the male imaginary by exposing the suppression of difference and female subjectivity over which it has been constructed. Indeed, in Irigaray's ledger, discovering the pervasiveness of the specular relation in which woman's desire is erased so that she may reflect man everywhere and uncovering and acknowledging the buried mother can lead women to begin to reclaim themselves as subjects of discourse or action. Why the mother and, more specifically, the buried mother? According to Irigaray, Western civilization remains "dominated by a destructive, death-oriented imaginary [. . .] constructed over a buried act of matricide," a matricide that would predate the parricide that Sigmund Freud posited as primary in *Totem and Taboo* (Whitford 33; Irigaray, "Bodily Encounter" 36). "Toute notre culture occidental repose sur le meurtre de la mère" (Irigaray, *Corps-à-corps* 81; "The mother's murder is the foundation of our entire culture in the West" [trans. mine]). Irigaray reinterprets the story of Orestes's murder of his mother, Clytemnestra, in the *Oresteia* as a myth recounting the establishment of the rule of patriarchy through its devastating appropriation of the "archaic powers of the mother" (Irigaray, "Bodily Encounter" 37). Irigaray's reading also focuses on elements of the story often neglected or passed over in silence: the tragic sacrifice of the daughters Iphigenia (by the father, Agamemnon, in the hope of winning the Trojan War) and Electra (who, while she does not perish, goes completely mad as a result of her mother's death). That the matricidal son, too, goes mad—his madness assuming the form of enraged Furies, those "ghosts of [the] mother" who pursue him relentlessly like a bad conscience—is precious proof that one does not murder the mother with impunity (Irigaray, *Corps-à-corps* 17). Divine intervention, however, does put a stop to the nightmare of Orestes's insanity, so that he may ultimately replace his father and found a new male order. Uncovering the buried mother thus represents the first step in recognizing woman as a primary underpinning of Western thought and in transforming a culture that has amply symbolized a paternal but not a maternal genealogy—the mother's relationship to her daughter. Although women's desire within a culture founded on its denial is profoundly threatening to that culture, the reduction of society to one sexual pole represents a tragic impoverishment of human potential. Both men and women students should therefore find interest in applying Irigaray's principles of cultural critique to guide them through a feminist reading of *Les Fleurs du Mal*.

Les Fleurs du Mal may well begin with some of Baudelaire's most famous but least interesting poems, as Leo Bersani maintains, but it would be a mistake for students to dismiss them as unimportant merely because the poems present an idealized and traditional view of the poet, a view that Baudelaire, according to many critics, does not sustain (Bersani 23). On the contrary, the content of these beginning poems, apparently so heterogeneous and unconnected to the more subversive poems that follow, in fact paves the way for our understanding of the more subversive poems. Three initial poems of *Les Fleurs du Mal*, when analyzed for the images of women they contain or appear to exclude, offer students fertile terrain from which to construct a feminist critique of Baudelaire.

The organizational logic to which I am referring bears little if any connection to what Baudelaire and others have called the work's secret architecture, unless by "secret architecture" we understand a coherence so deeply concealed, it escaped even Baudelaire's keen attention (Wing, "Exile" 740). The work's first poem seems founded on the ingenious concealment from self and reader of the restaging of what Irigaray calls the primordial crime of matricide. The camouflage is so successful, I tell students, that the representation of the poet's mother as seething with murderous rage against her son in "Bénédiction" (10–14; "Benediction") appears to enact the very opposite scenario. I examine the mechanism of this subterfuge shortly. In the space of three poems, "Au lecteur" (4–6; "To the Reader"), "Bénédiction," and "Elévation" (16; "Elevation;"), Baudelaire launches his poetic enterprise as an exchange among men; murders the mother (clearing the path for his coming to writing); and begins to establish a repertoire of hierarchical binary oppositions that reinforce the fundamental split of Western culture—man/woman—in which man symbolizes the valued term of the opposition and woman its negative, devalued reflection. In the second half of this essay, I examine the symptoms of the persecution anxiety to which guilt over the mother's murder gives rise. In Baudelaire, I argue, these symptoms surface as a form of deep-seated hostility toward the mother or, conversely, as an expression of helplessness and depression.

It is significant that, addressing and describing his ideal reader, Baudelaire identifies him as his same-sex twin, his brother in hypocrisy: "—Hypocrite lecteur, —mon semblable, —mon frère!" (6) ("—Hypocrite reader,—fellow man,—my twin!" [7]). This form of address would at the very least suggest that *Les Fleurs du Mal* seeks to promote a dialogue exclusively among men. In a male-dominated culture, Irigaray has argued, "women remain mute mediators," functioning only as objects of exchange or representation (Whitford 35; Irigaray, *Ce sexe* 172). In *Les Fleurs du Mal*, with few exceptions, only lesbian women are promoted to subjecthood and given the power of speech. Although the lesbian poems are not the focus of my analysis (see Schultz, this volume), they show in some ways an astonishingly positive attitude toward women whose refusal of heterosexuality and expression of sexual desire denote the possibility of breaking the mirror.

"Bénédiction" presents the allegory of the male poet's perilous attempts to accede to his calling. Having just excluded women as potential collaborators in his poetic project, Baudelaire here ushers them into the text as monstrous, deadly objects of representation. The poem stages the poet's coming to writing as a long trial by gauntlet; during the running of this gauntlet he barely escapes being burned to death by his mother and having his heart torn out and thrown to the dogs by his wife, both of whom are incensed at his choice of vocation. These brutal and vituperative women in fact do not speak; they only appear to. We are led to ask what might have motivated the creation of such a terrifying figure of the wife/mother—the cruelty linking these women arguably collapses their separate identities. While it is true that Baudelaire's own mother and stepfather vigorously opposed his desire to become a writer, the depth of the loathing expressed in the poem suggests that this portrayal is no mere biographical transposition. Through an uncanny reversal, the murder of the mother who subtends patriarchy becomes in *Les Fleurs du Mal* the murderous mother, the mother who like Jocasta, but somewhat more inexplicably, would like to rid herself of Oedipus, a son she loathes and fears. The psychoanalyst Julia Kristeva contends that this creation of a *mère mortifère* ("death-dealing mother") on the plane of fiction is a male cultural imperative, enacting a separation from the mother without which writing or any act of symbolization would be impossible (38). Unfortunately, the psychological individuation so essential to male creation requires the male imaginary to perpetuate a devastatingly negative stereotype of women.

The binary distinction male/female hinted at in Baudelaire's preamble intensifies and acquires definition as it shifts, in "Bénédiction," to the plane of ethics. Here the fundamental opposition is encoded as good/bad, with the innocent and aspiring male poet victimized by the bad wife/mother. With the third poem, "Elévation," we move to the axis of spatial representation, where oppositions continue to play out in a striking fashion as the pairs high/low and spirit/matter. Here Baudelaire depicts the life of the mind, the sphere of higher human activities, as a lofty male province where male pleasure ("mâle volupté" [16]) seems connected far more to the philosophical flight of ideas and the delights of the rational intellect than to the voluptuousness of sheer physical sensation. Indeed, he urges the poet to steer clear of morbid lowlands, vaporous regions, troubles and ennui, which by implication are female and linked to the body. These binary distinctions, which serve to oppose the material and spiritual planes, reinforce those already at work in the section titled "Spleen et idéal" ("Spleen and the Ideal") and announce oppositions that are presented in stronger terms by poems such as "Une Charogne" ("A Carcass"). In "Une Charogne," Baudelaire provides the stark description of a stinking, rotting carcass with the strange aim of exulting in his beloved's destiny to be a corpse. Comparing the carcass lying on its back to a "lecherous whore" (59), Baudelaire immediately feminizes decomposing nature and thus degrades it, refusing to contemplate the possibility, apparently, that the male corpse (and thus his own) is inevitably subject to a similarly disgusting deterioration.

"Elévation" presents the image of an airy masculine space that the poet strives to occupy, high above and cut off from the putrid, material world. Could he be seeking to avoid acknowledging certain burial sites? Or nurturing the illusion suggested in "Une Charogne," that only women's bodies decompose? "Man may think he is active, dynamic, propelling himself upwards from earth to sky," Margaret Whitford writes, "but he is in a sepulcher, while woman, like Antigone, is imprisoned and buried alive" (157). The terrible irony of the patriarchal imaginary is that while it seeks to dominate through the suppression of female subjectivity (burying woman alive), in fact it succeeds only in cutting itself off from life, in what amounts to self-imprisonment and a devastating sense of isolation (a sepulcher). Since the matricidal male fears retaliation, his repressed guilt over the mother's murder, like Orestes's guilt, resurfaces as persecution anxiety, symptoms of which manifest themselves in *Les Fleurs du Mal* in the guise of depression and the fear of women, which students should now be led to examine at length.

The three poems I next analyze present extreme solutions to the perceived threat of female desire. Each describes a drastic immobilization of femininity, a revenge carried out against a woman's body that is somehow experienced as insufficiently available to the male to fulfill his psychosexual needs. In "A celle qui est trop gaie" (86–88; "To One Who Is Too Cheerful"), the poet cannot tolerate his beloved's resplendent health and joyous sensuality, because these qualities are too abundantly expressive of her difference. Such wholeness and femininity do not belong to the passive woman the poet seeks to mirror his desire. His pernicious wish to bruise her breasts and carve out new genitalia in her abdomen or flank ("flanc" [88]) suggests that only a woman he himself has thus refashioned can adequately respond to his longings. Baudelaire's remark that he would like to "slip [his] venom" into this new set of fleshed-out lips shocked public morality during the book's trial as a scandalous reference to sexual intercourse (89). Far more troubling, we note, is the idea of poisonous sperm, from which, as Bersani has written, the woman will die (73). In a note, however, Baudelaire explained that "my venom" meant neither sperm nor syphilis but his melancholy disposition (see *Flowers of Evil* [McGowan] 362).

In "Les Métamorphoses du vampire" (252–54; "The Metamorphoses of the Vampire") the poem's initial dynamics are quite the reverse. Here, sex is fantasized not as a deadly male control over a woman's life and body but as an act in which a woman drains the poet of his virility, leaving him inert, feminized. But this theft does not renew her vitality. Indeed the vampire-prostitute, whom one might have expected to be as galvanized by the lovemaking as the poet is weakened by it, literally disintegrates while the poet looks on in "terror" (255), as though he were not implicated in this seemingly punitive transformation [which is inspired by Jacques Cazotte's *Le Diable amoureux*—LP]. As Laurence Porter has written in his splendid essay on Baudelaire's fictive audiences, "the motif of vampirism pervades Baudelaire's verse" and represents his fear of "engulfment" by the mother and a concomitant draining of his "independent identity" ("Baudelaire's Fictive Audiences" 115). The vampire-mother who has dared to drain the poet of his semen or lifeblood, symbols of his singularity, is metamorphosed into a mass of similar viscosity, punished, it would seem, by her own crime. Indeed, semen would appear to seal her annihilation, and in this her fate resembles that of the too cheerful woman. Two remarks are called for here. First, the so-called terror at the discovery of the prostitute's destruction conceals the poet's intense satisfaction that he is not himself the victim. Second, culturally constructed femininity, represented almost literally in "To One Who Is Too Cheerful" by Baudelaire's fantasized reworking of female anatomy, functions to protect the male subject from death. If the survivor is masculine, the corpse is by implication feminine, as Elisabeth Bronfen points out (65).

The female corpse leads us to what is arguably the ultimate—and most objectionable—expression of Baudelaire's poetics of the arresting of female desire. "Une Martyre: dessin d'un maître inconnu" (228–32; "A Martyr: Drawing by an Unknown Master") plays out amid images of intense beauty the unspeakable dramas of murder and necrophilia. Baudelaire's infamous statement about the prodigious power of art to transform horror into beauty seems particularly apposite here: "C'est un des privilèges prodigieux de l'art que l'horrible, artistement exprimé, devienne beauté" (*Curiosités* 682; "L'Art romantique") ("It is one of art's truly phenomenal prerogatives to transform through artistic means the hideous into the beautiful"). The prostitute's murder and the implied subjection of her body to necrophilic acts represent the sacrifice necessary to male self-affirmation. Decapitation signifies castration; here, the prostitute's symbolic castration and her lifeless and thus eminently available corpse doubly proclaim man's status as phallic. Furthermore, the poem ritualizing a dead, beautiful woman, Bronfen writes, functions "like the inscribed slab, relief sculpture or statue which stands, since classical antiquity, over tombs—as a 'sema' or sign to indicate the burial place of a 'heroine' by substituting the body of the deceased" (71). In "Les Métamorphoses du vampire" and "Une Martyre," it is a fear of the powerful buried mother that underlies both the expression of an acute distrust of female sexuality and the tyrannical exigencies of male sexual affirmation. More powerful dead than alive, the mother returns to claim an acknowledgment of the act of matricide.

The original matricide haunts not only what I call the fear-of-women poems. The unacknowledged crime, like an unspeakable secret enclosed within a crypt inside the male subject, never ceases its subversive activity, giving rise to images of an oppressive compression or containment that half conceal, half reveal its presence. Despite their having been preceded by numerous references to the airy, male provinces of poetry, Baudelaire's later poems are weighted down with sepulchers; some of his poems in fact seem to function *as* sepulchers. As he explains in the second of the "Spleen" poems, the poet's skull is a "giant vault," his entire being a "graveyard hated [more accurately, shunned] by the moon" (147). (Baudelaire's suggestive claim that the moon, symbol par excellence of femininity, hates him looks to be an inversion of his extreme ambivalence toward femininity.)

Despite the innovative genius of expressions of spleen in Baudelaire, their function is highly conservative: they seek to incorporate a loss. Incorporation, according to one definition, is "the refusal to acknowledge the full import of [a] loss, a loss that if recognized as such would effectively transform us" (Abraham and Torok 127). Were the mother's (fantasized) murder to be recognized as the base of Western culture, were her loss to be mourned rather than occulted, the male imaginary would no longer restrict her to the position of the mirroring other, and the representation of woman could assume another, more positive form.

I conclude with the analysis of a remarkable allegory of depression functioning simultaneously as the mother's burial site and the poet's sepulcher. "Spleen (4)" begins with an unusual image of compression: "Quand le ciel bas et lourd pèse comme un couvercle / Sur l'esprit gémissant en proie aux longs ennuis" (148) ("When low and heavy sky weighs like a lid / Upon the spirit moaning in ennui" [149]). Critics have found the utilitarian image of the lid an intriguing and unconventional poetic device. As an object found most commonly in a kitchen among the pots and pans, however, its striking metonymic use in this poem suggests nothing so much as an oppressive proximity to the mother.

Earth becomes a humid prison in the second stanza: "Quand la terre est changée en un cachot humide / Où l'Espérance, comme une chauve-souris, / S'en va battant les murs de son aile timide" (148) ("When earth is changed into a sweaty cell, / In which Hope, captured, like a frantic bat, / Batters the walls with her enfeebled wing" [149]). Associated by Baudelaire with the devalued feminine, earth, humanity's final resting place, is also commonly linked to the maternal, as may be evinced from expressions such as *earth mother* and *mother earth*. Here, earth-mother becomes the dank prison cell from which Hope— the poet?—represented in this poem by a bat, flutters in despair. The dynamics if not the detail of this scenario bring to mind "Bénédiction," in which, as we have seen, a rancorous mother seeks to destroy her poet-son. The mother's cruelty or, rather, her just anger may indeed reside in her refusal, like that of so many Furies, to let her son off the hook psychologically.

The third stanza depicts spleen as "a silent multitude of spiders" whose threads, deeply embedded in the vault that is man's brain, provoke disgust (151). We are reminded that after comparing woman to the cat, the humorist, and the great criminal, Freud compared her to that master weaver, the spider ("On Narcissism" 46), while other psychoanalysts have linked the spider to the phallic mother, a symbol wielding enormous power (Karl Abraham was one such analyst; see Kofman 83n63). To be inhabited by spiders may thus be understood as tantamount to housing the mother, stronger, and certainly more dangerous—from her occulted position beyond the grave. Depression, in fine, which Freud famously defined as anger turned inward, becomes in *Les Fleurs du Mal* the male poet's wholesale swallowing of the maternal object, giving rise to an outpouring of words that evoke his captivity and his undoing. Reading for Irigaray's foundational matricide, students of Baudelaire come away from his text with a heightened awareness of the human tragedy implicit in the workings of the male imaginary. Baudelaire's elaboration of a poetics of depression ultimately teaches us all to acknowledge the figure of the buried mother as a source of both man's extraordinary linguistic capabilities and his deepest despair.

Baudelaire's Lesbian Connections

Gretchen M. Schultz

Baudelaire's lesbian poems show lesbianism to be more than an isolated motif in *Les Fleurs du Mal*. In fact, they engage issues essential to Baudelaire's aesthetic project, most notably the representation of sexual difference and lyric subjectivity. They also allow the instructor to cover important contextual problems, including the genesis and reception of the collection and its relation to the proliferation of lesbian images in nineteenth-century French literature. The perspectives of gay and lesbian studies, a relatively new domain in university curricula, can provoke resistance in some students and enthusiasm in others, while enabling all to see how innovative approaches to canonical texts revitalize interpretive possibilities and shed light on unexplored aspects of well-known works.

Context

Baudelaire wrote his poetry within the context of a specific literary phenomenon, that of the emergence of the lesbian as a stock character in modern literature. Representations of lesbianism (such as Denis Diderot's *La Religieuse*, published in 1796, and Honoré de Balzac's *La Fille aux yeux d'or*, 1835) were in fact rare during the first half of the century, when fictional accounts of deviant sexuality tended to focus on gender ambiguity. Romantic literature, which preceded the "invention" of homosexuality by sexologists, was peopled with castrati (Balzac's "Sarrasine," 1830), transvestites (Théophile Gautier's *Mademoiselle de Maupin*, 1835), hermaphrodites (Gautier's "Contralto," 1852; Théodore de Banville's "Hermaphrodite," 1867), and androgynes (Balzac's *Séraphîta*, 1835; George Sand's *Gabriel*, 1843). In these texts, uncertain gender created the possibility of expressing same-sex desire and provided vehicles for the exploration of gendered subjectivities. More generally, the figures of the Romantic hero and poet incorporated what were considered the feminine qualities of physical delicacy and moral sensitivity. Through their texts and their characters, authors confronted their own alterity in relation to both masculine and feminine others. But such depictions of sexual indeterminacy did little to presage the rapid emergence of the literary lesbian that was to follow and that Baudelaire helped to inaugurate. The shift that occurred around 1850 with the waning of Romanticism not only opened up an entirely new field of representation—that of unambiguously lesbian eroticism—but also suggested a recasting of the artist's self-definition and new configurations of literary subject relations. In particular, lyric texts by male poets positing lesbian intersubjectivity indicated a departure from the centuries-old tradition of a masculine lyric "I" locked in an objectifying relation with a female beloved.

The literary fad of lesbianism began among a brotherhood of writers who composed texts in which Sappho played the principal role (see DeJean; Albert). The mid-century was marked by the publication of Baudelaire's poem "Lesbos" and by Philoxène Boyer's play *Sapho*. Numerous variations on Sappho and the figure of the modern lesbian followed, dominated by but not limited to symbolist lyric production. Poetic representations included Banville's chaste "Erinna" (1861), Paul Verlaine's erotic sonnet series *Amies* (1867), Stéphane Mallarmé's characteristically obscure allusion to the embrace of two nymphs in "L'Après-midi d'un faune" (1875), and Pierre Louÿs's *Chansons de Bilitis* (1894).

Works of fiction that featured lesbian coupling were fed by the realism and naturalism of the late nineteenth century for which, ostensibly, no subject was taboo. Emile Zola's *La Curée* (1871) and *Nana* (1879), Guy de Maupassant's story "La Femme de Paul" (1881), among other works, took up this theme. What these symbolist and realist texts have in common, besides their fascination with lesbianism, is their male authorship. Subjective representations of lesbians did not appear until the turn of the century, in the poetry of Renée Vivien.

I am obliged to engage in a bit of literary archaeology to place *Les Fleurs du Mal* within the context outlined above, since a number of events, both literary and legal, conspired to marginalize the lesbian images once central to Baudelaire's collection. During the mid-1840s, Baudelaire announced "Les Lesbiennes" as the title of his upcoming collection. Although this central reference to lesbians had long disappeared by the time *Les Fleurs du Mal* was published in 1857, the two titles are not unrelated. Marcel Proust, one of the first to address Baudelaire's interest in lesbians (see, more recently, Brunel; Fisher; Castle), suggested that both titles referred to the same aesthetic program, which Baudelaire summarized as "la tâche [. . .] d'extraire la beauté du *Mal*" ("Projets" 127) ("the task [. . .] of extracting beauty from *Evil*"). The lesbian would be, for Baudelaire, a kind of malevolent flower. Three poems form the kernel of what remained of "Les Lesbiennes" in the first edition of *Les Fleurs du Mal*: "Lesbos" and the two "Femmes damnées" ("Condemned Women"; the longer one subtitled "Delphine et Hippolyte" ["Delphine and Hippolyta"]). Although Baudelaire suppressed the original title, he grouped these poems along with several others in the section named after the entire collection's definitive title, "Fleurs du Mal." This association substantiates the suggestion that the titles are essentially synonymous, and that lesbians are somehow primary to the Baudelairean aesthetic summarized as "the flowers of evil."

But that centrality, first attenuated by the change in title, was then completely obscured by the censorship trial and judgment that immediately followed the publication of the collection. For although the Parisian literary community sanctioned and encouraged the portrayal of lesbians in literature, the bourgeois government of the Second Empire condemned and censored it. I ask students to read excerpts from the trial for a number of reasons (Baudelaire, *Œuvres* [Ruff] 723–34; "Le Procès des *Fleurs du Mal*"; see also Wing [*Limits*]; Leclerc). As well as inform students about the reception of the collection, these pages represent divergent reading styles and provoke a discussion of the role of legal authorities in determining artistic merit (analogies can be drawn to contemporary censorship debates in the United States concerning NEA funding, film and television content, song lyrics, Internet access, etc.).

After the denunciation of thirteen poems for "offense to public morals," the trial resulted in the striking of six poems from *Les Fleurs du Mal*, including "Lesbos" and "Delphine et Hippolyte." These "condemned women" were thus doubly damned, and only the shorter "Femmes damnées" (originally denounced) was left as a reminder of the prominent role that the lesbian initially played in Baudelaire's collection.

The court censored these poems on the basis of a literal reading. They were perceived as transparent representations of lesbians in the real world: a "paean of praise for the shameful love of women for other women" (qtd. in Pichois and Ziegler 224). The prosecuting attorney Ernest Pinard (who unsuccessfully prosecuted *Madame Bovary* the same year) turned his closing statements into an indictment of what he called Baudelaire's realism, which he characterized as the attempt to "fouill[er] la nature humaine dans ses replis les plus intimes" (Baudelaire, *Œuvres* [Ruff] 725) ("delve into the most intimate recesses of human nature"). He exhorted the court to "[r]éag[ir . . .] contre cette fièvre malsaine qui porte à tout peindre, à tout décrire, à tout dire" (726) ("react [. . .] against this unhealthy compulsion to paint everything, describe everything, say everything"). In their verdict the judges agreed with Pinard, condemning the incriminated poems for their "réalisme grossier et offensant pour la pudeur" (733) ("vulgar realism, an offense to decency").

Such a literalist reading is perhaps the predictable result of a trial in which both the prosecutor and the defense attorney agree that "le juge n'est point un critique littéraire" (725, 727) ("the judge is in no way a literary critic"). Given that literary questions had no place in this trial, the defense strategy was to defend the content of Baudelaire's poetry and to ignore its style. Baudelaire's lawyer, arguing that Baudelaire portrayed lesbians only in order to condemn them, proposed this recipe for reading the incriminated pieces:

> Transformez cela en prose, messieurs, supprimez la rime et la césure, recherchez ce qu'il y a au fond de ce langage puissant et imagé, [. . .] et dites-moi si nous ne trouverions pas les mêmes pensées [. . .] dans les homélies de quelque rude et sévère père de l'Eglise?   (728)

> Transform this poetry into prose, gentlemen, do away with rhyme and the caesura, consider the subject matter at the core of this strong and vivid language, [. . .] and tell me: would we not find the same thoughts [. . .] in the homilies of some harsh and severe father of the church?

The 1949 restitution of the condemned poems entailed not simply a new interpretation but what was also essentially a new method of analysis that emphasized the literariness of the poems. When the appeals court overturned the ban, it praised Baudelaire's originality and chided the earlier judges for their literalist approach, proposing a more sophisticated, symbolic reading: "The arbitrary nature of the first judges' ruling, drawing only upon a realistic interpretation of these poems and neglecting their symbolic meaning, has become evident" (qtd. in Leclerc 339; trans. mine).

It was thus the recognition of the aesthetic program behind Baudelaire's lesbians that permitted the legal restitution of these pieces. The move from a transparent reading to one that recognized the multivalence of Baudelaire's lesbians rendered the poems publishable by deeming them literary rather than obscene. However, since Baudelaire never reconstructed the lesbian cycle at the heart of *Les Fleurs du Mal*, it might be argued that this tardy restitution worked incompletely to remove its shroud of obscurity. Modern publishers (e.g., the Pléiade and Garnier Frères) usually defer to Baudelaire's augmented but expurgated second edition (1861), from which the condemned poems (literally ripped from the pages of the seized 1857 edition before the books were redistributed to the bookstores) were absent. Such editions typically relegate the censored poems to an annex entitled "Pièces condamnées" ("Condemned Pieces").

I propose to students that we read the sexual and gender configurations of *Les Fleurs du Mal* in a new way by granting these pieces their initial primacy, as does James McGowan and Jonathan Culler's bilingual edition. While there is little to learn from Baudelaire about "real" lesbians, his portrayal of lesbianism has quite a bit to teach us about how sexuality and sexual difference function in his modernist lyric project.

Baudelaire's Lesbians

The following exercise takes the lesbian poems as the starting point for an analysis of the relation in *Les Fleurs du Mal* between the male poet and the function of femininity. It demonstrates that lesbianism is more than the isolated theme of a cycle of three poems; it is, instead, a key to reading sexuality, gender, and subject positions in the collection. Students are asked to read the "Fleurs du Mal" section with the banned poems reinserted. In order to broaden the conclusions of the present discussion, reference is also made to poems from "Spleen et idéal" ("Spleen and the Ideal") and to passages from Baudelaire's journals and critical essays.

Dangerous women abound in Baudelaire's collection, above all in the "Fleurs du Mal" section. Baudelaire represents femininity in the guise not only of lesbians but also of vampires, corpses, and cruel women. He is, of course, known for his outspoken misogyny, and his prose writings contain much antifeminist invective, such as this passage from his *Journaux intimes*: "La femme ne sait pas séparer l'âme du corps. Elle est simpliste, comme les animaux" (*Œuvres* [Ruff] 635) ("Woman cannot distinguish the soul from the body. She is rudimentary, as are animals"). Woman, associated by Baudelaire with nature, animality, and impulsiveness, has neither the intellectual capacity of the poet nor his appreciation for artifice. Conversely, Baudelaire perceived women of letters as aping a masculine stance and therefore as monstrous as the "natural" woman. He reserved his most biting invective for "unnatural" literary women, writing that "nos yeux, amoureux du beau, n'ont jamais pu s'accoutumer à toutes ces laideurs compassées, à toutes ces scélératesses impies, [. . .] à tous ces sacrilèges pastiches de l'esprit mâle" (474; "Réflexions sur quelques-uns de mes contemporains"; "our eyes, in love with beauty, have never grown accustomed to this stiff and unnatural ugliness, to this ungodly wickedness [. . .] to this sacrilegious mimicry of the male mind"). Baudelaire's journals and criticism clearly figured *poet* and *woman* as mutually exclusive categories.

And yet in Baudelaire's poetry, the lesbian exists in a relation of equivalence with the figure of the poet. Their similarities are brought out in a number of pieces where sterility defines the sexual object relations of both poet and lesbian. Sterility is a positive attribute in *Les Fleurs du Mal*, where fecundity is aligned with abhorrent nature. Like the poet, called "ennemi des familles" (248) ("foe of families" [249]) and fecund only in a poetic sense, the lesbian is perceived as virgin and therefore barren. In "Lesbos," Sappho embodies lesbian virginity and poetic activity, femininity and masculinity: she is "la mâle Sapho, amante et poëte" (236) ("Sappho, male in poetry and love" [237]). The male poetic subject identifies with her, claiming that "Lesbos entre tous m'a choisi sur la terre / Pour chanter le secret de ses vierges en fleurs" ("I am Lesbos' choice from all on earth / To sing the secret of her flowering maids"). The modern lesbians depicted in the shorter "Femmes damnées," like the poet and his double, Baudelaire's splenetic lyric subject, strike a poetic stance and are ennobled as "Chercheuses d'infini" (246) ("seekers of the infinite" [247]). Unlike the judges before whom Baudelaire appeared, his lesbians are antirealists, described as "De la réalité grands esprits contempteurs" ("great spirits disdainful of reality" [trans. mine]).

How can we reconcile these contradictory figures, the exclusively masculine writer and the lesbian-identified poet of the "Femmes damnées" cycle? As an unnatural woman, a malevolent flower, the lesbian is elevated to a higher category than that of heterosexual women in Baudelaire's conceptual framework. But poetry belongs to the realm of fiction, and although Baudelaire's speaking subject often refers to himself as, or shares characteristics of, the masculine poet, the lyric also provides a place for this fictionalized hero to play dress-up and thereby to manipulate gender configurations with specific consequences for his poetic project.

A focused reading of "Femmes damnées: Delphine et Hippolyte" (238–44) allows students to work through Baudelaire's poetic investment in lesbianism. Point of view differentiates "Lesbos" and the shorter "Femmes damnées" from "Delphine et Hippolyte." The first two poems rely on apostrophe to situate a male speaking subject in relation to the personified isle of Lesbos and to the nameless group of lesbians he describes. "Delphine et Hippolyte," on the contrary, both offers portraits of two individual lesbians and allows them to speak. At the center of this tripartite poem lies an extensive dialogue, framed by two shorter segments, each having a strikingly different tone. The first segment offers an omniscient description, while the third segment reads like a fire-and-brimstone condemnation addressed directly to Delphine and Hippolyte.

In the initial section (sts. 1–6), a third-person narrator describes a sumptuous interior in which the women discuss what appears to have been their first sexual encounter. Delphine is majestic, ardent, and triumphant; Hippolyte timorous, passive, and confused. Baudelaire's narrator uses words such as "prey" and "victim" to describe the ingenuous Hippolyte, while Delphine is "a strong animal" who conquers Hippolyte as if in battle: "Ses bras vaincus, jetés comme de vaines armes" (238) ("Her conquered arms thrown down, surrendered in the field" [239]). The complementary opposition of strength and weakness returns in this symmetrical line, which seems to summarize the relationship between the two women: "Beauté forte à genoux devant la beauté frêle" (240) ("Strong beauty on her knees before frail beauty's couch" [241]). The poem is replete with suggestions of Hippolyte's youthful inexperience—"sa jeune candeur," "sa naïveté," "tes premières roses" (238, 240) ("her young innocence," "her naivety," "roses of your youth" [239, 241])—and passivity—"L'air brisé, la stupeur, la morne volupté / [. . .] Tout servait, tout parait sa fragile beauté" (238) ("The broken look, the stupor, the [lugubrious] voluptuousness, / [. . .] All strangely served her still, to show her fragile charm" [239]). The confident Delphine would seem to be Hippolyte's counterpoint: "Superbe, elle humait voluptueusement / Le vin de son triomphe, et s'allongeait vers elle" (240) ("Superb, luxurious, she breathed completely in / The wine of triumph, and she stretched out towards her love" [241]).

"Delphine et Hippolyte" is one of few poems in *Les Fleurs du Mal* (Fleurs du mâle?) where "woman" gets to speak, if only in quotations. The poem's dialogue in the central fifteen stanzas gives it a theatrical quality, heightened by references to curtains that rise at the beginning—"[les] caresses puissantes / Qui levaient le rideau de sa jeune candeur" (238) ("the thrilling touch / That spread apart the veil of her young innocence" [239])—and fall at the end— "Que nos rideaux fermés nous séparent du monde" (244) ("Let our closed curtains, then, remove us from the world" [245]). The two exchanges are initiated by Delphine, who first offers Hippolyte a choice between the brutality of a male lover and the delicacy of her own charms (sts. 7–10). Delphine employs a rhetoric of seduction that opposes a poetic vocabulary of ethereal communion ("ces éphémères," "les grands lacs transparents," "tes yeux pleins d'azur et d'étoiles" [240] ("mayflies on the wing," "great transparent lakes," "your eyes, so blue and full of stars" [241]) to prosaic, earthy images ("[les baisers] de ton amant creuseront leurs ornières / Comme des chariots ou des socs déchirants; // Ils passeront sur toi comme un lourd attelage") ("[the kisses] your lover gives dig out their cruel ruts / Like chariots, or like the farmer's biting plough; // They pass across you like a heavy, coupled team").

While Delphine's offer seems irresistible, the price that Hippolyte pays for choosing her includes fear, danger, and damnation. Instead of a delicate bliss, she foresees a heavy trampling more akin to Delphine's portrait of heterosexuality: "Je sens fondre sur moi de lourdes épouvantes / Et de noirs bataillons de fantômes épars" (240) ("I feel such heavy dread dissolving over me, / And black battalions of a scattered troop of ghosts" [241]). While Delphine's clear skies promise heaven, Hippolyte feels closed in by "un horizon sanglant" ("a bloody sky"), evocative of hell. In their final exchange (sts. 15–21), Delphine picks up on Hippolyte's vocabulary of damnation, insisting that judgment plays no role in love: "Qui donc devant l'amour ose parler d'enfer?" (242) ("Who in the face of love dares speak to me of Hell!" [243]). Nonetheless, their conversation crescendos into the closing condemnation (sts. 22–26), in which a judgmental voice addresses the two sterile women and sends them hurtling down to hell.

Students' reactions to "Delphine et Hippolyte" often reproduce the polemic of the trial, since students question whether or not to read the poem's ending as Baudelaire's condemnation of lesbianism. They are also interested in how Baudelaire depicts the lesbian couple, sometimes concluding that he offers a stereotypical opposition between Delphine's active masculinity and Hippolyte's passive femininity. But I encourage students to take a lesson from the 1949 court ruling and to read this relationship figuratively, as a metaphor for the lure of the forbidden. As such, the poem becomes a pretext for a meditation on the poet's quest for beauty, and the gendered dualism of masculine aggression and feminine passivity gives way to a discourse on the poet's vulnerability in the face of his overpowering task.

Barbara Johnson invites us to consider how this cliché falls apart in Baudelaire's work, concluding of Baudelaire's poetry, as of the Petrarchan tradition in general, that "There is [. . .] no simple correlation here between femininity and passivity, masculinity and action" ("Gender" 175). Indeed, Hippolyte does not stand for "the entirely feminine woman" (Paglia 427) but instead brings to mind the figure of passive masculinity in Baudelaire's *Les Fleurs du Mal* and suggests that masculinity and submission are not mutually exclusive.

A consideration of Baudelaire's choice of names for his heroines reveals the complexity of the gender positions in "Delphine et Hippolyte." Perhaps Baudelaire found a model in Germaine de Staël's 1802 novel *Delphine*, which presents a strong female character demanding recognition and defying conventions. Hippolyte's antecedents date further back, to Greek mythology. Normally a masculine given name in modern French, "Hippolyte" creates an ambiguity clarified in English by the gender-specific *Hippolyta* and *Hippolytus*. Hippolyta, queen of the Amazons, was said to have been slain by Hercules, whom she had befriended. Amazon, lesbian, conquered warrior: all these associations are reflected in the language of Baudelaire's poem. And yet perhaps a second Hippolyte—Hippolytus, the son of Theseus—is a more apt model for Baudelaire's timorous virgin. According to the myth (retold by Jean Racine in *Phèdre*), the young Hippolytus spurned the advances of his stepmother, Phaedra, who then wrought havoc that ended in Hippolytus's death. Not exclusively feminine in her antecedents, then, Hippolyte recalls stories of masculine victimization.

Within the context of *Les Fleurs du Mal*, the imperious Delphine reconfigures the overpowering woman of Baudelaire's heterosexual poems, whereas the fragile, passive Hippolyte is another version of an often masochistic masculine poetic subject (on Baudelaire's masochism, see B. Johnson, "Gender" 173–76). Indeed, one can interpret "Delphine et Hippolyte" as the lesbian version of several poems in which a male speaking subject addresses a highly aestheticized woman defined by her hard sterility and cold, cutting eyes: "La froide majesté de la femme stérile" (56; "Avec ses vêtements . . .") ("The sterile woman's frigid majesty" [57]). "La Beauté" ("Beauty") presents a personified figure that wounds docile poets who find her irresistible: "Et mon sein, où chacun s'est meurtri tour à tour" (38) ("And my breast, where you bruise yourselves all in your turn" [39]). Beauty's "larges yeux aux clartés éternelles" ("wide eyes gleaming with eternal light" [trans. mine]) reappear in "Le Chat" ("The Cat"), where the omnipresent cold gaze of femininity "coupe et fend comme un dard" (70) ("splits like a spear" [71]). The phallic aspect of this penetrating feminine gaze again calls into question normative associations between femininity and passivity, masculinity and aggression.

Delphine and Hippolyte themselves are described only from the neck up, here too largely in terms of their eyes. Hippolyte's betray her weakness and submission: we see "De ses yeux amortis les paresseuses larmes" (238) ("The heavy tears that fell from dull and weary eyes" [239]). In contrast, the aggressive fervor of Delphine's "yeux ardents" ("burning eyes" [trans. mine]) resembles the cutting coldness of Baudelaire's heterosexual vampire woman. Baudelaire himself suggests that these opposites are essentially the same: "Cruauté et volupté, sensations identiques, comme l'extrême chaud et l'extrême froid" (*Œuvres* [Ruff] 632; "Mon cœur mis à nu") ("Cruelty and sensual pleasure [are] identical sensations, like extreme heat and extreme cold"). The extremely hot Delphine would thus present a lesbian counterpart to the cold and distant Beauty for whom the self-ironic poet yearns.

Baudelaire's poetry raises the specter of menacing feminine sexuality that his most misogynist prose statements aim to neutralize. "Delphine et Hippolyte" functions as a kind of return of the repressed, where the male poet relinquishes control even of the subject position and comes into closer proximity to the threatening female figure. Ultimately, however, this theatrical poem performs lesbianism rather than engages it. It teaches us that Baudelaire's cult of beauty involved a more subtle attempt to control feminine sexuality by aestheticizing it, finally evacuating the lesbian of her femininity.

Invoking the collection's original title as did Proust, Walter Benjamin wrote that Baudelaire "reserved a place for [the lesbian] in the image of modernity" (*Baudelaire* 134; trans. mine). While recognizing the lesbian's importance, Benjamin nonetheless failed to analyze her symbolic position within the context of the collection's gender configurations. By heralding Baudelaire's lesbian

as the "heroine of modernity" (130), Benjamin acts in complicity with Baude-
laire's project of recuperating and defeminizing her. His and other critics' fail-
ure accurately to evaluate the literary lesbian suggests their blindness to a
crucial aspect of Baudelaire's lyric project: to purge femininity of its power.

It may well be that Baudelaire helped resolder for modernity the link (for-
gotten since Sappho) between lesbianism and the lyric; but it is also true that
his poems offer a vision of modernity in which the lesbian's elevation to a sym-
bol signals the containment of her sexuality and her femininity. Given the con-
text of intense interest in literary representations of lesbianism within which
Baudelaire wrote, students are invited to ask not only what role the lesbian
plays in lyric poetry but also what place she holds in modernist conceptions of
gender and sexuality—indeed, whether she exists at all within those concep-
tions, and what the ramifications of her absence might be.

Teaching the Devil

Jonathan Culler

T. S. Eliot called Baudelaire "the greatest exemplar in *modern* poetry in any language" ("Baudelaire" [1964] 377), and in universities the teaching of Baudelaire has, understandably, tended to stress his modernity. Unlike Victor Hugo, who today appears very much of his time and thus unlikely to appeal to undergraduates, Baudelaire can be presented as inclined in our direction: not only as the founder of modern poetry but also as the prophet of ennui ("Been there, done that"), of the alienated subject, of self-conscious sexuality, and of the quest for extreme experiences as the antidote to ennui. Recent critical discussions of Baudelaire have been greatly influenced by Walter Benjamin, who treats him above all as poet of the city, and graduate students who go on to become teachers have come to imagine Baudelaire as an urban flaneur, who strolls through the arcades of Paris, registering and parrying the shocks of modern experience. In short, Baudelaire can be presented as the writer who did more than anyone else to make people think of themselves as moderns; and since that possibility is available, it is hard to avoid being drawn to it, especially in undergraduate teaching.

But Baudelaire's collection of poems is called *Les Fleurs du Mal* (not, e.g., "*Beyond* Good and Evil") and offers, as the opening poem asserts, an explanation of the perverse condition of humanity: "C'est le Diable qui tient les fils qui nous remuent!" (4) ("It's the Devil who holds the strings that move us!" [trans. mine, here and throughout this essay]). Needless to say, this is scarcely a modern view. Even Christianity itself today seems to regard the Devil as a bit of outmoded mythological machinery. What could this creature of horns, hooves, tail, and pitchfork bring to a modern religion?

Resisting the resolute modernization of Baudelaire, I recently taught an undergraduate course entitled "Satan and *Les Fleurs du Mal*." Instead of placing

Baudelaire at the beginning of modern poetry, in that trajectory that runs, as Marcel Raymond's title has it, *Du Baudelaire au surréalisme* (*From Baudelaire to Surrealism*), I focused on the Devil and the problem of evil and thus inscribed Baudelaire in a different tradition—one that is new to many students but that proves of considerable interest to them: the tradition of satanic representations in the Romantic period, broadly conceived. Study of *Les Fleurs du Mal* becomes not investigation of the genealogy of the modern lyric and of modernity in general but reflection on the figuration of human agency or freedom and its relation to evil.

In addition to *Les Fleurs du Mal* and substantial selections from Baudelaire's prose writings, such as the *Les Paradis artificiels* (Artificial Paradises), *Mon cœur mis à nu* (My Heart Laid Bare), "De l'essence du rire" (On the Essence of Laughter), and the *Petits poèmes en prose* (Short Prose Poems), the course included Goethe's *Faust*, part 1, a work students seem not to encounter much these days. We also read Alfred de Vigny's "Eloa" and Byron's "Cain"—two excellent examples of Romantic satanism. Alphonse de Lamartine's *La Chute d'un ange* (The Fall of an Angel) and Victor Hugo's *La Fin de Satan* (The End of Satan) are other possibilities; we lacked the time to pursue them collectively, but they make excellent subjects for comparative term papers. (I would also have liked to use selections from Milton's *Paradise Lost*, the precursor of Romantic satanism). A number of Edgar Allan Poe's short stories, such as "The Black Cat" and "The Imp of the Perverse," which foreground questions about diabolical impulses that lead to self-destruction, are crucial to such a course. Excerpts from Honoré de Balzac's *Splendeurs et misères des courtisanes* (*The Splendors and Miseries of Courtesans*) and from Jules Michelet's *La Sorcière* (The Sorceress) illustrate different contemporary treatments of the diabolical. Jeffrey Burton Russell's *Mephistopheles* supplied background about the history of thinking about the Devil and, because of its rather simplistic and dismissive account of Romantic satanism, provided a useful foil for the study of these texts. (Students enjoy and benefit from discovering that the texts they are studying are more complex than is reported in well-regarded general surveys of the subject.) Finally, we read a number of other secondary works: "Toward a Romantic Iconology," from John Porter Houston's *The Demonic Imagination*; extracts from Mario Praz's *The Romantic Agony*; Sigmund Freud's "A Seventeenth-Century Demonological Neurosis," which takes up the psychoanalytic interpretation of the Devil; and Pope Paul VI's "Confronting the Devil's Power," which affirms that the Devil is not a symbol.

Thinking about the Devil provides a specific focus for reading the poems in a comparative perspective and highlights new aspects of *Les Fleurs du Mal*. In traditional scenarios the Devil tempts those who are bored or dissatisfied; he appears to those who are in a state of ennui and proposes to rescue them from it, by offering knowledge, power, or sensual satisfaction—at the cost of their immortal soul. In Baudelaire, however, the Devil leads his victims not out of ennui but into it. In "La Destruction" ("Destruction"), Baudelaire's Devil "prend [. . .] / La forme de la plus séduisante des femmes" (228) ("takes the form of the most seductive of women") but leads the speaker not to nights of pleasure but into "Des plaines de l'Ennui, profondes et désertes" ("the plains of ennui, deep and deserted"), where he throws blood and destruction at him. And in "L'Irrémédiable" ("The Irremediable"), seven stanzas describing night-marish entrapments of different figures are summed up as

> — Emblèmes nets, tableau parfait
> D'une fortune irrémédiable,
> Qui donne à penser que le Diable
> Fait toujours bien tout ce qu'il fait!   (160)

> Clear emblems, a perfect tableau
> Of an irremediable fortune,
> Which makes us think that the Devil
> Always does well anything he does.

What the Devil does, it seems, is not to tempt with knowledge and power but to oppress and confine. The Devil of "Au lecteur" ("To the Reader") pulls our strings so that we find repugnant objects attractive and descend through stink-ing darkness, snatching furtive pleasures from which, like a shrivelled orange, we try to squeeze some enjoyment (4). If we haven't committed rape, murder, or arson, it is only because Satan has "vaporized our will" and our soul is not sufficiently bold. In Baudelaire the Devil is less a spur to wicked, self-serving acts than the agent of hopeless entrapment and paralysis.

Baudelaire was certainly touched by the Romantic satanism that, identifying the Devil with revolution, embraced the energy of his doomed revolt against despotic rule. Baudelaire speaks, for instance, of Milton's Satan as the most perfect type of virile beauty (*Œuvres* [Ruff] 626; "Mon cœur mis à nu"). Romantic Satanism presents satanic characters—either Satan himself made a character in a substantial narrative (as in Hugo and Vigny) or other characters identified as satanic surrogates (as in Byron or Balzac). Baudelaire, however, does not make Satan a character in a narrative, and he participates very little in the reversals of value that would make the Devil a hero. Baudelaire's "Les Litanies de Satan" ("The Litanies of Satan"), which substitutes Satan for the Virgin Mary in its liturgical refrain, "O Satan, prends pitié de ma longue mis-ère!" (268–72) ("O Satan, take pity on my misery!" [269–73]) makes Satan not a heroic rebel but a figure who might offer consolations to social outcasts.

A passage of Romantic satanism from Balzac's *Splendeurs et misères des courtisanes* compares satanic characters of vast destructive potential, such as Robespierre, to venomous plants that fascinate and kill. "C'est la poésie du mal" (474) ("This is the poetry of evil"). This passage contains the possible seed of Baudelaire's title, *Les Fleurs du Mal*, but strikingly, Baudelaire does not in the least take up the possibilities it describes. He does not create satanic characters and, unlike many of his immediate precursors, does not participate in the rehabilitation of the Devil that structures such efforts as Vigny's "Eloa," Lamartine's *La Chute d'un ange*, and, eventually, Hugo's *La Fin de Satan*. The historian Ernest Renan wrote in 1855, two years before the publication of *Les Fleurs du Mal*: "Of all the previously accursed beings whom our century in its tolerance has relieved of their curse, Satan is undoubtedly the one who has most profited from the progress of enlightenment and of universal civilization" (49). Baudelaire was not an agent of the progress of enlightenment, as emerges clearly in this comparative perspective.

The question of Baudelaire's relation to Poe is also sharpened by focus on the Devil. Despite Poe's Gothic scenarios and interest in the fate of the soul, the Devil plays little role in Poe's fiction, and we can conclude that the Devil in *Les Fleurs du Mal* is not something Baudelaire acquired from Poe but Baudelaire's distinctive formulation of an engagement with questions of evil and agency.

Within *Les Fleurs du Mal* itself, concentration on the Devil enables one to begin by focusing on a small group of poems in which the problem of the Devil's role is posed. The opening poem, "Au lecteur," blames our condition on Satan, who has vaporized our will and who pulls the strings. But after presenting us as the Devil's puppets too weak for real sin, the poem shifts to a different allegorical space that it calls "la ménagerie infâme de nos vices" ("the infamous menagerie of our vices") where beasts that are also demons clamor, groan, prance, or yawn.

> Mais parmi les chacals, les panthères, les lices,
> Les singes, les scorpions, les vautours, les serpents,
> Les monstres glapissants, hurlants, grognants, rampants,
> Dans la ménagerie infâme de nos vices,
>
> Il en est un plus laid, plus méchant, plus immonde!
> Quoiqu'il ne pousse ni grands gestes ni grands cris,
> Il ferait volontiers de la terre un débris
> Et dans un bâillement avalerait le monde;
>
> C'est l'Ennui! — l'œil chargé d'un pleur involontaire,
> Il rêve d'échafauds en fumant son houka.
> Tu le connais, lecteur, ce monstre délicat,
> — Hypocrite lecteur, — mon semblable, — mon frère!   (6)
>
> But among the jackals, panthers, hounds,
> The monkeys, scorpions, vultures, snakes,
> The yowling, yelping, groaning, crawling monsters,
> In the infamous menagerie of our vices,

There is one that is more nasty and disgusting!
Although he makes no grand gestures nor great cries,
He would willingly devastate the earth
And in one yawning swallow all the world.

It's Ennui. An involuntary tear in his eye,
He dreams of scaffolds while smoking his hookah.
You know this finicky monster, reader.
—Hypocritical reader, my like, my brother.

Though the Devil pulls the strings, he is no longer on the scene when the poem turns to this zoo and to the ugliest, meanest, most disgusting of these monsters, Ennui, who dreams of executions and wouldn't mind swallowing the world in a yawn.

Is the presence of this monster in our world the work of the Devil or not? One can't be sure. The allegorical scene of yawning Ennui puffing his hookah like an oriental pasha seems far removed from that of Satan manipulating human puppets. Is it that, with the Devil pulling the strings and vaporizing our will, we are left vulnerable to this finicky monster? Is the very promotion of ennui to a fearsome monster of our inner life an example of the Devil's control? This is certainly possible but far from certain.

This poem, in its development, poses the problem of the Devil. The poem announces, as though it were the explanation of the human predicament described in the first two stanzas, that the Devil holds the strings that move us. It then proceeds to offer further description of human complicity with vice in a scenario that reaches its climax with the worst monster, without telling us whether we know this finicky monster and lodge him in the menagerie of our vices *because* the Devil controls us or whether, on the contrary, as critics have sometimes suggested (and this is indeed the common scenario in the literary tradition), it is the overpowering presence of ennui that gives the Devil his power to seduce.

What happens in the opening poem happens in the collection as a whole: the poems with an important framing function claim that the Devil is ubiquitous, always at work, pulling our strings or prompting our desires. Thus "La Destruction," the opening poem of the collection's titular section, "Fleurs du Mal" declares:

Sans cesse à mes côtés s'agite le Démon;
Il nage autour de moi comme un air impalpable;
Je l'avale et le sens qui brûle mon poumon
Et l'emplit d'un désir éternel et coupable. (228)

The Demon moves about ceaselessly at my side;
He swims about me like intangible air.
I swallow him and feel him burn my insides
And fill them with an eternal, guilty desire.

The introductory poems assert the Devil's continuous presence, but subsequent poems do not tell us whether the scenes or movements they narrate are examples of the Devil's work or not. Sometimes they raise the question and leave it unresolved: the speaker of "Les Sept Vieillards" ("The Seven Old Men"), for instance, does not know whether he is victim of an infernal plot or whether it is just "méchant hasard" (178) ("a nasty form of chance") that is driving him crazy. Is Satan responsible for what is described in poems where he makes no obvious appearance? What is most diabolical about the Devil, I am tempted to conclude, is that we can never be sure when he is at work.

The Devil, then, is the name of a problem that can be formulated in various ways: Is there a meaning or purpose in the things that befall us? Is there agency in the world apart from human will? Are there forces that make things go wrong, that frustrate our purposes and serve other ends, leading us, for instance, to act against our own interests, or is this idea just a self-serving delusion? To personify such forces as the Devil is not to relieve humans of responsibility or guilt—Baudelaire, notoriously, insists on guilt. To speak of the Devil is, however, to posit that there are forces that make things go wrong for us, that failure is meaningful, not meaningless accident. Everyone senses the Devil, but no one believes in him, wrote Baudelaire: "Tout le monde le sent mais personne n'y croit" (Œuvres [Ruff] 127; "Projets de préface").

But if the Devil is the name of a force that works on us against our will—if, as Baudelaire says in "Au lecteur," "le riche metal de notre volonté / Est tout vaporisé par ce savant chimiste" (4) ("the rich metal of our will is wholly vaporized by this clever chemist")—isn't he just a personification of the unconscious or the id, forces that make us do what our conscious self might reject? This is a question about the rhetoric that best enables us to think about our condition. Baudelaire had, in fact, considered the possibility of a psychological or medical interpretation of the Devil and in his prose poem "Le Mauvais Vitrier" ("The Bad Glazier") speaks of "cette humeur, hystérique selon les médecins, satanique selon ceux qui pensent un peu mieux que les médecins, qui nous pousse sans résistence vers une foule d'actions dangereuses ou inconvenantes" (152) ("this humor, which doctors call 'hysterical' but which those who think a bit better than doctors call 'satanic,' that pushes us, unresisting, to a host of dangerous or inappropriate acts"). The satanic hypothesis is superior thinking, one surmises, because it adduces not an individual neurotic disorder but impersonal structures and forces. But we might ask what is lost—to thought, but above all to poetry—when the Devil vanishes and is replaced by psychoanalytic discourse.

Christian theology introduces the Devil to account for the presence of evil in the world. If God is not to be held responsible for evil, there must be another creature whose free choice in deviating from good introduced evil. The Devil, thus, is not a *symbol* of evil but an agent or personification whose ability to act is essential. Just as God is not a symbol of good but, if he is anything, an agent, a creator or ruler, so the Devil is the name for evil agency—evil as a positive force, not evil as the absence of God, as modern theologians are wont to suggest. *Les Fleurs du Mal* makes the Devil an actor, along with other unexpected agents, such as Prostitution, which lights up in the streets, Anguish, which plants its black flag in my skull, Ennui, who puffs on his hookah and dreams of the gallows. To dismiss Satan as *just* a "personification" of evil, though, and thus a fiction requires remarkable confidence about what can and what cannot act, about what forces are in fact at work in the universe. Behind the wish to dismiss him as personification may lie the wishful presumption that only human individuals can act, that they control the world, and that there are no other agents. But the world would be a very different place if this were true. Much of its character, its difficulty, its mystery, comes from the effects produced by actions of other sorts of agents, which our grammars may or may not personify: "history," "the market," "the establishment," "public opinion"—forces that are not graspable at the level of the empirical actions of individuals but seem to control the world and give events meaningful and often oppressive structures.

Baudelaire's poems, in which Anguish, Autumn, Beauty, Ennui, Hope, Hate, and others do their work, pose questions about the constituents and boundaries of persons, about the forces that act in the world, and about whether this level of allegorical action does not in fact best capture the realities of body, spirit, and history. The figure of the Devil—a figure who never becomes a character in the mode of Romantic satanism—helps focus attention on this level of rhetorical action and on the question about the sort of rhetoric best suited to explore our bizarre modern condition.

After *Les Fleurs du Mal* had been condemned for offense to public morals, Baudelaire wrote an "Épigraphe pour un livre condamné" ("Epigraph for a Condemned Book") for the second edition of the collection—though in the end he did not include it. This poem claims that readers who haven't studied with Satan, that crafty dean, should throw away his book:

> Lecteur paisible et bucolique,
> Sobre et naïf homme de bien,
> Jette ce livre saturnien,
> Orgiaque et mélancolique.
>
> Si tu n'as fait ta rhétorique
> Chez Satan, le rusé doyen,
> Jette! tu n'y comprendrais rien.
> Ou tu me croirais hystérique.   (330)

> Calm and bucolic reader,
> Sober and naive, respectable fellow,
> Throw away this saturnine book,
> Orgiastic and melancholic.
>
> If you didn't do rhetoric
> With Satan, the crafty dean,

> Get rid of it, you'll not understand a word
> Or you'll think me hysterical.

Since the *classe de rhétorique* is the sixth form or terminal year of *lycée*, to study rhetoric with Satan is to complete your education. Studying the Devil can do that too. It helps one focus on the strangely archaic rhetoric of Baudelaire, with its myriad apostrophes, personifications, and hyperboles, and on what I take to be Baudelaire's wager that modes of allegorical action provide, in the end, the most telling representations. Finally, one of the particular virtues of a course on Baudelaire focused on the Devil is that it helps students confront the entanglement of questions about style and questions about content. In courses on poetry, teachers usually tell students that form and content are inseparable, but they often have trouble convincing them that talk about poetic form and rhetorical devices is indeed integrally related to questions about the nature of experience and the meaning of life. Students find it all too easy to evade the former for the latter. But the figure of the Devil makes questions about the nature of freedom, evil, and human agency inseparable from questions about such poetic techniques as personification and allegory. Is it a personification to say that the Devil tempts us? If so, what is the effect of that rhetorical strategy? Concentration on the effects of poetic style is a surprising reward of teaching the Devil in Baudelaire.

Teaching the Ethical Baudelaire:
Irony and Insight in *Les Fleurs du Mal*

Edward K. Kaplan

Ask the students what they know about Baudelaire . . . Our discussion will probably start with his reputation as a poet of evil who led a debauched life and died of syphilis—and who has little to teach us beyond his own shame. My classroom method is to explore in depth major poems at strategic points in *Les Fleurs du Mal* in order to reveal the collection's overall unity, progression, and internal contradictions. In undergraduate courses on French poetry I have taught Baudelaire as the last Romantic and the first modern poet, followed by Paul Verlaine, Arthur Rimbaud, Stéphane Mallarmé, leading through Guillaume Apollinaire and surrealism to Yves Bonnefoy. Or I have ended a course in French Romanticism with Baudelaire to emphasize the irony, or self-critical awareness, we sometimes find in predominantly lyrical Romantic works. The humor of Alfred de Musset and Stendhal typifies such distancing but lacks Baudelaire's innovative provocations.

I focus on Baudelaire's approach to basic human situations that should concern everyone. Baudelaire appears to offer impassioned (and often shockingly "perverse") judgments on sin and personal accountability, violence, poverty, love relationships (including homosexuality), attitudes toward women, God, the Devil, beauty, and the practical uses of art and poetry. With tact, the instructor can help students address issues of principle (and their political entanglements), current then as now, to show how Baudelaire is relevant.

What I mean by ethics involves more than standards of conduct or moral judgment. The ethical includes our manner of perceiving—intellectually and emotionally—both the real world and the quality of our relationship to other people. This approach heuristically regards *Les Fleurs du Mal* as a spiritual autobiography retracing the poet-persona's struggles—but within an often elusive perspective. As a poet, Baudelaire was not a moralist who usually expressed his values directly; he deplored "the heresy of didacticism" ("l'hérésie de l'enseignement," as he wrote in his essay on Edgar Allan Poe ["Notes" 332]), which he associated with Victor Hugo, lesser writers, and the officially endorsed painters of his era. Authentic poetry, as Baudelaire practiced it, highlights the problematics of morality itself.

My teaching strategy applies the notion of ethical irony: Baudelaire's feigned cruelty or criminal attitudes, disturbing and inconsistent moods that arouse readers to anger but also, eventually, to self-reflection, critical insight, and dialogue with the poet. (Baudelaire parodies this risky technique in his prose poem, "Assommons les pauvres!" [*Œuvres* (Ruff) 182–83] ["Let's Beat Up the Poor!"], where the narrator tests an ideological maxim all too literally on a beggar's back.) Ethical irony is Socratic; it challenges complacency and moralistic stereotypes, forcing us to face life's harsh contradictions and the inadequacy or tyranny of doctrine (see 362; "Exposition universelle 1855").

Students and teacher, from the beginning of this unit, must remain alert. First and foremost, the collection's very title is ambiguous, since *flowers* could be a supreme expression of evil or its lovely antithesis. Inspired by Simone Weil's reflections on existential *malheur* as a parallel to original sin (124), I encourage the class to consider the word *mal* as a synonym of *misfortune* or *suffering* as well as *evil*. We may thus translate *Les Fleurs du Mal* as "The Flowers of Affliction," suggesting that people who act badly are not essentially malicious but fallible (Paul Ricoeur's term), potentially depraved but responsible for their actions. The last line of the collection's original epigraph from Agrippa d'Aubigné—"la vertu n'est pas fille de l'ignorance" (Baudelaire, *Œuvres* [Ruff] 126) ("Virtue is not the daughter of ignorance")—can guide the class's progressing discernment of what Baudelaire called his "horrible morality" (724; "Notes et documents pour mon avocat").

Ethical Irony as Dialogue

Our interpretive model is the threshold poem, "Au lecteur" ("To the Reader"), which at first depicts humankind as morally feeble, manipulated by the Devil, and actively relishing vice: "Aux objets répugnants nous trouvons des appas" (4) ("In repulsive objects we find charms" [5]). As various sins are depicted, students may feel discomfited by the poet's apparent alliance with offenders. The poem ends, however, by asserting that vice is not simply a moral issue, since crimes may be motivated by ennui, the greatest vice. Ennui is more than boredom; it is a psychological or existential capitulation of personal will. As depicted in the poem, ennui is a suicidal apathy as a defense against anxiety.

"Au lecteur" ends by asserting Baudelaire's full range of attitudes: first, contemptuous challenge to the "Hypocrite lecteur" (6) ("hypocrite reader" [7]), the bourgeois who cannot deny his or her penchants toward vice; then, tender identification that leads to intimacy ("mon semblable, — mon frère!") ("my companion, my brother" [trans. mine]). This memorable final line (cited by T. S. Eliot in *The Waste Land* as the epitome of the fragmented modern self) surprisingly declares the poet's compassion for afflicted persons whose distressing imperfections he shares.

The class's journey through *Les Fleurs du Mal* thus emphasizes the key problem of ambiguity. Reading Baudelaire is an adventure of passion and cognition, moral judgment and aesthetic pleasure, and, above all, self-knowledge. Ethical irony undermines self-deception, a denial mechanism more radical than common hypocrisy, which is the disguising of one's true feelings from others. The collection's overriding topic is the struggle with personal responsibility rather than the inevitable submission to the Devil or original sin.

I confirm the ethical Baudelaire textually by emphasizing the changes he made between the 1857 and 1861 editions of *Les Fleurs du Mal*. His regrouping of poems—which highlights major pieces added in 1861—adds an explicitly ethical focus. I have found it pedagogically expedient to follow the collection's order by sections. As we examine major poems in detail, we gradually clarify the general structure of these groupings and, eventually, of the collection as a whole, facilitating directed debates on the relations among literature, imagination, and personal conduct.

Shared awareness of death is Baudelaire's ethical premise, as "Au lecteur" suggested. The collection as a whole gathers energy through various conflicts between the aesthetic (hedonistic self-involvement or escape through fantasy) and the ethical (recognition of finite reality as well as of a reciprocal relation between two human beings). As we enter the long, diverse, somewhat disorganized—yet resolutely dialectical—first section, "Spleen et idéal" ("Spleen and the Ideal"), I stress how Baudelaire modifies (or revises) his quest for perfection, which dominates the original edition, by introducing direct expressions of mortality and compassion.

Differing images of women mark the contrast: "La Beauté" (38; "Beauty"), a widely taught staple of anthologies, represents woman as statue, a transcendent, aloof idealization; "Le Masque" (40–42; "The Mask"), added in 1861, rejects that heartless prototype and asserts the poet's identification with the person beneath Art's mask: "Elle pleure, insensé, parce qu'elle a vécu!" (42) ("The reason, fool, she cries is that she's lived!" [43]). (See Kaplan, *Prose Poems* 4–9; Zimmermann, "Expression") The complementary piece, "Hymne à la Beauté" ("Hymn to Beauty"), further revises "La Beauté" by promoting Art's ameliorative function: "[rendre] L'univers moins hideux et les instants moins lourds" (44) ("[to make] the world less dreadful, and time less oppressive" [trans. mine]). Students should also savor Baudelaire's radically escapist position in "Parfum exotique" (48; "Exotic Perfume") and "La Chevelure" (50–52; "Head of Hair"), celebrated examples of Baudelairean synaesthesia.

The second section, "Tableaux parisiens" ("Parisian Pictures" [trans. mine]), added in 1861 (although many of its poems were composed much earlier: see Baudelaire, *Œuvres* [Pichois] 1: 811; Robb), applies the previous section's ethical allegories (as in "The Mask") to daily urban life. "Le Soleil" ("The Sun") reinforces the poet's use of art by which he "ennoblit le sort des choses les plus viles" (168) ("lends a grace to things that are most vile" [169]). Students ponder how the poet, inspired by the city's poverty and the unexpected ("Flairant dans tous les coins les hasards de la rime" ["Stumbling on words as over paving stones"]), acts like the sun to cure illnesses and soothe anxieties: "Il fait s'évaporer les soucis vers le ciel" ("He sends our cares in vapour to the skies"). A valuable discussion might occur here. How can art or poetic idealization really help us live? (The prose poem "Le Mauvais Vitrier" [*Œuvres* (Ruff) 151–52; "The Bad Glazier"] parodies the claim that art can improve life.)

Three poems dedicated to the exiled Victor Hugo consolidate Baudelaire's ethical position. I try to devote at least one class period to "Le Cygne" (172–76; "The Swan"), which summarizes Baudelaire's inspirational pathos of temporality.

My ethical reading depends on our interpretation of the final part linked by a long series of "Je pense à [. . .]" (176) ("I think of [. . .]" [177]). Yet the undeniable tenderness of these lines, and the self-absorption it also includes, is ambiguous. How do we understand the two final lines? "Je pense aux matelots oubliés dans une île, / Aux captifs, aux vaincus! . . . à bien d'autres encor!" ("I think of sailors left forgottten on an isle, / Of captives, the defeated . . . many others more!"). Is the tone positive (a remembering process that inspires politically engaged poetry) or negative (a yielding to oblivion)? As crude as the categories of pessimistic and optimistic may be, they are stimulating for class discussion.

Temporality—the fragility of all life and the prospect of death—energizes Baudelaire's compassion. The diptych "Les Sept Vieillards" ("The Seven Old Men") and "Les Petites Vieilles" ("The Little Old Women"), poems 90 and 91 in the collection and first published together in the September 1859 *Revue contemporaine*, presents two different responses to the aged: terror at the men, paternal solicitude for the women. More subtle is the brief tableau "A une passante" (poem 93; "To a Woman Passing By") in which the poet dreams of love. The final line, "O toi que j'eusse aimée, ô toi qui le savais!" (188) ("O you I might have loved, as you well know!" [189]), expresses what I call Baudelaire's loving in the pluperfect subjunctive—technically, the second form of the conditional perfect (a brief grammar review might be in order here for the verb tenses). We can ask students to discuss how love can be both a feeling, internal to one person, and a dialogue, a mutuality that affirms both individuals as subjects. In practical terms, the poet's preference for hypothetical or imagined desire defeats his ability to love. For there to be love, as I insist in discussion, two people must make contact and develop reciprocal communication.

The class can now explore some problematic aspects of the ethical. (In so doing, we put the entire venture at risk.) Baudelaire as critic and thinker knew that compassion, productive as it might be, was not exempt from selfish aesthetic gratification. The poet of "Les Petites Vieilles" indeed implied that his empathy with the little old women was both detached and hedonistic: "Mais moi, moi qui de loin tendrement vous surveille, / [. . .] Je goûte à votre insu des plaisirs clandestins" (186) ("But I, who from a distance mark your steps / With tenderness [. . .] / Unknown to you I taste a secret joy" [187]). Distance, paradoxically, makes his compassion possible, and so it becomes an aesthetic pleasure, inspiring poetic creation. (The prose poem "Les Fenêtres" ["Windows"] confirms Baudelaire's self-judgment as an urban writer in search of inspiration.)

Must we then collapse the ethical into the aesthetic? Must readers respond only as sensualists to this proclamation in the prose poem "Enivrez-vous" ("Get High"): "Pour n'être pas les esclaves martyrisés du Temps, enivrez-vous; enivrez-vous sans cesse! De vin, de poésie ou de vertu, à votre guise" (*Œuvres* [Ruff] 174) ("So as not to be the martyred slaves of Time, get high; get high constantly! On wine, on poetry, or on virtue, as you wish")? I think not. Ethical irony surpasses binary categories and, in the present example, the joys of solipsism and escape can coexist with a recognition of temporality, of the limits of desire.

Compassion, therefore, is a first step toward moral action, but it is not a full commitment. To test the boundaries between the aesthetic (what is imaginative) and the ethical (what requires relationship), we end this crucial section with analyses of "Le Crépuscule du soir" (192–94; "Dusk") and "Le Crépuscule du matin" (210; "Dawn"), both Parisian poems in which Baudelaire evokes a benevolent community of working people, regardless of their civil or moral status: criminals, scholars, prostitutes, debauchees, people dying in hospitals—and writers. Baudelaire suggests that recognition of our banal toil enhances the possibility of collective responsibility. But the section's penultimate poem, "Rêve parisien" (204–08; "Parisian Dream"), radically separating fantasy from the real, prevents us from succumbing to hermeneutic complacency, ethical or otherwise.

The Hidden Dignity of Rebellion

The next three sections specify some ways to resist or reject personal responsibility. Does Baudelaire sanction nihilism and deny his ethical ideals? The five pieces of "Le Vin" ("Wine"), any of which might be examined, view intoxication as an understandable though fleeting deliverance from anguish and also from social obligations. The class can address the consequences of alcoholism, drug abuse, gambling, the compulsive search for entertainment, and other forms of diversion in today's culture. (However, this debate may widen the classroom generation gap.)

For Baudelaire's contemporaries, the irony of the next two sections, "Fleurs du Mal" and "Révolte" ("Revolt"), was not easily perceived. Now that the class is trained to detect the probable discrepancy between the poet's manifest coldness and his compassion, issues of sexuality and violence in the section "Fleurs du Mal" can be discussed—but with age-appropriate caution (see Kaplan, "Baudelaire and the Vicissitudes"). "Une Martyre" (228–32; "A Martyr") is a graphic (almost pornographic) masterpiece of ethical irony: it lures readers into relishing an attractive young victim's body before it states that she had been decapitated by her lover. The "marriage" evoked in the final lines is clearly ironic, since the poet refers to her assassin as her husband. We are left not with a savor of sadistic distraction but with sorrow at the murder of this loving teenage woman by a man, like herself, frustrated by unassuaged desire.

After exploring how Baudelaire uncovers the violence fomented by heterosexual love, the class examines same-sex passion in the one poem about lesbians not condemned by the tribunal, "Femmes damnées" (244–46; "Damned Women" [my trans.]). This piece, beginning "Comme un bétail pensif [. . .]" ("Like pensive cattle [. . .]"), demonstrates how Baudelaire displaces the focus from behavior conventionally judged as deviant to the sinners' dignified inner lives; it may lead to a discussion of Baudelaire's trial and the censuring of the first edition. At the end, the poet-narrator again admits his benevolent identification with women's "mornes douleurs" and "soifs inassouvies" (246) ("dismal griefs" and "unslaked thirsts" [trans. mine]); in a word, he praises their longings for the infinite, thus explaining, if not excusing, their sexual preference as another form of religiosity misconstrued by bourgeois obtuseness. Another discussion topic: Can we judge social and intimate behavior apart from the integrity of one's inner life? Condemn the sin but not the sinner?

A parallel love poem but one of broader consequence is the famous anthology piece "Un Voyage à Cythère" (254–58; "A Voyage to Cythera"). I bring out less obvious ethical insights (see Kaplan, "Baudelaire and the Vicissitudes" 124–25) by examining the poet's interpretation of a castrated corpse hanging from a gallows as an allegory of the poet's failed life: "Ridicule pendu, tes douleurs sont les miennes" (258) ("Hanged man, ridiculous, your sorrows are my own!" [259]). Again, judgment of Baudelaire's ethics depends on ambiguous final lines: "— Ah! Seigneur! donnez-moi la force et le courage / De contempler mon cœur et mon corps sans dégoût!" ("Ah, Lord! I beg of you the courage and the strength / To regard my body and my heart without disgust!" [trans. modified]). In my view, the poet accepts responsibility for his failings and utters a sincere prayer. He does not reject sexual pleasure as such, nor does he sublimate it. His higher morality accepts carnal desire and seeks an integration of spirit and flesh. Advanced students can consider distinctions between symbol and allegory raised by Paul de Man's now classic essay "The Rhetoric of Temporality. De Man's refusal to consider the ethical and religious dimensions of literature (see Kaplan, *Prose Poems* 171–73) marks a major divide in our hermeneutical commitments.

At this point in the collection, we can almost conclude that the villain of *Les Fleurs du Mal* is not the drive to enjoy evil or a diabolical force exterior to the person. Rather, antisocial behavior may be self-assertion (or rebellion) aroused by the inevitable frustration of infinite desire. That natural limits might explain these apparent crimes is confirmed by the emblematic poem "L'Amour et le crâne: vieux cul-de-lampe" (258–60; "Passion and the Skull: An Old Colophon"), which closes the section. Human fragility surpasses the categories of good and evil. Finitude is our common denominator, and so our fear of death, the anxiety of mortality, should bind us together.

The class can now discuss Baudelaire's notice inserted before the first edition of "Révolte" ("Revolt"), the penultimate section: "Fidèle à son douleureux programme, l'auteur des *Fleurs du Mal* a dû, en parfait comédien, façonner son esprit à tous les sophismes comme à toutes les corruptions" (*Œuvres* [Ruff] 127) ("Faithful to his distressing procedure, the author of *The Flowers of Affliction* was constrained to conform his mind, like a consummate actor, to every sophistry as to all forms of corruption"). Government censors, however, distrusted this authorial confession of ethical irony and judged his pastiche of anti-Christian anger to be sincerely blasphemous. Careful reflection explains why: these poems (as do William Blake's "Holy Thursday" poems in *Songs of Innocence and of Experience*) deplore the hypocrisy of the church and other sanctioned institutions that tolerated poverty. Students should consider what it means to utter blasphemy (or to question divine justice) in the name of humanistic principles.

Some examples from the Bible can be discussed: Abraham pleading with God to save Sodom and Gomorrah, the Book of Job.

The final section, "La Mort" ("Death"), recapitulates Baudelaire's insight that dread of extinction underlies much antisocial behavior, which is too readily condemned as willfully evil. The grand, sprawling, and somewhat disorganized but impressive final poem, "Le Voyage" (282–92; "Voyaging"), which was added in 1861, summarizes many of the previous topics (imagination and disillusion, sin and sexual love, utopias, etc.), while insisting on the inescapable fact, now completely acknowledged, of human finitude or death.

This concluding poem provides a decisive test of ethical irony, especially the two last stanzas, which begin, "O Mort, vieux capitaine, il est temps! levons l'ancre!" (292) ("O Death, old captain, time to make our trip!" [293]). The ethical Baudelaire thrusts readers before two opposing but equally plausible perspectives: Does the poet mean to embrace suicide as a desperate escape from frustrated idealism, or does he embrace chance (i.e., a responsible life) as such, realistically, or even heroically? (see Kaplan, "Courage" and "Baudelaire and the Battle"). Interpreted in terms of its ethical seriousness, "Le Voyage" implies that death has been integrated into an unremittingly energetic life, just as fallibility and self-deception coexist with our drive toward righteousness and truth. Do the two final stanzas celebrate the poet's surrender to suicide—or his courageous faith in the unknown? The class does not have to conclude.

General Applications

The notion of interpretive undecidability, which became fashionable with deconstructive textual analysis, should form a starting point (not an end to) an ethical reading of Baudelaire and other literature. His poetry and especially the self-analytic prose poems (see Kaplan, *Prose Poems*) do not prescribe what to think; they demonstrate how to think, that is, dialogically, Socratically. Ethical irony forces us, obliquely, to examine ourselves, to judge critically how we react to Baudelaire's performances. An analysis of ethical irony explains in large part why his writings affect us deeply, stirring up complicated emotions and subtle judgments.

Ethical irony is one broadly applicable category of narrative ambiguity that underscores the historical and personal content of literature. A focus on the ethical Baudelaire helps contrast the didactic aspects of, say, Alphonse de Lamartine and Victor Hugo's poetry with the cool or ironic works of Baudelaire, his contemporary Gustave Flaubert, and, later, Arthur Rimbaud. Contradictions between the putatively realistic or naturalistic narratives of Honoré de Balzac and Emile Zola, for example, and their mythical or erotic lyricism also emerge from a contrast of ethical and aesthetic elements. Our implicit agenda may be fulfilled when the students can appreciate the complexity of moral judgments while realizing that the responsibility for making them cannot be avoided.

Teaching *Les Fleurs du Mal* with CD-ROM: Visual and Verbal Art

Rosemary Lloyd

With the new technologies of the CD-ROM and the World Wide Web, teaching literature in a culturally enriched context has suddenly become not only far easier but also far more stimulating. In the past, teachers could help students enter the demanding, rewarding, somewhat enigmatic poems of *Les Fleurs du Mal* by gathering dictionaries to guide them through the complexities of the lexicon; encyclopedias to elucidate proper names; slides to illustrate the works of artists who inspired particular poems; tapes of first language speakers reading the poem, to facilitate an exploration of the intricacies of sound patterning, syllabification, and rhyme play; and a selection of translations to sensitize students to the extraordinary complexity of Baudelaire's use of language. Now all this and more can be gathered together on a CD-ROM that can be explored in class by projecting from a computer screen and also be made available for individual use and further exploration outside the classroom. Although all this information could have been posted directly onto the World Wide Web, I preferred the sound qualities of a CD-ROM at the present state of technological development. The enormous advantage of the CD-ROM over conventional methods is that it enables students simultaneously to see images and hear readings or musical settings of texts. It also gives them instant, easy access to a wealth of supporting documents.

Given the cultural baggage the aesthete Baudelaire expected his readers to possess and given the little of art or music history our own students often know, a CD-ROM can allow prompt, satisfying, unintimidating entrance into a rich interartistic context where visual and verbal artists collaborate and where the pleasure of the text depends largely on an enthusiastic response to that collaboration.

Moreover, this technology both encourages and rewards individual exploration, allowing students to take responsibility for their own learning.

A passionate interest in art pervades both the critical and creative writing of Baudelaire, in ways that we as teachers can exploit—not merely to allow our students to penetrate more deeply into the complexity and richness of his thought and expression but also to give them greater enjoyment and confidence while reading the poems. Baudelaire's literary criticism shows him honing his own skills as a writer, through parody and pastiche as well as through analysis. His art criticism offers him a forum where, in more general terms and with less rivalry, the synthesizing sweep of his mind can explore representational possibilities, question the direction of modern art, and begin to establish an intricate network of correspondences between the written word and the visual arts. Art criticism also allows him to question the notion of genre, to throw into doubt the rigid divisions between the critical and the creative, in ways that illuminate his experiments with genre and the extent to which his poetry is inspired by the visual arts. Indeed, the line between art criticism and poetry in Baudelaire's work is often hard to discern.

This seamless transition between creative and critical writing is also part of an essential characteristic of Baudelaire's poetry: that everything is interconnected, pervaded, and subtended by a symbolic system that gives *Les Fleurs du Mal* its harmony and sense of unity. Images that describe or respond to works of art are themselves wrought with secondary images intimately connected to this system. As a result, close exploration of poems that offer verbal transpositions of works of visual art, and even more so of poems that include several such transpositions, allows us a privileged access to many other poems in the collection.

As Baudelaire puts it, the aim of the *transposition d'art* is not to illustrate but to explain the subtle pleasure the work arouses (*Œuvres* [Ruff] 423; "Salon de 1859") by transposing it from the visual to the verbal field. It is, then, a uniquely personal, intellectual response, demanding techniques that point forward to Stéphane Mallarmé's insistence on the need not to describe but to suggest. What Baudelaire seeks in these transpositions is a form that, as he argues in his unfinished article on philosophical art, creates a suggestive magic, containing both the outside world (the source of inspiration) and the inner world (the temperament or sensitivity through which that outer source is reflected and subtly altered) (*Correspondance, 1862–1871* 206). The CD-ROM facilitates a far deeper awareness of that suggestive magic, since, through its rich labyrinths and intricate architecture of symbols, it sets the student more swiftly on the interface between inner and outer worlds.

We can detect several essential stages in the mechanism of the *transposition d'art* if we combine this mingling of inner and outer worlds with Baudelaire's definition of beauty as something a little vague, leaving room for conjecture (*Œuvres* [Ruff] 626; "Mon cœur mis à nu" ["My Heart Laid Bare"]). In "Le Squelette laboureur" (188–90; "Skeletons Digging"), his interest is seized first by an image, then his curiosity is aroused by how and why it should interest him, and finally his mind moves on to seeing in it a symbol or allegory bearing (but not imposing) a broader message. Those stages illuminate our reading, and our teaching, of the poems in *Les Fleurs du Mal* that respond in complex and multiple ways to the plastic arts.

In teaching such poems, I find it helps to focus first on a couple of fairly straightforward transpositions, beginning, for example, with "Le Masque" (40–42; "The Mask"). CD-ROM technology enables students to see a series of slides of Christophe's statue *Le Masque*, now in the Musée d'Orsay, while listening to a reading of the poem. They realize how much the poem engages in a conversation with the statue and thereby enacts that constant desire to transform emotion into understanding that Baudelaire adumbrates in his phrase "transformer ma volupté en connaissance" (*Œuvres* [Ruff] 514; "Richard Wagner et *Tannhäuser* à Paris") ("convert my pleasure into knowledge"). The technology gives the viewer the illusion of moving around the statue and discovering its deception at the same time as the narrative voice does. I like to add a link here that sets the poem in the grittier, more demanding context of the section of the *Salon de 1846* entitled "Pourquoi la sculpture est-elle ennuyeuse?" (257) ("Why Is Sculpture Boring?") and of those passages in "Mon cœur mis à nu" that explore the notions of human duality, the dual impulse to good and to evil, and the horror of sexuality that finds expression in misogyny. Given his jibe about the boring nature of sculpture, it is surely significant that what Baudelaire indicates as its negative characteristic is precisely what Christophe has been able to turn to advantage here: "In vain the sculptor struggles to place himself at a single viewpoint; the viewer, walking around the figure, can choose a hundred different viewpoints, except the right one" (Baudelaire, *Salon* 257). The spectator's disruptive movements are presented here as a quintessential part of the statue's force and meaning. Moreover, the narrative voice presents an exemplary reading of the statue as text that illuminates the reading practices Baudelaire expects of readers of his poetry.

As Christophe's original title, *The Human Comedy*, indicates, "Le Masque" represents the human condition, the way society forces us into modes of behavior that we adopt to hide our real grief, our suffering, our private emotions. Like the woman in "Confession" who laments:

> Que c'est un dur métier que d'être belle femme,
> Et que c'est le travail banal
> De la danseuse folle et froide qui se pâme
> Dans un sourire machinal; [. . .]   (94)

> Being a beauty is a hard affair,
> A banal business, vanity,
> The swoons of mad and frigid dancers, where
> The smiles are done mechanically.   (95)

the woman in "Le Masque" is painfully aware of the horror of life, but has the *pudeur* ("delicacy") the dandy Baudelaire so valued to keep her feelings to herself, hidden behind her mask.

Baudelaire leads us around the statue, inviting us to contemplate, not just to look at it, goading us into a response by qualifying his adjectives with what appear hackneyed adverbs: she is "[d]ivinement robuste" (42) ("[d]ivinely robust" [43]) and "adorablement mince" ("adorably slim"). He focuses on elements of beauty that have most appeal for him—his love of the undulating line, for example—while simultaneously suggesting an undercurrent of irony by the rather precious alliteration of "pontife" ("pope") and "prince." This preciosity, intensified by the expression "charment les loisirs" (literally, "charm the idle moments"), reflects the baroque preciosity of the statue; but, more important, it acts as a mask veiling a qualitatively different appreciation. This quite different response is laid bare when Baudelaire takes us through the surprise and shock of the spectator's realization that the beautiful face is in fact a mask. Again the poet refracts the work of art through his artistic temperament and shows how it sparks his nervous reactions: "Pauvre grande beauté! Le magnifique fleuve / De tes pleurs aboutit dans mon cœur soucieux" (42) ("O beauty, how I pity you! the great / Stream of your tears ends in my anxious heart" [43]). And he claims, in two terms very close to the heart of Baudelairean aesthetics, the lie and intoxication: "Ton mensonge m'enivre" ("Your lie transports me"). The *transposition d'art* here serves above all as the basis for deeper questioning and for reaching a generalized conclusion about the human condition: "Elle pleure [. . .] comme nous!" ("She weeps [. . .] And so will we!" [trans. modified]). The harshness of sounds—the repeated p, k, and s—prepares the explosive nature of the closing words. We should stress that while Baudelaire sees the statue as a source of philosophical questioning, he does not condemn it as didactic, since it poses and prompts that questioning without presupposing or limiting a response. After all, the response of the poetic persona here is steeped in Baudelairean world-weariness and melancholy; the response's refraction through a particular temperament is so obvious that the reader, goaded by being addressed as "insensé" ("fool") in the final lines, may well be led to a very different interpretation.

In "Le Masque" the specific work of visual art is very much present in the transposition. In other poems, however, the work of art is relegated to a minor role, presented more as the initial stimulus for the poet's more wide-ranging meditations. One could consider, for example, the moral lesson Baudelaire extracts from an engraving by Hendrik Goltzius in "L'Amour et le crâne" (258–60; "Passion and the Skull") or the similarities and differences between "Le Rebelle" (340–42; "The Rebel") and Eugène Delacroix's murals in Saint-Sulpice. Students can compare the comments in "Le Rebelle" with the brief but powerful descriptions Baudelaire gives of the murals in his 1861 article "Les Peintures de Delacroix à Saint-Sulpice" (*Œuvres* [Ruff] 526–29), or they can compare a series of Delacroix nudes—for instance, the *Woman with a Parrot* or the *Woman with White Stockings*—with *Les Bijoux* (*The Jewels*), where sound patterning and the suggestive power of rhyme are strikingly manipulated to respond to the challenge set by the painter's evocative use of color, light, and shade. Following some of the labyrinthine connections to contemporary art and to statements made in Baudelaire's critical writing, as well as exploring some of the rhetorical devices exploited in these transpositions, lays the groundwork for a more fruitful student response to "Les Phares" (20–24; "The Beacons"; see Porter, "Anagogic Structure").

Indeed, of all Baudelaire's *transpositions d'art*, "Les Phares" sets the greatest challenge in the classroom, since it takes for granted the reader's familiarity with the works of a wide range of painters and sculptors, as well as with the composer Carl Maria von Weber. Yet "Les Phares" is also an essential expression of the artist's function as witness, warning, and guide. Its position so early (sixth) in "Spleen et idéal" suggests that the poem acts as a lighthouse, a beacon illuminating the collection as a whole. Whatever else Baudelaire meant by his claim in his letter to Alfred de Vigny that *Les Fleurs du Mal* possessed a deliberate architecture, that claim confers on these early poems a crucial role in preparing the reader for what follows.

In creating my own CD-ROM, I was eager to enrich my students' experience without denying the role played by the imagination. The lexicon, accessible through hot links from each word in the text, reveals that the poem's title draws on a word that, before it took on more general significance, began as the name of a specific building, the lighthouse at Alexandria, one of the seven wonders of the ancient world. Just as the lighthouse evokes a specific building as well as the general class of such structures, each of the artists to whom the poem devotes a thumbnail sketch is of interest both for his specific contribution and for how he contributed more generally to the transformation of human existence through art. Making the leap from the specific to the universal demands an act of imagination, but the leap can be greatly prepared and facilitated by the technological possibilities of a CD-ROM.

The central part of this section of the CD-ROM consists of two first language speakers' reading the poem. Listening, the students can follow the text and watch a series of slides. They can choose which voice they want to hear, can compare and contrast the speakers' accents, and can stop at any point to consult the linked dictionary and encyclopedia entries. Providing two different accents, one from the south of France and one from Belgium—one voice male and one female—serves two practical functions. First, increasing students' familiarity with accents other than that of Paris, it better prepares them for encounters with the French and with Francophones. Second, it releases them from the notions that there is only one way to read the poem and that the voice of only one gender has authority.

Enabling students to hear the poem read aloud while they see both the text and a series of illustrations reveals how suggestive sound patterning underpins the statements. Examples in the Delacroix stanza, for instance, would be the repetition of *lac* (already present in the artist's name), the repeated nasals, and the concatenation of *b*'s and *p*'s, together with the enjambment of "fanfares étranges / Passent" (22) ("fanfares pass away / And disappear"), where the device echoes the meaning to suggest unstoppable movement. Hearing the poem is particularly effective in drawing students' attention to some of the suggestions embedded in the rhymes. If we take the following stanza:

> Ces malédictions, ces blasphèmes, ces plaintes,
> Ces extases, ces cris, ces pleurs, ces *Te Deum*,
> Sont un écho redit par mille labyrinthes;
> C'est pour les cœurs mortels un divin opium! (22)

> These curses, blasphemies, these maledictions, groans
> These ecstasies, these pleas, cries of *Te Deum*, tears
> Echo respoken by a thousand labyrinths,—
> An opium divine for hungry mortals' hearts! (23)

we can't help being struck by the sardonic implications of rhyming *opium* with *Te Deum*, as if in an ironic reworking of Karl Marx's dictum that religion is the opiate of the masses. Similarly the rhyme of *plaintes* with *labyrinthes* intensifies the visual image of endless corridors filled with curses, cries, and weeping.

The selection of slides to accompany the reading was determined both by a wish to respond to suggestions and hints in the text and a need to indicate something of the range and variety of each artist's work. Where possible, I included a self-portrait of the artist, showing, for example, Peter Paul Rubens's self-portrait with his first wife, Isabella Brant; and one of the many Rembrandt self-portraits. The allusion in the Rubens stanza to a pillow of flesh prompted a reproduction of the painting *Samson and Delilah* as well as a detail from *The Erection of the Cross*. In the Leonardo da Vinci stanza, the metonymic reference to the mirror was illustrated by the delicate portrait of Ginevra de' Benci, which suggests both the mimetic and the symbolic function of art. The allusion to the mystical dimension of the painter's work justified the choice of *The Virgin of the Rocks* and several *Angel Musicians* from the da Vinci workshop, just as the reference to the gentle smile demanded both the *Mona Lisa* and the *Saint John*. To illustrate the assimilation of Rembrandt's work to a hospital, I chose *The Anatomy Lesson of Dr. Nicholas Tulp* by Rembrandt; for the reference to Jesus, I used his *Christ on the Cross*; while the allusion to prayers arising from ordure prompted his *The Apostle Paul in Prison*. The stanza on Michelangelo requires images of statues inspired by both classical and Christian mythology, Hercules as well as *The Risen Christ* and the *Pietà*, and invites slides of the slaves, especially *The Heroic Captive* and *The Dying Captive*, where the figures are still emerging from the marble; as Baudelaire puts it,

"Déchirent leur suaire en étirant leurs doigts" (22) ("[they] stretch their fingers out, and tear their winding-sheets" [23]). (The lower left-hand corner of Michelangelo's *The Last Judgment* may be what Baudelaire had most in mind. From 1837 on, a copy of it was on view at the Ecole des Beaux-Arts.) Reproductions of Pierre Puget's muscular statues, some housed in the new wing of the Louvre, others in the Marseilles museum, also facilitate the reading of what can prove to be a disconcerting stanza for those more accustomed to seek beauty rather than range and impudence in art: I chose *Hercules and Cerberus*, *Milos of Croton*, and the leering and cynical *Faun*. Similarly, the Antoine Watteau stanza suggests a series of his fêtes champêtres, notably the *Venetian Fêtes*, *The Elysian Fields*, and *The Embarkation for Cytherea*.

Focusing on the two stanzas of Francisco Goya and Delacroix reveals much about Baudelaire's response to art, but it is also clear that Baudelaire's aim was to convey the atmosphere of their work instead of confining himself to a single theme or, even less, to a single work. With the Goya stanza, for instance, Baudelaire follows the viewer's reaction to, say, Goya's *Caprichos* or the war pictures. The initial response brings a sense of terror, the unknown, something horrible yet undetermined. The eye then picks out details, the intensity of Goya's treatment of them reflected by the obsessive sound patterning in, for instance, "des fœtus qu'on fait cuire" ("foetuses one cooks") or by juxtapositions that highlight the incongruity instantly evident in the painting or etching: *Old Woman at the Mirror*, for example. In addition to Goya's *Satan Devouring His Son* and *The Bewitched* I included several of the *Caprichos*, the *Clothed Maja*, and *Naked Maja*. In the Delacroix stanza, Baudelaire, fascinated as we know from the *Salon of 1846* by combinations of red and green and convinced that in a good painting the mood would be conveyed by color before the eye picked out details, centers instantly on the reds, with their connotations of blood, suffering, and death. I illustrated these with Delacroix's *The Death of Sardanapalus*, *The Bride of Abydos*, and *Rebecca*. Baudelaire transposes Delacroix's ability to suggest mood and emotion through nature by attaching the adjective *chagrin* ("gloomy") to *ciel* ("sky") in an expression that I chose to illustrate by the painting of Hamlet against a wild, romantic sky. The last stanzas, in which no particular artist is mentioned, were accompanied by Delacroix's *Liberty Leading the People*, *The Fire*, and *The Women of Algiers*, while the final stanza, with its reference to the search for human dignity and its transformation of art into a sob rolling down the ages, was illustrated with Delacroix's *The Massacre at Chios*. Some of these choices are arbitrary: encouraging students to find illustrations more appropriate to their individual readings is part of the aim of this CD-ROM.

Given Baudelaire's fascination for the music of Wagner, it would be interesting to include in a CD-ROM an exploration of the relations between Baudelaire's text and Wagner's music, accompanying annotated readings of Baudelaire's *Tannhäuser* article with passages from the opera. For "Les Phares," however, the fleeting reference to Weber may have been determined by the exigencies of rhyme. Be that as it may, I accompanied the allusion with a brief passage from Weber's romantic opera *Der Freischütz*.

The technological resources of CD-ROMs and the Internet provide us with an outstanding way of offering students an enriching entry into the complexities of *Les Fleurs du Mal*, an entry, moreover, that enables them to share what Baudelaire describes as his great, unique, and oldest passion, "le culte des images" (*Œuvres* [Ruff] 638; "Mon cœur mis à nu") ("the cult of pictures").

Hypermedia Approaches to Baudelaire's Poetry
Eugene F. Gray

The popularity of the multimedia computer has soared in recent years; the computer has found applications in games, scientific modeling, architectural and engineering design, and illustrated encyclopedias. As supplements to their beginning language textbooks, publishers have begun to offer not only workbooks of exercises but also dialogues, exercises, and video clips of cultural situations on CD-ROM.

The successor to the CD-ROM, DVD, holds up to two and a half hours of high-quality video accompanied by several sound tracks, offering heretofore undreamed-of storage space for cultural materials. Challenged by these developments, teachers of the humanities have begun to ask, How can we use this technology effectively for teaching literature? Will it enhance learning? Can it take over the routine, repetitive aspects of teaching literature (e.g., the rules of French prosody, *style indirect libre* ["free indirect style"], the vocabulary of rhetoric), thereby freeing class time for more innovative activities? The answer to the last two questions is a qualified yes. The power and flexibility of the multimedia computer offer tremendous opportunities for teachers and learners, but we are still seeking answers to the first question. Not only is computer technology much more complex than what we have used in the classroom up to now, it is of a different type, requiring teachers to organize their class materials in radically different ways.

The above mention of storage space underscores a seemingly banal yet important use of the computer—maintaining an archive. I have often confronted the problem of how to make available to students all the materials that I would like them to consult. These materials are not only the basic texts to be read—selections from the *Fleurs du Mal* and Baudelaire's art criticism, for example—but also illustrations of the art, science, philosophical thought, and social customs of Baudelaire's day; of the architecture of Paris; of Baudelaire's travels; and so forth (for examples of illustrations, see the books *Album Baudelaire* [Pichois] and *Baudelaire/Paris* [Pichois and Avice]). Many illustrations are reproductions of paintings and lithographs, some difficult or impossible to obtain, others buried in anthologies and journals. The traditional method of placing assigned books on reserve in the library is inefficient and awkward. How much better it would be to have all Baudelaire's works (including variants) archived in a computer, along with reproductions of all the artworks to which Baudelaire refers (if permission can be obtained, of course); photographs, lithographs, and street plans of nineteenth-century Paris; reproductions of official documents; biographies of people he knew; personal impressions of people who knew him; contemporary reviews of his publications; contemporary illustrations of Lyon, Mauritius, Reunion, Brussels, Paris; and so forth. Once such an archive was in place, the instructor, using what is known as an authoring program, would construct a *fil d'Ariane* ("guiding thread") through just those materials deemed essential to the course. The remaining materials would be available for student research projects.

But this thread is nonlinear, multidimensional, if you forgive the paradox; it contains an unlimited number of potential branching points. While reading a biography of Baudelaire or one of his essays or poems, a student will encounter words, names, and allusions that need to be explained. For the poems "Le Cygne" and "L'Albatros" how many students will take the time to look up in an encyclopedia references such as "Andromaque," "Simoïs," "Carrousel," "l'homme d'Ovide," "Pyrrhus," "Hector," "Hélénus"? How many students will know the words "chapiteaux," "fûts," "flaques," "voirie," "palmés," and "phtisique"? How many will understand the implications of "nouveau Carrousel" and "Ce Louvre?" (The Place du Carrousel was closed off by a new wing of the Louvre, dedicated 14 August 1857, along the Rue de Rivoli, a project begun under Louis-Philippe. Until the Second Empire the area had been a slum, described by many authors of the day, e.g., Honoré de Balzac in *La Cousine Bette* [99-100]. See Richard Terdiman's essay in this volume for the powerful emotional and political associations that Baudelaire had with this neighborhood). Of course it is possible to distribute annotated handouts to the class, as we have always done. But with the text and annotations stored in the computer, the student need only click on a word to obtain a definition, explanation, illustration, or recording. This way of structuring knowledge is known as hypertext, if only text is involved, or hypermedia, when different media are combined. It may well be that an explanation will contain names, references, and words that in turn need explaining: the student can then click on them, moving from item to item as needed in order to understand the text fully. (It would perhaps be wise to limit the number of levels of explanation in undergraduate classes, so as not to frustrate the student.) The advantage of the computer is that it offers, in contrast to the paper handout or a student edition of *Les Fleurs du Mal*, a network of explanations (not all of which every student may need to consult), explanations that can consist of photographs, illustrations of various sorts, and sound as well as of words.

How many people have ever seen an albatross? How much more enlightening and engaging than a bare definition it would be to click on the word and obtain not only a scientific description but also photographs and even a film clip of the bird in flight. Popular references, too, can add dimension to Baudelaire's text, as the following excerpt from a novel of Patrick O'Brian:

> They will abide a great deal, sailors, but not a Jonah. It's like a white crow—the others peck him to death. Or an albatross. You catch an albatross—it's easy, with a line—and paint a red cross on his bosom, and the others will tear him to pieces before the glass is turned. Many's the good laugh we had with them, off the Cape.   (168)

Might Baudelaire have witnessed a similar event off the cape?

Understanding the family life and upbringing of Baudelaire can be crucial to understanding his poetry and his attitudes. Much has been written about his conflicts with his mother and his stepfather, General Jacques Aupick. But it is important to realize that the general had a distinguished military and diplomatic career, as Gustave Vapereau's *Dictionnaire universel des contemporains* will attest (78–79; see also Pichois and Ziegler 56–63 [French ed.]). The general's views seem typical of the French middle class of that day. His posting to Lyons during the 1831 riots there led to an event that must have marked the young Baudelaire indelibly. At the beginning of 1832, after things had calmed down, Mme Aupick and the ten-and-a-half-year-old Charles joined the general in Lyons. Later that year a second series of riots broke out, and Baudelaire's school was caught in the middle of the fighting. Contemporary accounts and illustrations of this and other tense episodes in the poet's life underscore the intense personal elements of his poetry.

Baudelaire spent almost his entire life in Paris. During that period the city underwent a radical transformation, finally assuming the form that foreigners most often envision when they think of Paris. The installation of gas lighting in 1825 (Place Vendôme) shifted much of the intellectual and social activity of the city from the salons to the cafés and theaters. Many of Baudelaire's poems reflect the street scenes of the modern city. Enid Starkie called him "the greatest of city poets" (545). The importance of the city to Baudelaire is evident in remarks such as "Je t'aime, ô capitale infâme!" (*Œuvres* [Le Dantec] 362; epilogue to *Le Spleen de Paris*") ("I love you, O infamous capital") and "La vie parisienne est féconde en sujets poétiques et merveilleux" (679; *Salon de 1846*) ("Parisian life is rich in poetic and marvelous subject matter"). "[L]a forme d'une ville / Change plus vite, hélas!, que le cœur d'un mortel" (174) ("The shape of a city, alas, / Changes more quickly than a mortal's heart" [trans. mine]).

How can we become familiar with a cityscape and a way of life that have disappeared but that Baudelaire knew so well? One way is to use the images and descriptions of the day. The computer allows the instructor to choose the items that best illustrate the Parisian poems: photographs by pioneers of photography like Charles Nègre and Charles Marville (Nègre lived on the Ile Saint-Louis, not far from Baudelaire; Baron Haussmann hired Marville to document the old buildings before they were demolished), engravings, lithographs, and extracts from memoirs. References to social customs and clothing, such as these extemporaneous lines by Baudelaire:

A force d'empois et de serge
Et d'aciers contournés en rond
La crinoline, en potiron
Avait transformé cette asperge.

By means of starch and serge
And pieces of steel bent into circles
The crinoline, in the shape of a pumpkin
Had transformed that asparagus.

> (qtd. in Pichois and Ziegler 174)

remain obscure unless accompanied by contemporary illustrations—for example, lithographs by Gavarni (Paul Chevalier) and Bertall (Charles-Albert d'Arnoux), who specialized in depicting everyday life. Bertall's *La Comédie de notre temps* is full of illustrations of fashion and etiquette as well as of whimsical texts with titles like "Le Monde" ("Society"), "L'Habit" ("The Dress Suit"), "Le Gilet" ("The Vest"), "Le Pantalon" ("Trousers"), "Le Gommeux" ("The Fop"), "La Crinoline" ("Crinoline"), "Du Chic" ("On Being Fashionable"), and many others that would be invaluable in any general humanities course that includes nineteenth-century literary texts.

Caricature is a rich source of background materials on the nineteenth century, a source unfortunately underutilized in literature courses. Baudelaire himself prized caricature and several caricaturists of his day. Of Carle Vernet he wrote:

> Son œuvre est un monde, une petite *Comédie humaine*; car les images triviales, les croquis de la foule et de la rue, les caricatures, sont souvent le miroir le plus fidèle de la vie.
>
> (*Œuvres* [Ruff] 378; "Quelques caricaturistes français")

> His work is a world, a miniature *Human Comedy*; for the commonplace images, the sketches of crowds and streets, the caricatures, are often the most faithful mirror of life.

Baudelaire considered Charles-Joseph Traviès de Villers, the creator of that strange creature Mayeux, "un artiste éminent et qui ne fut pas dans son temps délicatement apprécié" (386) ("an eminent artist who was not appreciated"). But Honoré Daumier, who with Charles Philipon adapted the character of Robert Macaire from the theater to the art of caricature, was for Baudelaire "l'un des hommes les plus importants, je ne dirai pas seulement de la caricature, mais encore de l'art moderne" (380) ("one of the most important men, not only of caricature but of modern art"). Fortunately, scanning the black-and-white line art of lithographic prints or engravings into a computer is a relatively easy matter; thus the student can be provided with a valuable resource for the study of nineteenth-century France.

Thematic studies that cut across genre boundaries (literature, social history, painting, music) are readily constructed from such archives, allowing students to pursue research in areas that interest them. One example among many might be tobacco. Gustave Courbet painted Baudelaire smoking a pipe, and the last poem of "Spleen et idéal" is a sonnet titled "La Pipe." Tobacco as a literary subject dates back at least to the seventeenth century (e.g., in a sonnet by Saint-Amant: "Assis sur un fagot, une pipe à la main, / Tristement accoudé contre une cheminée" [279] ["Seated on a log, a pipe in my hand, / Sadly leaning back against the fireplace"]). But for the young Romantics, the pipe had become an essential accessory. Many of Gavarni's drawings depict young men with a pipe. Gustave Flaubert's correspondence abounds in dithyrambic references to his pipe:

> Il m'est arrivé un grand malheur. On m'a perdu une pipe dans mon déménagement de la rue de l'Est: un beau tuyau noir rapporté de Constantinople et dans lequel j'ai fumé pendant sept ans. C'est avec lui que j'ai passé les meilleures heures de ma vie. N'est-ce pas un épouvantable chagrin de le savoir perdu, profané!   (*Correspondance* 210)

> I've suffered a great disaster. They lost my pipe during the move from the Rue de l'Est. It was a beautiful black pipe that I brought back from Constantinople and that I smoked for seven years. It's terribly sad to know that it's lost, defiled!

Gavarni, who often depicted fashionable young men with pipes, mocked this excessive attachment in a well-known drawing. As a young man is packing his bags, presumably to leave Paris forever, he says to his friend, "Adieu, mon bon homme. Je te laisse ma pipe et ma femme . . . t'auras bien soin de ma pipe" (plate 6) ("Goodbye, old friend. I'm leaving you my pipe and my girlfriend. Take good care of my pipe").[1] Later in the nineteenth century, Jean Moréas wrote a poem on the same subject, containing the lines "Compagne de l'éther, indolente fumée / Je te ressemble un peu" (78) ("Companion of the ether, lazy smoke / I'm a little bit like you"). Students can be asked to compare the public's view of tobacco in different periods or to compare the techniques of different artists treating the same subject.

A computer-based study can also illuminate a poem's phonological structure. First the student should be able to hear at will the recitation of any part of a poem, so as to develop a sense of the rhythms and sound patterns of French poetry. The text could appear on the screen at the same time, even accompanied by multiple translations if the instructor desires (in the fashion of Douglas Hofstadter).

A computerized tutorial on basic French prosody would spare the instructor from having to present this material in class. Such a tutorial would enable students, guided by graded exercises stored on the computer, to attempt simple interactive analyses of selected poems. The simplest elements are of course the rhymes, the placement of pauses, internal rhymes, and phonological figures such as anaphora (e.g., "Quand [. . .] Quand [. . .] Quand" in "Spleen (4)" [148–50]) and epizeuxis (e.g., "Jamais, jamais!" in "Le Cygne" [176]). Examples of more complex patterns can be found in *Baudelaire and the Poetics of Craft*, by Graham Chesters. In "Le Cygne," for example, Chesters calls attention to the internal rhymes with *douleur*, affirming that "the phonetic rubrication confirms it as a key word in the metaphorical weave of these lines and in the thematic development of the whole poem" (22). He devotes considerable space to sound patterns that reinforce syntactic structure, as in the following examples. (I use boldface type to indicate the phonological repetitions. Chesters employs a different system, but boldface is more concise. In these examples, the second page number is from the James McGowan edition of *Flowers of Evil*; the translations are mine.)

Comme après un noc**tu**rne et **terr**ible repas (43; 240)

As after a fearsome, nocturnal feast

De sa fourrure **b**londe et **b**rune (45; 104)

From its blond and brown fur

Je poserai sur lui ma **fr**êle et **f**orte main (45; 12)

I will place on him my frail and powerful hand

A more complex category that Chesters dubs "phonetic logic" provides a transition from purely phonological studies to imagery. He explains:

> To illustrate what is meant by phonetic logic it is merely necessary to take the simplest form of image, the direct comparison:
> A is like B
> and then take the simplest form of phonetic pattern:
> phoneme A is the same as phoneme B
> and then combine these two facts:
> A (containing phoneme A) is like B (containing phoneme B)
> and we obtain a parallel structure, an example of which is:
> Le **P**oète est semblable au **p**rince des nuées (49; 16)
> The poet is similar to the prince of the clouds

Chesters has found many such examples; they can easily be incorporated into a set of computerized exercises. To heighten student interest, the search for phonological patterns could be structured like a game. Different rewards would be based on the number or the complexity of phonological patterns discovered. The most important result, however, would be the student's gaining a better appreciation of the fundamentals of poetic style.

Students sometimes have difficulty grasping the syntax of a complicated sentence or recognizing syntactic patterns such as parallelism and chiasmus.

Because elements of text can easily be programmed to move or be moved on the screen, the computer provides a convenient way to help the student perceive syntactic structure. The ending of "Recueillement" ("Meditation") provides an example:

> [. . .] Vois se pencher les défuntes Années,
> Sur les balcons du ciel, en robes surannées;
> Surgir du fond des eaux le Regret souriant;
>
> Le Soleil moribond s'endormir sous une arche,
> Et, comme un long linceul traînant à l'Orient,
> Entends, ma chère, entends la douce Nuit qui marche.   (346)

> Look, as the Years lean down
> From heaven's porches, clothed in ancient gowns;
> Regret, in smiles, looms from the water's depths;
>
> Under an archway sleeps the dying Sun.
> And, like a shroud swept to the Orient,
> Listen, my dear, the sweet Night walks along.   (347)

The student could be asked to show the structure of this sentence by highlighting the complements of the verb *vois* or by rearranging the text. If unable to do either, the student, by clicking on a screen button, could ask the computer to outline the structure. One possible computer response could be that *vois* and its complements would first be highlighted in color on the screen within the poem, then would move to form the following pattern:

> Vois se pencher les défuntes Années
> [Vois] Surgir le Regret
> [Vois] Le Soleil s'endormir
> Entends la douce Nuit

A grammar reference could also be incorporated into the program, so that a student needing to review the structure "verb of perception + infinitive" could do so at the click of a button. Once sensitized to various syntactic patterns, students could seek other examples of them and discuss their poetic effects.

The study of variants, as well, becomes easier once Baudelaire's corpus has been stored in a computer. Exercises based on well-chosen variants can help students see that writing involves making choices and that the text of even such a great writer as Baudelaire often improves with revision. The third verse of "L'Albatros" ("The Albatross") is a case in point: "Qui suivent, indolents compagnons de voyage" (14) ("That follow, like idle traveling companions"). In an earlier version Baudelaire wrote: "Qui suivent, curieux compagnons de voyage" ("That follow, like curious traveling companions"). Henk Nuiten's excellent discussion of this earlier version (222–23) could easily be transformed into an exercise in which the student evaluates alternative versions of the line ("curieux," "indolents," or other choices) according to the definitions of the words and the student's interpretation of the poem. Although this exercise can be presented on paper, the student is more likely to reflect on word choice if the definitions are available at the click of a mouse. In fact, since the *Dictionnaire Robert* (both the full version and the *Petit Robert*) has appeared on CD-ROM, the student can have at hand a powerful tool for analysis.

The computer, then, provides a means to solve two problems confronting the teacher of literature. It allows the teacher to construct a multimedia archive of interesting and often unobtainable materials about Baudelaire's milieu and Baudelaire's writing, together with essential reference materials such as dictionary and encyclopedic extracts. And it permits the teacher to construct a series of interactive lessons and exercises with which students can review the basics of French prosody and French history and then see how well they have mastered the material. The instructor can receive summaries of this feedback to guide students more effectively, while saving much class time previously spent on routine and often repetitive drill.

These interactive lessons can easily be made available on the World Wide Web, so that the student can access them from a residence hall room. Links to resources on the Web such as the ARTFL database at the University of Chicago (limited at the moment to Baudelaire's *Salons* of 1845 and 1846, the *Paradis artificiels*, and the *Petits poèmes en prose*, but it is rich in other nineteenth-century texts) can then be integrated into the lessons. A discussion group for the class can even be set up on a local network, so that students can exchange ideas about particular poems at any time of day or night. In principle, the student then comes to class much better prepared, and class time is used to better advantage. Greatly to be desired is a collaborative project in which Baudelaire specialists around the world would contribute original scanned materials and sample lessons. The whole corpus would be made available at a central site on the World Wide Web. Such a site would benefit both scholars and teachers of Baudelaire.

NOTE

[1] Plate 6 of Gavarni's *Les Etudiants de Paris* may be viewed on the Web page http://polyglot.cal.msu.edu/efg/curiosities/gavarni/adieu.htm.

CONCLUSION

The Classroom versus Poetry; or, Teaching Transportation

Ross Chambers

[. . .] les transports de l'esprit et des sens.
—"Correspondances"

When it comes to Baudelaire, I'm in no position to write one of those satisfy-ing essays in which an expert teacher demonstrates that seemingly intractable pedagogical problems can be dissolved with a few tricks of the trade. What I remember most vividly about my earliest attempt to teach *Les Fleurs du Mal* is the earnest delegation of students that came to me, asking, "Why do we have to read this morbid stuff?" And the last time I taught Baudelaire to graduate students, the seminar was such a flop that I wrote a book in compensation for it. In short, I have reasons to think that teaching *Les Fleurs du Mal* is no open-and-shut proposition. My essay therefore is in the nature of a think piece and should be read in hypothetical mode: it's about problems to which I'm groping, optimistically, for solutions. Take the ambivalence of my title—proposing an incompatibility, suggesting the possibility of overcoming it—as evidence of my desire not to admit defeat on an issue I can't resolve.

One of the defining problems of teaching arises from a categorical paradox: teaching is about "life" (its purpose is education) but it is "not life" to the extent that it is only teaching (or, from the students' viewpoint, only learning). Teach-ing/learning is a mode of interaction that's mediated, and so determined, by a whole set of pedagogical institutions, settings, and genres (drilling, testing, stu-dent evaluation, and the like) that are definitionally not the contexts and inter-active modes of everyday, nonpedagogical existence. Nor, if it comes to that, do the genres and contexts of pedagogy correspond to the discursive modes we classify as literary: the play we read in class, the novel on which students must write a report (or risk a failing grade), the poem encountered in a language-learning textbook or school edition (or on a photocopied sheet or overhead transparency, today's versions of the ditto paper of yesteryear)—these aren't plays, novels, or poems so much as they're classroom exercises. Indeed they're not so much classroom exercises as mere supports and pretexts for the real business of the classroom: Q and A, analysis, commentary, practices that are governed by complicated rules that it's a teacher's business to know and the student's task, more or less actively pursued, to internalize. That's why I speak of the classroom as poetry's antagonist.

But a conscientious teacher, who knows that these pedagogical constraints can't be dispensed with (they're the condition of possibility for education itself, because they produce teacherly authority), will still struggle—knowing that the real stakes of teaching lie elsewhere—to "get the classroom out" of pedagogical practices so that to some degree education may take place. The gamble of teaching, in other words, is that the categories and contexts we call pedagogical and nonpedagogical are permeable, that genres can be made to mix so that slippage can occur—can be made to occur—between them: teaching wants to be transportational. If I can't remember Gérard de Nerval's "El Desdichado" without recalling the crummy Classiques Larousse edition in which I first encountered it, it's also true that when I was nine, Miss Hunter's voice reciting not Nerval or William Butler Yeats but Hugh McCrae and Walter de la Mare brought strange and fascinating sensations, for me, into an Australian bush classroom, full of chalk dust and the odor of Clag—a vital intimation of otherness. (Ask me sometime about Clag.) And if classrooms can be visited by poetry, as Miss Hunter knew, it must be equally possible to transport their denizens out of class in the direction of extrapedagogical landscapes (indeed, the two operations are presumably one and the same). I'm going to look at Baudelaire, then (Miss H. having not passed on her secrets), for some pointers about teaching as transportation, in the sense of an exploitation of the permeability of genres that can get the classroom out—maybe even leave it behind—when poetry is on the pedagogical agenda.

One thing Baudelaire made perfectly clear is that he considered poetry and teaching to be absolutely incompatible: for him, poetry that teaches was a contradiction in terms, and although his particular target was the didactic poem, aiming to teach a moral lesson (see "Notes nouvelles sur Edgar Poe," esp. in fine), we can extrapolate and realize that in his eyes poetry that is made to teach anything other than itself is no longer poetry but some other thing: a moral doctrine, a lesson in metrics, a literary-historical exposition, or whatever. This fierce insistence on the purity of poetry as a genre—on poetry as the genre of aesthetic purity—coincides in him, logically enough, with the perception that the drama of modernity lies in the detachment of poetry from the sphere of existence in which history is made (the sphere of politics, of work, of urban existence), a detachment that has resulted in turn in the marginalization of both poetry and poets.

This second separation, though, is one that Baudelaire does not perceive to be irremediable. Much of his reflection revolves, therefore, around the problem of how, following Balzac, to make poetry (and not novelistic prose) the site and vehicle of what in chapter 18 of *Salon de 1846* he had called "the heroism of modern life" (how to make poetry central to the conditions of modern existence that have marginalized it), but without falling into the posturing and moralizing—in short, the didacticism—of a Victor Hugo. Out of Baudelaire's thinking on this issue, thinking of which various aspects and stages can be traced throughout *Les Fleurs du Mal*, emerges eventually the experiment in poetic prose that is *Le Spleen de Paris*. But my purpose here is to use part of Baudelaire's reflection in *Les Fleurs du Mal* on the problematic relation of poetry and the modern everyday—his passionate belief that they are reconcilable—in order to explore the possibility of reducing the distance between teaching and the poetic that Baudelaire himself regards as absolute. If that's a perverse project, so be it.

Two observations are worth making in this connection. One is that the detachment of the poetic, as an autonomous domain of the beautiful, is for Baudelaire both a factor of pleasure and a source of pain. On the one hand, the poetic provides a domain of rhythmic harmony and sensuous delight that's safely remote from the sordid, difficult world of the everyday; it's a destination for dreams and a place of escape, the *là-bas* of "L'Invitation au voyage": "Mon enfant, ma sœur, / Songe à la douceur / D'aller là-bas vivre ensemble!" (108) ("My sister, my child / Imagine how sweet / To live there as lovers do!" [109]), and so on. The question, then, is only how to discover a means of transportation from the dreary here-and-now to this ideal place of "Luxe, calme et volupté" (110) ("Luxury, tranquillity, and sensuous delight" [trans. mine]) that is situated elsewhere. On the other hand, and this is where the question of transportation becomes urgent, the separation of the beautiful from the ordinary is not only a painful circumstance in itself, it's also the model of all the discontinuities and disconnections, the failures of coherence and system, the uncontrolled contingencies, social inequities, and conflicts that make up modern life in general and urban existence in particular. Baudelairean dualism, with its manifold ironies and other *grincements* ("dissonances"), is grounded in this sense of the failure of things to come together and form a world that would be materially, morally, socially, and aesthetically in harmony with itself. If transportation is a concept in this connection, it's only to the extent that the word refers to the endless movement of the mind—what will memorably be called "les soubresauts de la conscience" (*Œuvres* [Ruff] 146; in the preface to *Le Spleen de Paris*) ("the somersaults of consciousness")—as the mind attempts, but fails, to encompass in a single totality a world experienced as irremediably disconnected, because fallen: the world Baudelaire calls evil, the site of *le mal*, because he understands it (see "Au lecteur," 4) as being in the grip of the Devil.

That's one point. The second is that this metaphysical dominance of evil in the form of disconnectedness is itself, in Baudelaire's eyes, a product of human moral responsibility: Baudelaire uses traditional terms like hypocrisy, complacency, pusillanimity, but "Au lecteur" specifies that the Devil reigns only because human beings practice what psychoanalysis calls *Verneinung* (sometimes translated as "denegation"), that is, the denial of what one nevertheless knows to be the case (in everyday English, one might say "disavowal": in the *American Heritage Dictionary*, "disclaim[ing] knowledge of, responsibility for, or association with," although that choice weakens the implication of bad faith). The liminal poem of *Les Fleurs du Mal* angrily diagnoses the bourgeois world as dominated by ennui (the in-difference or indifferentiation that arises from the unconnectedness of things), because that world denies the principle of evil. By implication, only the marginalized poet is left—his social disconnection being fortunate in this circumstance, because it preserves his lucidity—to denounce the Devil's domination and attempt to awaken the poet's hypocritical readers from their moral numbness. There's thus a double lesson in "Au lecteur." The first is that the separation of genres (e.g., the disconnectedness of poetry from the genres of everyday life) is part of the general state of disconnectedness that signals the Devil's mastery and that generic disconnection is therefore itself a product of denegation. (We might extrapolate that, in every genre, the "traces"—to use Derrida's word (*Positions* 26)—of other genres would be perceptible and the genres no longer disconnected, if only we did not, in order to make life livable, or, as Baudelaire would say, out of pusillanimity, blot the traces from our consciousness.) But the second lesson is that the separation of genres, when it is experienced as a source of pain, can make poetry an agency of clear-sightedness and exert an impact capable of countering (although not of countermanding) the numbing effect of denegation, that is, of "Ennui." That poetry, although itself disconnected, might be able to awaken us to the alienating effect of universal disconnectedness is the hope that underlies "Au lecteur" and gives the poem its rhetorical point. But poetry enacts this purpose in a paroxysmic, angry way that has nothing in common with the "luxe, calme et volupté" of poetry conceived as *là-bas*, a distant but beckoning elsewhere.

If poetry is imagined in this way both as a site of beauty—a factor of pleasure—and as a factor of pain (the pain that accompanies the dissolution of our moral torpor through the combatting of denegation), then the transportations of which poetry is capable are in turn of two kinds. Poetry can lead us away from the everyday world toward a destination defined as aesthetically harmonious, or it can be a vehicle of lucidity and an agent of exploration. In this second role, it inflicts a salutary pain, by making us aware of the startling connections that exist, or can be made, within the ordinary, disconnected world, a world that nevertheless, and despite these more or less aleatory connections, resists totalization, let alone harmonization, because disconnection—the product of denegation experienced as numbness, torpor, "Ennui"—is the law of the Devil's regime. Transportation, in other words, as a way of making connections that oppose disavowal, can also take the form of "les soubresauts de la conscience," the phrase used by Baudelaire to suggest the restlessness of an *ironic* consciousness, unable either fully to harmonize things or to exist in the state of indifference that is ennui, a consciousness corresponding to transportation as an expression of pain. (Pain has only recently become a topic in the critical conversation about Baudelaire. The most challenging discussion is in Ramazani. See also Chambers, "Perpetual Abjuration"; Maclean. Finally, schizoanalysis is highly relevant: see Holland.)

Since in Greek *metaphorein* is to transport (and in the modern language, *metaphor* can be a vehicle, e.g., a bus or a shuttle), we can say, then, that Baudelaire is proposing a metaphoric theory of poetry as both the pleasurable object or goal of practices of displacement whose destination is *là-bas* (or anywhere out of the world) and the dysphoric vehicle of restless mental displacements whose function, in the damped-down world of moral complacency, is to keep alive the sense of pain that signifies a consciousness at work, even if all the consciousness can perform is somersaults. I suggest that the second of these propositions about poetry derives from the failure of the first: poetry can't be a destination of transportation, only its vehicle, because the *là-bas* poetry creates is itself only a metaphor (i.e., a figuration) of the elsewhere that is the object of desire. It is therefore poetry in the second sense—poetry expressive of pain—that is in touch, albeit in a critical sense, with everyday existence.

We as teachers of poetry are confronted with a double requirement by this Baudelairean theory: to teach the poetry of "escape" and to teach the poetry of lucidity that is consequent on the failure of escape. The double requirement might be brought into quite fruitful contact with the homologous educational imperative, of constructing a positive outcome (called education) from what we experience as our inability to escape the pedagogical, that is, to transport students "anywhere out of the *classroom*." By what means of transportation can we induce our students to escape the boundaries of their classroom world in the direction of a more poetic destination? But also, how—within the classroom—can we abet the function of poetry as itself a vehicle of transportation, but of transportation in the sense of unending participation, without final destination, in the "soubresauts de la conscience" that are both an expression of pain and the sign of a critical intelligence that puts lucidity above pleasure?

Both questions, at bottom, assume that a poetic education is an exploration of the condition of being human in the specific sense, as I explain below, of being a desiring subject. But neither question suggests ready answers, and the second—how to teach pain—is, on the face of it, particularly difficult. In the belief that Baudelaire's poetry, contrary to his expostulations, *is* a "poésie enseignante," a poetry that teaches, and that what it teaches is a double art of transportation, I simply take a brief look here at two poems and ask how we can learn from them. What is to be learned from "Parfum exotique" (48–49; "Exotic Perfume") and "Le Cygne" (172-77; "The Swan") about teaching (poetry as) transportation?

Desire is the motor of transportation, and it is the character of desire—its production of imaginary objects, its failure ever to be satisfied—that makes transportation a dubious business. "Parfum exotique" and "Le Cygne" are explorations of "les transports de l'esprit et des sens" ("Parfum exotique" relating to the senses, "Le Cygne" to the mind) as a product of desire.

Desire is deviationary. A friend once startled me by reporting that, although right-handed, he likes to masturbate left-handed, because "it feels like someone else." Partners in sexual congress have been known to close their eyes the better to imagine that they're coupling not with Mary Higgins or Joe Bloggs but with X or Y (supply your own icon of sexual desirability). When meetings get boring, I take off my glasses: instantly—thanks to myopia—the surroundings blur, and I can daydream myself right out of there. This deviationary (sometimes deviant) character of desire illustrates the familiar law that what you possess can't be desired whereas what you desire can't be possessed. For desire needs props, devices, and aids, mediatory agents (one's left hand, the closing of the eyes, glasses on or off) to transport us into its world—but as a result (the closing of eyes as an enactment of denegation figures this well), the realm of desire becomes a domain of figments and illusions. You can get there from here, and transportation does occur; it's just that there's no real there when you get there. Baudelaire seems to have understood poetry, as an ideal object of beauty, in this transportational sense. Certainly "you can('t) get there from here" might be the motto of "Parfum exotique."

> Quand, les deux yeux fermés, en un soir chaud d'automne,
> Je respire l'odeur de ton sein chaleureux,
> Je vois se dérouler des rivages heureux
> Qu'éblouissent les feux d'un soleil monotone;
>
> Une île paresseuse où la nature donne
> Des arbres singuliers et des fruits savoureux;
> Des hommes dont le corps est mince et vigoureux,
> Et des femmes dont l'œil par sa franchise étonne.
>
> Guidé par ton odeur vers de charmants climats,
> Je vois un port rempli de voiles et de mâts
> Encor tout fatigués par la vague marine,
>
> Pendant que le parfum des verts tamariniers,
> Qui circule dans l'air et m'enfle la narine,
> Se mêle dans mon âme au chant des mariniers.   (48)
>
>
> When, eyes closed, on a pleasant autumn night,
> I breathe the warm scent of your breast, I see
> Inviting shorelines spreading out for me
> Where steady sunlight dazzles in my sight.

An idle isle, where friendly nature brings
Singular trees, fruit that is savoury,
Men who are lean and vigorous and free,
Women whose frank eyes are astonishing.

Led by your fragrance to these charming shores
I see a bay of sails and masts and oars,
Still wearied from the onslaught of the waves—

While verdant tamarind's enchanting scent,
Filling my nostrils, swirling to the brain,
Blends in my spirit with the boatmen's chant.   (49)

This is a poem about deviation in which the *je* of the text praises his mistress, but only for providing a set of props that function as vehicular stimuli, transporting him, "les deux yeux fermés" (of course), from a presumably Parisian *alcôve* on a warm fall evening to an imagined tropical island. The narrative, then, allegorizes transportation as a matter of deviation. The woman's main prop—her "sein chaleureux"—is, thanks to its odor, metaphorically transformed, in the mind's eye, into "une île paresseuse" (note the series of transformations: "sein chaleureux," "rivages heureux," "charmants climats"), an island in which (quatrain 2) nature reigns in the form of lush vegetation and frank human sexuality. But simultaneously, and accordingly, the (natural) odor that sets off the transportational daydream is sublimated into something more delicate (if not less natural), "le parfum des verts tamariniers," which mingles "dans mon âme" with music, a metonym for art(ifice) since the music is by implication the work song of sailors in the island's port. The allegedly natural world of beauty and sensuality is accessible only through artifices like shutting one's eyes or taking a ship, which means that it is only illusorily natural, and the poem is thus not only a poem about poetry but also one in which transportation is described in terms of distance from its goal: the subject is not the island but a vision of the island, and a mental vision at that. By the end of the poem, the *je* is still only within sight of the desired island (note the repeated "Je vois [. . .] Je vois [. . .]"), within olfactory and auditory range of its sounds and perfumes. The I is within poetry but not on the island itself.

If I were teaching "Parfum exotique," I would take the poem's hint, then. It's the deviation of (minds and) senses that matters, not arriving at an actual destination. So I might begin by proposing to my students that we write a collective poem about the classroom and its environment (What kind of space is the classroom? What does it smell like? How does it feel to sit in class?). Either our collective effort will produce a dysphoric (realist) poem, about contained settings, disciplined bodies and minds, forced and hierarchical interpersonal relations (in which case I have a ready-made contrast with the themes of "Parfum exotique"), or it will produce a more euphoric poem of deviation and/or sublimation, in which, for example, surrealist techniques (or just plain adolescent cheerfulness) may exert a transformative effect on the classroom's more or less carceral reality (in which case I have a potential point of direct comparison with "Parfum exotique"). Having thus drawn attention to the classroom as the frame of our activities, I would then invent some deviationary exercises, as preparation for grasping what the poem is saying about poetry.

I could use films and music, of course—but filmic and musical representations of the "exotic" tropics are now so sanitized for the tourist trade that they miss the bodily down-to-earthness that Baudelaire celebrates. I'd certainly encourage my students to sit on the floor ("for a change"), to make themselves comfortable, to remove their shoes and wiggle their toes (in the rhythm of a sea shanty, perhaps, or an alexandrine line). They could do eye-closing exercises, where I would allow time for their minds to wander and then ask, "Where did you go?" They could practice hearty yawning, generous stretching, a good belly laugh, all by contrast with the constraints put on these and other bodily manifestations under the conventions of classroom discipline. That same day I'd have invited them, perhaps, to wear something to class that they consider beautiful instead of, or in combination with, the uniform(ity) of jeans and sneakers, and the next day there could be a general discussion of who was wearing what and why it was beautiful (Did it make class more interesting? more fun? more pleasant? Was it a distraction?).

But ultimately there would have to be an olfactory show-and-tell. I'd ask the students to bring in their favorite—or least favorite—"perfume or odor," and to be prepared to share it with the group and talk about the personal associations it might have. I myself would make sure to bring a cloying tropical perfume (say, vanilla or frangipani) and to mention that sailors once knew they were close to the Spice Islands before they could even see them, so strong was the smell of cloves or cinnamon on the prevailing wind. I'd also bring a strong, musky perfume so as to be able to draw attention to the difference between our present preference for floral-based scents and the nineteenth-century love of animal-based perfumes. (I'd mention the smell of leather in a new car as a latter-day example of an animal perfume.) Olfactorily deprived as they are, North American students may need a little pushing to realize the degree of that deprivation (with luck, a student or two may be moved to describe the atmosphere in the Paris metro at rush hour on a hot summer's afternoon). Issues like the biological role of the sense of smell as a sexual stimulant may or may not arise spontaneously. But my musk, and the association with cars, would probably have done its job subconsciously, and that's all I'd need. (Of course, I'd be sure to produce a can of pine-scented "air freshener" at the end and to do an ostentatiously ironic job of aerosoling away all the accumulated stench.)

By the time we come to read and discuss "Parfum exotique," then, we should be in a position to frame our reading in terms of parallel questions about the class itself: Does being in class encourage daydreaming (and if so, why)? Did we open a window in our classroom? How far did the window opening actually succeed in taking the classroom out of our work? Or did it all just boil down to yet another pedagogical exercise? If the students grasp the idea that Baudelaire's poem understands itself, and so defines poetry, as the verbal equivalent of the *parfum exotique* it describes and thus as something like the deviational practice of wearing a particularly beautiful silk scarf to class one day (or spending a half hour on olfactory show-and-tell between an hour of physics and an hour of accountancy), I will have set them on the way of thinking about the conditions of their own education, about their education as itself a deviationary practice with respect to the peculiar genres of pedagogy and the constraints, disciplines, and formalisms of the classroom.

A consequence, however, of the structure of desire—its ability to achieve only substitute, and so illusory, satisfactions—is that transportation tends to resolve into an apparently limitless *series* of transportations, as deviations arise from what was already an initial deviation, each of them constituting a further deferral of desire's ultimate object. Baudelaire's poetry cannot escape Paris (and education correspondingly fails to elude the classroom). As a consequence, the tendency, visible in the cohesive patterning and closed structure of "Parfum exotique," to produce the poetic as an autonomous island of beauty becomes, in "Le Cygne," a looser, more elongated, listlike form more capable of accommodating "les soubresauts de la conscience," that is, the proclivity of frustrated desire to resolve into a series of shifts, deviations, transports. This form is figured in the poem itself as a stream, the fake river ("Simoïs menteur" [172] ["fraudulent Simois" (173)]) that Andromache has "transported" from Troy into the fallen circumstances of her exile in Epirus and that she swells with her tears. There's no need to resist the temptation, therefore, of applying to "Le Cygne" the modernist metaphor of the stream of consciousness. But another, more implicit, model for a list-poem like "Le Cygne" is the urban street, with its restless traffic and its open-endedness, each street opening onto the grid of other streets (Chambers, "Baudelaire's Street Poetry"). Both street and stream, furthermore, are clearly metaphoric of the flow of historical time, which is the poem's most fundamental subject matter. "Le Cygne," then, begins as the poem of desire's energetic somersaulting, when desire finds itself confined to the fallen world of historical time.

The poem's figure of desire's unattainable object is, of course, the lost city of Troy (which, when Baudelaire wrote, had not been archaeologically recovered). It is Andromache's fall, as she is carried ignominiously back to Greece, a spoil of war, that signals the fall into historical time that is marked by the onset of insatiable desire, with its pattern of deviation and further deviation. All the pseudo Troys that have substituted for Troy itself, beginning with Andromache's patriotic Troy replica in Epirus, as reported by Vergil, all the historical capitals of empire, that is, from Greece and Rome through to France's First and Second Empires, are thus situated by the poem as places of exile and sites of historical pain, the list culminating in Baron Haussmann's new Paris—not only the most recent but, in Baudelaire's eyes, also the most degraded, the most pompously deceitful of them all. My task as teacher is therefore to help my students obtain some sense of the historical pain that is implied by the poem's recourse to a double list-structure: the list of the poet's "soubresauts de la conscience" superimposed on the (partly implied) list of Troy substitutes. Like Baudelaire's task as a poet, mine as a teacher consists in trying to induce a certain painful lucidity in a classroom world defined by a kind of anesthetizing torpor—not the torpor induced, in Baudelaire's mythology, by the reign of the Devil but the torpor produced by the deadening effect of routine pedagogical practices. But I must take note also of the complicating factor that the poem's two-part structure clearly points to. Lapsing in part 2 from the mental excitement of part 1 into a kind of obsessive mulling over of its themes, "Le Cygne" indicates that transportational techniques, used as a factor of lucidity, can themselves degenerate into melancholy and a sort of monotony, in which the consciousness of pain degenerates to something more like a dull ache: "Aussi devant ce Louvre une image m'opprime" (176) ("So at this Louvre an image weighs on me" [trans. mine]).

In the first part of the poem, we are given access to the poet's mind as it moves in vast swoops between three apparently unrelated figures—himself, ancient Andromache, a swan in a gutter—figures who turn out, however, to share a common circumstance: their strandedness, their historical exile, the pain of their unsatisfied desire. They thus make the titular swan a "mythe étrange et fatal" (174) ("a strange, inevitable myth" [trans. mine, here and throughout this paragraph]). Such a myth is valuable, the poem suggests, because it produces insight into the nature of human existence. Although transportation works, in its zigzag fashion, in a way that is quite painful, the pain is salutary, given the lucidity it creates. In part 2 of the poem, the list begins to swell—myself, Andromache, the swan, but now also a "négresse" ("Negress"), then "quiconque a perdu ce qui ne se retrouve / Jamais" (176) ("whoever has lost what can be recaptured / Never"), the "maigres orphelins" ("skinny orphans"), the "matelots oubliés dans une île" ("sailors forgotten on an isle"), the "captifs" and the "vaincus" ("captives," "vanquished")—and finally reveals itself to be open-ended ("Je pense [. . .] à bien d'autres encor!" ["I think (. . .) of many others too"]). It is here that the initial excitement subsides into depression, and the opening flash of insight degenerates into an obsessive perception of universal exile and abandonment. There is still consciousness, so this melancholy is not a mere variant of bourgeois Ennui as described in "Au lecteur," but it shares with Ennui a defeated quality that contrasts with the breakthrough feeling permeating part 1.

The point to retain, though, is this. Just as one can occasionally stand in the street and have one's imagination tickled by an odd sight (say, a swan in a gutter), while at other times the traffic flow might suggest grim and depressing uniformity, so a list of consciousness's acrobatics can vary between maximally transportational excitement, like that of part 1 of "Le Cygne," and minimally transportational melancholy. In either case, the endless movement of the mind, whether maximally or minimally transportational, forms a cognitive response to a world of historical pain, a world in which desire is denied closure. And it is that response to the evidence of pain, to which the Devil ordinarily blinds us by clouding our minds with Ennui, that Baudelaire regards as morally superior and recommends therefore, implicitly, as educationally valuable (I am rethinking here my reading in Chambers, *Mélancolie* 167–86).

Classrooms are a lot like the world as seen by Baudelaire, provided we substitute pedagogy for the Devil. It's the dreariness of our torpor-inducing pedagogical routine that inhibits education by discouraging students from making deviationary, transportational moves, in the course of which they might discover the pain of their own historical situation (e.g., as seekers after education who have been turned over to us pedagogues). So, in preparing to teach "Le Cygne," I don't need to employ heroic means of transportation "out of the classroom," as in the case of "Parfum exotique": nothing maximal is really necessary. I can rely on what my classroom, as a microcosm of my students' experience as subjects of (subjected to) an educational institution, offers in its own commonality with the poem's world. It will be enough for me to interrupt the comforting torpor of class a bit and to encourage the students to think what their own existence is like. For example, I could ask them to jot down, using infinitive verb phrases, what they "have to do" immediately after class, listing their phrases on the board:

> retourner au dortoir ("go back to the dorm")
> aller au travail ("go to work")
> téléphoner à maman ("call Mom")
> terminer mon devoir de comptabilité ("finish my homework in
>   accounting")
> essayer d'emprunter $5 à quelqu'un ("try to borrow $5 from
>   someone") . . .

Discussing this little game, I'd have two main lines of questioning. First, what kind of picture of student life emerges from our list? Euphoric? Exotic? Agreeable? Comfortable? Humdrum? Tedious? Painful? (Sometimes it might be worth probing a little into what underlies the need to call Mom or the urgency of borrowing five bucks.) Second, with those phrases, have we written a poem (a monotonous poem? an interesting poem? a traditional poem? a modern poem? a fantasy poem? a poem about life?)? For the following class, the assignment might be to bring in either a list they've been led to make, for real purposes, in their everyday life or an invented list that might, in some sense, constitute a poem. Discussion would again center on two issues: Is there a difference between the two kinds of lists (a great opportunity here to raise the issue of genre and of genre expectation)? and Under what kind of circumstances are people led (driven?) to make lists? To the second question I'd hope for responses like "When things get out of control," "Around exam time," "When I have too many tasks and they make competing claims on me." We might discuss whether list making has a calming effect or whether it exacerbates anxiety (perhaps it does both). But my general emphasis would be on the peculiar way lists bring things together—sometimes things that seem quite remote—without being able to draw them into a fully closed unity.

Because "Le Cygne" is a demanding poem, I'd also illustrate the ubiquity of listing in modern poetry and show something of the wide range of its effects by introducing a couple of shorter and simpler list-poems (Jacques Prévert is an obvious source). And I'd consider approaching Baudelaire's poem itself in two sessions, treating part 1 first as if it were a complete (closed) poem and one that's only incipiently listlike, to gain maximum effect from the unexpectedness of the poem's turning back on itself in part 2 and then opening out into endless melancholy. But my leading questions would go something like this: Remember what we said about lists in our own experience. Why is this man making lists in his head as he walks the streets of Paris? What accounts for his intellectual excitement at the start? Why does it lose steam? What kind of frustration does the poem record? A very natural follow-up would be to clinch the connection between student pain and the pain in the poem by asking class members to write individual poems, in which their persona "walks" in the street (on the way to class?), "notices" things, makes "connections," and attempts to "take stock" of his or her life. (In French I'd encourage them to use the *penser à* construction, which suggests thinking "toward" something, making sure they understand its transportational implications.)

So is it really the classroom versus poetry? I've worked my way through to the position that, at least as far as Baudelairean understandings go, the classroom isn't as remote as one might think either from poetry (the aesthetic domain) or from the city (what students call the real world without realizing they are already living in it). What Baudelaire has taught me is that teaching poetry can be an educational enterprise when it becomes a way of teaching also about living in the world—more particularly, about what it's like to be a desiring subject, under the conditions of modernity. But the condition of success in such an enterprise, I've also extrapolated, is that for a routine pedagogy, productive of "Ennui" and *inconscience*, we substitute a pedagogy of transportation, a pedagogy that—just like poetry—can't attain its (probably unknowable) goal, called education, but knows what it needs to move away from and also understands that, in the end, deviation is as good as having a destination, is in fact the only destination one can have. Education, in other words, is just pedagogy when the pedagogy is transportational. Thus we can teach (poetry as) both the utopian desire for another and better world and the dystopian consciousness that we inhabit a world of pain, in the understanding that those two impulses (the aesthetic, the critical) aren't incompatible, but allied, having in common their deviational structure.

Everything else is just a matter of invention. Traveling, I learn from "Le Voyage" (282-92; "Voyaging"), is not about arriving but about departing (or deviating): "les vrais voyageurs sont ceux-là seuls qui partent / Pour partir" (282) ("True travelers are those only who depart / To depart" [trans. mine]). We're invited, then—as the very last line of *Les Fleurs du Mal* has it, in both the 1857 and the 1861 editions, exercising the privilege of the last word—to plunge into the Unknown. To plunge into the unknown, but not, like the chicken in the joke, with a view to getting to some putative other side. For the Unknown has no other side. Our task is to

> Plonger au fond du gouffre, Enfer ou Ciel, qu'importe?
> Au fond de l'Inconnu pour trouver du *nouveau*!   (292)

> Plunge to the depths, be they Heaven or Hell!
> Plumb the Unknown to encounter the *new*!   (trans. mine)

NOTE

I gratefully acknowledge that this essay recalls, responds to, and deviates from some invaluable recent conversations with Anne Freadman, whose 1994 Sonia Marks Memorial Lecture, with its injunction to "renew our imagination of the possibilities of the classroom itself, to intervene and modify its standard generic properties" (25) has been my major point of departure.

NOTES ON CONTRIBUTORS

Anna Balakian, to whom this volume is dedicated, died suddenly in August 1997. She taught French and comparative literature at New York University since 1953, chairing the comparative literature department for nine years and playing a leading role in the International Comparative Literature Association. She had published over a hundred essays on modernism, surrealism, symbolism, and poetic theory, in addition to six books on symbolism (at New York UP and Princeton UP), surrealism (Cambridge UP, U of Chicago P, and Oxford UP), and the zeitgeist of contemporary literary criticism (*The Snowflake on the Belfry: Dogma and Disquietude in the Critical Arena*, Indiana UP, 1994). See her autobiographical essay in *Building a Profession* (State U of New York P, 1994) for details of her numerous additional awards, distinctions, and instances of outstanding service.

Ross Chambers is Marvin Felheim Distinguished University Professor of French and Comparative Literature at the University of Michigan. His major interests are critical and cultural history and literature in European languages since 1789. His early work concentrated on poetry and visionary literature in nineteenth-century France. Two later books, *Story and Situation: Narrative Seduction and the Power of Fiction* (U of Minnesota P, 1984) and *Room for Maneuver: Reading Oppositional Narrative* (U of Chicago P, 1991) integrated pragmatic narratology with cultural critique. He has two recent books: *Facing It: AIDS Diaries and the Death of the Author* (U of Michigan P, 1998) and *Loiterature* (U of Nebraska P, 1999). His major current project examines witnessing writing (testimony) as a cultural practice, with special attention to AIDS witnessing; the working title is "Discourses of Extremity."

Jonathan Culler is Class of 1966 Professor of English and Comparative Literature at Cornell University. His major current project is a book, "The Devil's Part: Baudelaire's Poetry." As analyst of French critical theory, he won the James Russell Lowell Prize of the MLA for *Structuralist Poetics* (Cornell UP, 1975), which was followed by *Ferdinand de Saussure* (Harvester, 1976; Cornell UP, 1986); *The Pursuit of Signs: Semiotics, Literature, Deconstruction* (Cornell UP, 1981); *On Deconstruction: Theory and Criticism after Structuralism* (Cornell UP, 1982); *Roland Barthes* (Oxford UP, 1983); *Framing the Sign: Criticism and Its Institutions* (U of Oklahoma P, 1988); and *Literary Theory: A Very Short Introduction* (Oxford UP, 1997). He has also published the study *Flaubert: The Uses of Uncertainty* (Cornell UP, 1974).

Eugene F. Gray is professor of French and director of the Language Learning Center at Michigan State University, specializing in nineteenth-century literature, French stylistics, and literature and technology. He is also developing computerized materials for the study of French literature and culture and of nineteenth-century French caricaturists. Originally trained as an engineer, he designed two modern multimedia laboratories at Michigan State and serves as science and technology editor for the *French Review*. With Laurence M. Porter, he edited *Approaches to Teaching Flaubert's* Madame Bovary (MLA, 1995) and contributed the Flaubert chapter to *A Critical Bibliography of French Literature: The Nineteenth Century* (Syracuse UP, 1994). He has written other studies of *Madame Bovary* and numerous articles on technology and teaching.

Deborah A. Harter received her doctorate in comparative literature from the University of California, Berkeley, and currently is associate professor of French studies at Rice University, where she has won four prizes for outstanding teaching, including the Phi Beta Kappa Prize. She is the author of the comparative study *Bodies in Pieces: Fantastic Narrative and the Poetics of the Fragment* (Stanford UP, 1996). She has also published articles and chapters on Baudelaire, Kafka, Maupassant, and the theory of the fantastic. Her current projects include a book, "Framing Madness: Figures of Excess in Balzac, Géricault, Melville, Maupassant, and Kafka," and work on Baudelaire's prose poems, narrative poetics in the art story, nineteenth-century fiction and criminality, representations of madness in art and literature from the late eighteenth century to the present, and the visual art of Géricault, Fuseli, and Goya.

J. A. Hiddleston, professor of French at Oxford University, has published many articles in nineteenth-century French studies and for decades has contributed to the intellectual life of scholarly conferences in North America and the United Kingdom. Among his books are *Essai sur Laforgue et les* Derniers vers, *suivi de* Laforgue et Baudelaire (French Forum, 1980), *Baudelaire and* Le Spleen de Paris (Oxford UP, 1988), and *Baudelaire and the Art of Memory* (Oxford UP, 1999). He edited the collection *Laforgue aujourd'hui* (Corti, 1988).

Judd Hubert taught at Harvard University and the University of Illinois, Urbana. He is currently professor emeritus of French and Italian at the University of California, Irvine, where he and Renée Rièse Hubert have played a leading role in developing doctoral programs. His *L'Esthétique des* Fleurs du Mal (1953) was a major contribution to aesthetic theory. He also published books on Corneille, Molière, and Shakespeare, and over seventy articles. Written in collaboration with Renée Rièse Hubert, his latest study is *The Cutting Edge of Reading: Artists' Books* (Granary, 1999). He continues to pursue research on the aesthetics of literature.

Edward K. Kaplan is professor of French and comparative literature at Brandeis University. His translation of Baudelaire's prose poems, *The Parisian Prowler* (U of Georgia P, 1997), won the Lewis Galantière Prize of the American Translators Association. He interpreted these modern fables in *Baudelaire's Prose Poems: The Esthetic, the Ethical, and the Religious in* The Parisian Prowler (U of Georgia P, 1990). He is also author of articles on Hugo, Nerval, Desbordes-Valmore, Rimbaud, Bachelard, Jabès, Bonnefoy; books on Jules Michelet; and a biography of the Jewish philosopher and social activist Abraham Heschel.

Rosemary Lloyd is Rudy Professor of French and Italian at Indiana University, Bloomington. She previously taught at the University of Cambridge. She held an NEH Fellowship for College and University Teachers during 1998. Her comparative study of jealousy in literature, *Closer and Closer Apart* (Cornell UP, 1995), was a *Choice* Outstanding Academic Book for 1996. Besides having had published numerous translations, editions, and essays, she has written *The Land of Lost Content: Childhood in Nineteenth-Century French Literature* (Clarendon, 1992), books on Flaubert and on Mallarmé, and two books on Baudelaire with Cambridge University Press. Her current research project is an intellectual biography of Mallarmé and his age, using original sources such as letters and diaries.

Ainslie Armstrong McLees teaches French at the Governor's School for Government and International Studies in Virginia. She is the author of *Baudelaire's "Argot Plastique":*

Poetic Caricature and Modernism (U of Georgia P, 1989). She has also contributed to *Teaching Poetry and the Other Arts* (MLA, 1990) and published articles in *Mosaic* and *Symposium*. Having received several major grants for curriculum development and for research, she currently is developing a seminar on the anthropology of language and writing a book on teaching foreign language to the gifted student.

William Olmsted, professor of humanities at Valparaiso University, works on nineteenth-century French literature and art, on censorship, and on the history of the body. His current research project is "Censorship and the Foundations of Modernism: Baudelaire and Company." Among his earlier publications are a reading of "Une Charogne" in *Understanding* Les Fleurs du Mal, edited by William Thompson, and the study "Subversive Taxonomies: Remarks on Baudelaire's Groups and Lists" in *Michigan Romance Studies*.

Laurence M. Porter is professor of French and comparative literature at Michigan State University, where he received the Distinguished Faculty Award in 1995. With Eugene F. Gray, he edited *Approaches to Teaching Flaubert's* Madame Bovary (MLA, 1995). He has contributed essays to the Approaches to Teaching World Literature volumes on Balzac and on Goethe. His *The Crisis of French Symbolism* (Cornell UP, 1990) was nominated for the James Russell Lowell Prize. His *Victor Hugo* (Twayne) appeared in 1999. Holding an NEH Research Fellowship for University Teachers in 1998, he is completing the comparative and theoretical book "Happening, Knowing, and Telling: How Stories Work in Life and Art," which includes examples from jokes and popular culture.

Laurence Risser has taught in the Minneapolis Public Schools. He served two terms as president of the statewide Association of International Baccalaureate Schools. He also taught the citywide course Humanities on Location, funded by the NEH, at the Minneapolis Institute of Art. He served on the editorial board for volumes 1 and 2 of 25 *Minnesota Poets* and was the photographer for those volumes as well as for the National Textbook Company. He has won a statewide prize for writing. He now teaches reading for adults and serves on the board of the Center for Arts Criticism in Minneapolis.

Peter Schofer is professor of French and Italian at the University of Wisconsin, Madison, where he holds a chair in French studies. His interests include film and pedagogy as well as nineteenth-century French poetry. With William Berg and Tom Rice, he was responsible for the poetry sections of the anthology *Poèmes, Pièces, Prose* (Oxford UP, 1973). He is coauthor of *Rhetorical Poetics: Theory and Practice of Figural and Symbolic Reading in Modern French Literature* (U of Wisconsin P, 1983). His book "The Teaching of Literature" is forthcoming. Current projects include a study of remakes in film and literature and a critical edition of *Les Types de Paris* (1895).

Gretchen M. Schultz, associate professor of French studies at Brown University, has written articles on Baudelaire, Desbordes-Valmore, Verlaine, Nina de Villard, and Valéry. She is author of *The Gendered Lyric: Subjectivity and Difference in Nineteenth-Century French Poetry* (Purdue UP, 1999). Her current projects include an anthology of nineteenth-century French women poets and a study of lesbian literature in nineteenth-century France.

Roger Shattuck, University Professor Emeritus at Boston University, began his career at Harvard University and also taught at the University of Texas, Austin, and at the University of Virginia. He served as president of the Association of Literary Scholars and

Critics. A distinguished scholar of literature and the other arts, Proust, and cultural studies, he has published *The Banquet Years* (Harcourt, 1958), *The Forbidden Experiment: The Story of the Wild Boy of Aveyron* (Farrar, 1980), *The Innocent Eye: On Modern Literature and the Arts* (Farrar, 1984), and *Forbidden Knowledge: From Prometheus to Pornography* (St. Martin's, 1996), in addition to numerous book chapters and articles. He has also published a volume of original poetry and coedited a volume on translation. His *Marcel Proust* (Princeton UP, 1974) won the National Book Award. *Candor and Perversion: Literature, Education, and the Arts* (Norton, 1999) is his most recent book.

Sonya Stephens is senior lecturer in French at Royal Holloway, University of London. She is author of *Baudelaire's Prose Poems: The Practice and Politics of Irony* (Oxford UP, 1999) as well as of numerous articles (in such journals as *Australian Journal of French Studies, French Studies*, and *Modern Language Review*) and book chapters on Baudelaire and nineteenth-century culture. She has edited the forthcoming volume *A History of Women's Writing in France* (Cambridge UP). She is currently working on two projects: the aesthetic of the unfinished in nineteenth-century France and the prose poem genre from 1820 to the present.

Richard Terdiman, professor of French literature and history of consciousness at the University of California, Santa Cruz, works on the literary and cultural history of France from the Enlightenment to the present and on critical theory. His books include *The Dialectics of Isolation: Self and Society in the French Novel from the Realists to Proust* (Yale UP, 1976); *Discourse / Counter-Discourse: The Theory and Practice of Symbolic Resistance in Nineteenth-Century France* (Cornell UP, 1985); and *Present Past: Modernity and the Memory Crisis* (Cornell UP, 1993). His current book projects include "Body and Story: Diderot Discovers Postmodernism" and "Taking Time: Temporality, Modernity, and Theory."

Timothy Unwin is James Barrow Professor of French at the University of Liverpool, specializing in nineteenth-century French literature and in critical theory. His major current project is a book on reflexivity in nineteenth-century French literature. Among his other books are *Flaubert et Baudelaire: affinités spirituelles et esthétiques* (Nizet, 1982); *Constant,* Adolphe (Grant and Cutler, 1986); and *Art et infini: l'oeuvre de jeunesse de Gustave Flaubert* (Rodopi, 1991). He also edited *The Cambridge Companion to the French Novel: 1800 to the Present* (1997).

Susan L. Wolf teaches French language and francophone studies at the University of Massachusetts, Boston. She frequently serves as resident director of the Paris Program. She regularly creates courses on feminism and psychoanalysis and has written essays on Flaubert (in the MLA volume *Approaches to Teaching Flaubert's* Madame Bovary); Dumas *fils*; Roumain; and Pynchon, Flaubert, and Irigaray. Her current research project is an intercultural study of French and Italian theater (Natalia Ginzburg and Ionesco).

Eléonore M. Zimmermann, professor emerita, taught French and comparative literature at the State University of New York, Stony Brook. Her books include *Magies de Verlaine* (Corti, 1967; rpt. Slatkine, 1981); *La Liberté et le destin dans le théâtre de Jean Racine* (Anma, 1982; rpt. Slatkine, 1999); and *Poétiques de Baudelaire dans* Les Fleurs du Mal, *rythme, parfum, lueur* (Minard, 1998), a major reappraisal of Baudelaire's achievement and originality. Her current research includes two projects on Baudelaire in relation to other poets. Her articles have appeared in *Comparative Literature, MLN, Revue des sciences humaines*, and *Studi francesi*.

SURVEY PARTICIPANTS

The following scholars and teachers generously agreed to participate in the survey of approaches to teaching *Les Fleurs du Mal*. Without their assistance, this volume would not have been possible.

Nicolae Babuts, *Syracuse University*
Anna Balakian, *New York University*
Dorothy M. Betz, *Georgetown University*
Elizabeth S. Blake, *University of Minnesota, Morris*
Ross Chambers, *University of Michigan, Ann Arbor*
Jonathan Culler, *Cornell University*
Sima Godfrey, *University of British Columbia*
Eugene F. Gray, *Michigan State University*
Stirling Haig, *University of North Carolina, Chapel Hill*
Deborah A. Harter, *Rice University*
J. A. Hiddleston, *Oxford University, Exeter College*
Judd Hubert, *University of California, Irvine*
Edward K. Kaplan, *Brandeis University*
James Lawler, *University of Chicago*
Norman H. Lewis, *City University of New York, Queens College*
Rosemary Lloyd, *Indiana University, Bloomington*
Ainslie Armstrong McLees, *The Governor's School, Virginia*
Frances Novack, *Ursinus College*
William Olmsted, *Valparaiso University*
Mary Anne O'Neil, *Whitman College*
Timothy Raser, *University of Georgia, Athens*
Larry Risser, *Minnesota Public Schools*
Ronald René Saint-Onge, *College of William and Mary*
Beryl Schlossman, *Carnegie Mellon University*
Peter Schofer, *University of Wisconsin, Madison*
Gretchen Schultz, *Brown University*
Roger Shattuck, *Boston University*
Sonya Stephens, *University of London, Royal Holloway*
Raymonde Tadros, *California State University, Los Angeles*
Richard Terdiman, *University of California, Santa Cruz*
Timothy Unwin, *University of Liverpool*
Thomas R. Vosteen, *Eastern Michigan University*
Jeanne Theis Whitaker, *Wheaton College, MA*
Adelia Williams, *Pace University*
Susan L. Wolf, *University of Massachusetts, Harbor Campus*
Eléonore M. Zimmermann, *State University of New York, Stony Brook*

WORKS CITED

A list of further reference materials follows this list.

Abraham, Nicolas, and Maria Torok. *The Shell and the Kernel*. Trans. Nicholas T. Rand. Vol. 1. Chicago: U of Chicago P, 1994.

Abrams, M. H. *Natural Supernaturalism: Tradition and Revolution in Romantic Literature*. New York: Norton, 1973.

Adatte, Emmanuel. Les Fleurs du Mal *et* Le Spleen de Paris: *essai sur le dépassement du réel*. Paris: Corti, 1986.

Albert, Nicole. "Sappho Mythified, Sappho Mystified; or, The Metamorphoses of Sappho in Fin de Siècle France." *Gay Studies from the French Cultures*. Ed. Rommel Mendès-Lette and Pierre-Olivier de Busscher. New York: Haworth, 1993. 87–104.

The American Heritage Dictionary of the English Language. 1969.

Arendt, Hannah. *Eichmann in Jerusalem: A Report on the Banality of Evil*. New York: Viking, 1963.

Atget, Eugène. *A Vision of Paris: The Worlds of Marcel Proust*. New York: Macmillan, 1980.

Auerbach, Erich. "The Aesthetic Dignity of the *Fleurs du Mal*." *Scenes from the Drama of European Literature: Six Essays*. Trans. Ralph Manheim. New York: Meridian, 1959. 201–26. Rpt. in *Baudelaire: A Collection of Critical Essays*. Ed. Henri Peyre. Englewood Cliffs: Prentice, 1962. 149–69.

Balakian, Anna. *The Symbolist Movement: A Critical Appraisal*. New York: Random, 1967.

Balzac, Honoré de. *La Cousine Bette. Œuvres complètes*. Vol. 7. Ed. Pierre-Georges Castex. Paris: Gallimard, 1977. 55–451.

———. "La Messe de l'athée." *La Comédie humaine*. Ed. Marcel Bouteron. Vol. 2. Paris: Gallimard, 1951. 1148–63.

———. *Splendeurs et misères des courtisanes*. Ed. Antoine Adam. Paris: Garnier, 1987.

Baudelaire, Charles. *Charles Baudelaire, 1821–1867: Selected Poems*. Trans. Felix W. Leakey. 2nd ed. London: Greenwich Exchange, 1997.

———. *Charles Baudelaire:* Les Fleurs du Mal. Ed. Jacques Dupont. Paris: Flammarion, 1991.

———. *Correspondance*. Ed. Claude Pichois and Jean Ziegler. 2 vols. Paris: Gallimard, 1973.

———. *Correspondance, 1862–1871*. Ed. Bertrand Marchal. Paris: Folio, 1995.

———. *Curiosités esthétiques:* L'Art romantique *et autres œuvres critiques*. Ed. Henri Lemaître. Paris: Garnier, 1962.

———. *Les Fleurs du Mal*. Ed. Antoine Adam. Paris: Garnier, 1994.

———. *Les Fleurs du Mal*. Ed. Philippe Semichon. Paris: Larousse, 1993.

———. *Flowers of Evil*. Trans. Richard Howard. Brighton, UK: Harvester, 1982.

———. *Flowers of Evil*. Ed. James Laver. London: Fanfare, 1940.

———. *The Flowers of Evil*. Trans. and ed. Marthiel Matthews and Jackson Matthews. New York: New Directions, 1955.

———. *The Flowers of Evil*. Oxford World's Classics. Trans. James McGowan. Introd. Jonathan Culler. Oxford: Oxford UP, 1993.

———. *From* Flowers of Evil *and* Paris Spleen. Trans. William Holmes Crosby. Brockport: BOA, 1991.

———. "Notes nouvelles sur Edgar Poe." Baudelaire, *Œuvres* [Ruff] 346–53.

———. *Œuvres complètes*. Ed. Yves Le Dantec. Paris: Gallimard, 1954.

———. *Œuvres complètes*. Ed. Claude Pichois. 2 vols. Paris: Gallimard, 1975–76.

———. *Œuvres complètes*. Ed. Marcel A. Ruff. Paris: Seuil, 1968.

———. "Projets de préface [pour *Les Fleurs du Mal*]." Baudelaire, *Œuvres* [Ruff] 127–29.

———. *The Prose Poems and* La Fanfarlo. Oxford World's Classics. Trans. and ed. Rosemary Lloyd. Oxford: Oxford UP, 1991.

———. *Salon de 1846*. Ed. David Kelley. Oxford: Clarendon, 1975.

———. *Selected Poems from* Les Fleurs du Mal: *A Bilingual Edition*. Trans. Norman R. Shapiro. Chicago: U of Chicago P, 1998.

Benjamin, Walter. *Charles Baudelaire: un poète lyrique à l'apogée du capitalisme*. Paris: Payot, 1982. Trans. as *Charles Baudelaire: A Lyric Poet in the Era of High Capitalism*. Trans. Harry Zohn. London: NLB, 1973.

———. "On Some Motifs in Baudelaire." *Illuminations*. Trans. Harry Zohn. Ed. Hannah Arendt. New York: Harcourt, 1968. 155–200.

Berg, Alban. "Der Wein" [concert aria for soprano and orchestra, 1929], J. Blegen, soprano, and Pierre Boulez, conductor. Sony Classical CD SMK 45838 [DDD].

Bernard, Suzanne. *Le Poème en prose de Baudelaire jusqu'à nos jours*. Paris: Nizet, 1959.

Bernheimer, Charles. *Figures of Ill Repute: Representing Prostitution in Nineteenth-Century France*. Cambridge: Harvard UP, 1989.

Bersani, Leo. *Baudelaire and Freud*. Berkeley: U of California P, 1977.

Bertall [Charles-Albert d'Arnoux]. *La Comédie de notre temps*. Paris: Plon, 1874.

Bishop, Michael. *Nineteenth-Century French Poetry*. New York: Twayne, 1993.

Blake, William. *Songs of Innocence and of Experience*. Princeton: Princeton UP, 1991.

Bonnefoy, Yves. *Entretiens sur la poésie*. Paris: Mercure de France, 1990.

Bourdieu, Pierre. *Distinction: A Social Critique of the Judgement of Taste*. Trans. Richard Nice. Cambridge: Harvard UP, 1984.

Bronfen, Elisabeth. *Over Her Dead Body: Death, Femininity, and the Aesthetic*. New York: Routledge, 1992.

Broome, Peter, and Graham Chesters. *The Appreciation of Modern French Poetry, 1850–1950*. New York: Cambridge UP, 1981.

Brunel, Pierre. "Lesbos." Les Fleurs du Mal: *l'intériorité de la forme*. Ed. Max Milner. Paris: SEDES, 1989. 85–92.

Burton, Richard D. E. *Baudelaire and the Second Republic: Writing and Revolution*. Oxford: Clarendon, 1991.

——. *Baudelaire in 1859: A Study in the Sources of Poetic Creativity*. Cambridge: Cambridge UP, 1988.

——. *The Context of Baudelaire's "Le Cygne."* Kendal, Eng.: U of Durham, 1980.

Byron, George Gordon. *Poetical Works*. New York: Oxford UP, 1997.

Calvin, William H. *Cerebral Code: Thinking a Thought in the Mosaics of the Mind*. Cambridge: MIT Press, 1996.

Campbell, Linda, Bruce Campbell, and Dee Dickerson. *Teaching and Learning through Multiple Intelligences*. Needham Heights: Allyn, 1996.

Castle, Terry. *The Apparitional Lesbian*. New York: Columbia UP, 1993.

Cazotte, Jacques. *Le Diable amoureux*. Paris: Ricci, 1978.

Chabrier, Emmanuel. "L'Invitation au voyage: mélodie pour chant et piano." 1913. Accord CD ACD 201392 [ADD].

Chambers, Ross. "Baudelaire's Street Poetry." *Nineteenth-Century French Studies* 13.4 (1985): 244–59.

——. *Loiterature*. Lincoln: U of Nebraska P, 1999.

——. *Mélancolie et opposition: les débuts du modernisme en France*. Paris: Corti, 1987. Trans. as *The Writing of Melancholy: Modes of Opposition in Early French Modernism*. Trans. Mary Siedman Trouille. Chicago: U of Chicago P, 1993.

——. "Perpetual Abjuration: Baudelaire and the Pain of Modernity." *French Forum* 15.2 (1990): 169–88.

——. "Relevance, Meaning, and Reading." *Approaches to Teaching Flaubert's Madame Bovary*. Ed. Laurence M. Porter and Eugene F. Gray, New York: MLA, 1995. 144–52.

Chesters, Graham. *Baudelaire and the Poetics of Craft*. Cambridge: Cambridge UP, 1988.

Cohen, Jean. *Le Haut Langage: théorie de la poéticité*. Paris: Flammarion, 1979.

——. *Structure du langage poétique*. Paris: Flammarion, 1966.

Collins First Harper. 1991.

Culler, Jonathan. Introduction. Baudelaire, *Flowers of Evil* [trans. McGowan] xiii–xxxvii.

Debussy, Claude. *Ariettes oubliées*. Werner Von Mechelen, baritone, and Marc Declaro, piano. Phaedra CD 292003 [DDD].

——. *Cinq poèmes de Baudelaire*. Hughes Cuénod, tenor, and M. Isepp, piano. Nimbus CD NI 52312 [ADD].

——. *Songs*. Dalton Baldwin, piano, and several singers including Frederica Von Stade and Elly Ameling. Angel CDMC-64095.

DeJean, Joan. *Fictions of Sappho, 1546–1937*. Chicago: U of Chicago P, 1989.

Delbanco, Andrew. *The Death of Satan: How Americans Have Lost the Sense of Evil*. New York: Farrar, 1995.

de Man, Paul. "The Rhetoric of Temporality." *Blindness and Insight: Essays in the Rhetoric of Contemporary Criticism*. London: Methuen, 1983. 179–203.

De Quincey, Thomas. *Confessions of an English Opium Eater*. New York: Dover, 1995.

Derrida, Jacques. *Given Time: I. Counterfeit Money*. Trans. Peggy Kamuf. Chicago: U of Chicago P, 1992.

——. *Positions*. Trans. and annotated by Alan Bass. Chicago: U of Chicago P, 1981.

Driskel, Michael Paul. *Representing Belief: Religion, Art, and Society in Nineteenth-Century France*. University Park: Pennsylvania State UP, 1992.

Eliot, T. S. "Baudelaire," *Selected Essays*. New York: Harcourt, 1964. 371–81.

——. "Baudelaire." *Selected Essays: 1917–1932*. 1st ed. New York: Harcourt, 1932. 335–45.

——. *The Sacred Wood*. 1920. London: Methuen, 1928.

——. *The Waste Land*. New York: Boni, 1922.

Emmanuel, Pierre. *Baudelaire: The Paradox of Redemptive Satanism*. Trans. Robert T. Cargo. University: U of Alabama P, 1970.

Fairlie, Alison. *Baudelaire: Les Fleurs du Mal*. Barron's Educ. Ser. Woodbury: Barron's, 1960.

——. "Reflections on the Successive Versions of 'Une Gravure fantastique.'" *Imagination and Language*. Cambridge: Cambridge UP, 1981. 216–27.

Fisher, Dominique. "The Silent Erotic/Rhetoric of Baudelaire's Mirrors." *Articulations of Difference: Gender Studies and Writing in French*. Ed. Fisher and Laurence Schehr. Stanford: Stanford UP, 1997. 34–51.

Flaubert, Gustave. *Correspondance*. Ed. Jean Bruneau. Vol. 1. Paris: Gallimard, 1973–.

——. *Madame Bovary*. Ed. Bernard Ajac. Paris: Flammarion, 1986.

Foucault, Michel. *The Uses of Pleasure*. Trans. Robert Hurley. New York: Pantheon, 1985. Vol. 2 of *The History of Sexuality*.

Freadman, Anne. *Models of Genre for Language Teaching: The 1994 Sonia Marks Memorial Lecture*. Sydney: U of Sydney P, 1995.

Freud, Sigmund. "On Narcissism: An Introduction." 1914. *Collected Papers*. Vol. 4. Ed. Ernest Jones. Trans. under the supervision of Joan Riviere. London: Hogarth and Inst. of Psycho-analysis, 1948. 30–59.

——. "A Seventeenth-Century Demonological Neurosis." Freud, *Standard Edition* 19: 67–105.

——. *The Standard Edition of the Complete Psychological Works*. 24 vols. Ed. and trans. James Strachey. London: Hogarth, 1953–74.

Friedrich, Hugo. *The Structure of Modern Poetry: From the Mid-Nineteenth to the Mid-Twentieth Century*. Trans. Joachim Neugroschel. Evanston: Northwestern UP, 1974.

Froman, Robert. *Venn Diagrams*. New York: Crowell, 1972.

Gardner, Howard. *Multiple Intelligences: The Theory in Practice*. New York: Basic, 1993.

Gavarni [Sulpice-Paul Chevalier]. *Les Etudiants de Paris*. *Œuvres choisies de Gavarni*. Vol. 2. Paris: Hetzel, 1846. 3rd section. n. pag.

Genette, Gérard. *Figures III*. Paris: Seuil, 1972.

——. *Mimologiques: voyage en Cratylie*. Paris: Seuil, 1976.

Grammont, Maurice. *Le Vers français, ses moyens d'expression, son harmonie*. Paris: Delagrave, 1947.

Greenblatt, Stephen, and Giles Gunn, eds. *Redrawing the Boundaries: The Transformation of English and American Studies*. New York: MLA, 1992.

The Handbook to the Lutheran Hymnal. Saint Louis: Concordia, 1942.

Hiddleston, James. *Essai sur Laforgue et les Derniers Vers, suivi de Laforgue et Baudelaire*. Lexington: French Forum, 1980.

Hofstadter, Douglas. *Le Ton Beau de Marot: In Praise of the Music of Language*. New York: Basic, 1997.

Holland, Eugene. *Baudelaire and Schizoanalysis. The Sociopoetics of Modernism*. Cambridge: Cambridge UP, 1993.

Houston, John Porter. "Toward a Romantic Iconology." *The Demonic Imagination: Style and Theme in French Romantic Poetry*. Baton Rouge: Louisiana State UP, 1969. 43–69.

Hugo, Victor. *Les Contemplations*. Ed. Léon Cellier. Paris: Garnier, 1969.

——. *La Fin de Satan*. La Fin de Satan; La Légende des siècles; Dieu. Ed. Jacques Truchet. Paris: Gallimard, 1967. 767–942.

——. *Œuvres poétiques*. Vol. 1. Bibliothèque de la Pléiade. Paris: Gallimard, 1964.

Hurtgen, André O. *Tous les poèmes pour le cours avancé*. New York: Longman, 1992.

Hyslop, Lois. *Baudelaire, Man of His Time*. New Haven: Yale UP, 1980.

Irigaray, Luce. "The Bodily Encounter with the Mother." Trans. David Macey. *The Irigaray Reader*. Ed. Margaret Whitford. Oxford: Blackwell, 1991. 34–46.

——. *Ce sexe qui n'est pas un*. Paris: Minuit, 1977. Trans. as *This Sex Which Is Not One*. Trans. Catherine Porter and Carolyn Burke. Ithaca: Cornell UP, 1985.

——. *Le corps-à-corps avec la mère*. Montréal: Pleine Lune, 1981.

James, Henry. "Charles Baudelaire." *French Poets and Novelists*. London: Macmillan, 1878. 57–65.

Johnson, Barbara. *Défigurations du langage poétique: la second révolution baudelairienne*. Paris: Flammarion, 1979.

——. "Gender and Poetry: Charles Baudelaire and Marceline Desbordes-Valmore." *Displacements: Women, Tradition, and Literatures in French*. Ed. Nancy Miller and Joan DeJean. Baltimore: Johns Hopkins UP, 1990. 163–81.

Johnson, Nancy L. *The Faces of the Gifted*. Dayton: Creative Learning Consultants, 1989.

Jones, John. *The Egotistical Sublime: A History of Wordsworth's Imagination*. London: Chatto, 1970.

Kaplan, Edward. "Baudelaire and the Battle with Finitude: 'La Mort,' Conclusion of *Les Fleurs du Mal*." *French Forum* 4.3 (1979): 219–31.

——. "Baudelaire and the Vicissitudes of Venus: Ethical Irony in *Les Fleurs du Mal*." *The Shaping of Text: Style, Imagery, and Structure in French Literature: Essays in Honor of John Porter Houston*. Ed. Emanuel Mickel. Lewisburg: Bucknell UP, 1993. 113–30.

——. *Baudelaire's Prose Poems: The Esthetic, the Ethical, and the Religious in* The Parisian Prowler. Athens: U of Georgia P, 1990.

——. "The Courage of Baudelaire and Rimbaud: The Anxiety of Faith." *French Review* 52.2 (1978): 294–306.

Kimura, Doreen. *Neuromotor Mechanisms in Human Communications*. New York: Oxford UP, 1993.

Kofman, Sarah. *The Enigma of Woman*. Trans. C. Porter. Ithaca: Cornell UP, 1985.

Kramsch, Claire. *Context and Culture in Language Teaching*. New York: Oxford UP, 1993.

Kristeva, Julia. *Soleil noir: dépression et mélancolie*. Paris: Gallimard, 1987.

Kselman, Thomas A. *Death and the Afterlife in Modern France*. Princeton: Princeton UP, 1993.

Lagarde, André, and Laurence Michard. *XIXième siècle*. Paris: Bordas, 1964.

Lamartine, Alphonse de. *La Chute d'un ange. Œuvres poétiques complètes*. Ed. Marius-François Guyard. Paris: Gallimard, 1963. 803–1081.

Larousse Dictionnaire Compact Français-Anglais, Concise Dictionary English-French. 1999.

Leclerc, Yvan. *Crimes écrites: la littérature en procès au 19e siècle*. Paris: Plon, 1991.

Maclean, Marie. *Narrative as Performance: The Baudelairean Experiment*. London: Routledge, 1988.

Mallarmé, Stéphane. *Œuvres complètes*. Ed. Henri Mondor and G. Jean-Aubry. Paris: Gallimard, 1970.

McLuhan, Marshall. *The Gutenberg Galaxy: The Making of Typographic Man*. Toronto: U of Toronto P, 1962.

McLuhan, Marshall, and Eric McLuhan. *Laws of Media: The New Science*. Toronto: U of Toronto P, 1988.

Michelet, Jules. *La Sorcière*. Paris: Union Générale d'Edition, 1960.

Miller, Christopher. *Blank Darkness*. Chicago: U of Chicago P, 1985.

Moréas, Jean. *Œuvres*. Vol. 2. Paris: Mercure de France, 1926.

Morier, Henri. *Dictionnaire de poétique et de rhétorique*. Paris: PUF, 1983.

Mossop, D. J. *Baudelaire's Tragic Hero: A Study of the Architecture of* Les Fleurs du Mal. Oxford: Oxford UP, 1961.

Nerval, Gérard de. *Œuvres complètes*. 2 vols. Paris: Gallimard, 1989.

The New Catholic Encyclopedia. 17 vols. New York: McGraw, 1967–79.

The New Oxford Companion to Literature in French. Ed. Peter France. Oxford: Clarendon, 1995.

Nisbet, John Donald. *Learning Strategies*. Boston: Routledge, 1986.

Nuiten, Henk. *Les Variantes des* Fleurs du Mal *et des* Epaves *de Charles Baudelaire*. Amsterdam: Holland UP, 1979.

O'Brian, Patrick. *Master and Commander*. London: Collins, 1970.

Paglia, Camille. *Sexual Personae*. New Haven: Yale UP, 1990.

Patty, James S., and Laurence M. Porter, with L. Cassandra Hamrick. "Charles Baudelaire." *A Critical Bibliography of French Literature: Volume V: The Nineteenth Century*. Ed. David Baguley. Vol. 2. Syracuse: Syracuse UP, 1994. 711–800.

Paul VI [Giovanni Battista Montini]. "Confronting the Devil's Power." *The Pope Speaks* 17 (1973): 315–19.

Le Petit-Larousse illustré. 1991.

Le Petit Robert. 3rd ed. 1968.

Pichois, Claude, comp. *Album Baudelaire*. Paris: Gallimard, 1974.

Pichois, Claude, and Jean-Paul Avice. *Baudelaire/Paris*. Paris: Musées, 1993.

Pichois, Claude, and François Ruchon, comps. *Iconographie de Charles Baudelaire*. Geneva: Cailler, 1960.

Pichois, Claude, and Jean Ziegler. *Baudelaire*. Paris: Julliard, 1987. Abr. and trans. Graham Robb. London: Penguin, 1989.

Poe, Edgar Allan. "The Black Cat." Poe, *Poetry* 597–606.

———. "The Imp of the Perverse." Poe, *Poetry* 826–32.

———. *Poetry and Tales*. New York: Lib. of Amer., 1984.

Pope, Alexander. *The Rape of the Lock*. *The Norton Anthology of English Literature*. 6th ed. Gen. ed. M. H. Abrams. Vol. 1. New York: Norton, 1993. 2234–52.

Porter, Laurence M. "The Anagogic Structure of Baudelaire's 'Les Phares.'" *French Review* 46.5 (1973): 49–54.

———. "Baudelaire's Fictive Audiences." Porter, *Crisis* 113–90.

———. *The Crisis of French Symbolism*. Ithaca: Cornell UP, 1990.

———. "Decadence and the Fin de Siècle Novel." *The French Novel: From 1800 to the Present*. Ed. Timothy Unwin. Cambridge: Cambridge UP, 1997.

Praz, Mario. *The Romantic Agony*. Trans. Angus Davidson. 2nd ed. London: Oxford UP, 1951.

Prendergast, Christopher, ed. *Nineteenth-Century French Poetry: Introductions to Close Reading*. Cambridge: Cambridge UP, 1990.

Prévost, Jean. *Baudelaire: essai sur la création et l'inspiration poétiques*. Paris: Mercure de France, 1953.

Proust, Marcel. *A la recherche du temps perdu*. 3 vols. Paris: Gallimard, 1954.

———. *Contre Sainte-Beuve*. Paris: Gallimard, 1971.

Ramazani, Vaheed. "Writing in Pain: Baudelaire, Benjamin, Haussman." *Boundary 2* 23.2 (1996): 199–224.

Raymond, Marcel. *De Baudelaire au surréalisme*. 2nd ed. Paris: Corti, 1969. Trans. as *From Baudelaire to Surrealism*. London: Avon, 1961.

Renan, Ernest. "La Tentation du Christ de M. Ary Scheffer." *L'Artiste* 27 May 1855: 47–50.

Ricoeur, Paul. *Fallible Man*. Trans. Charles Kelbley. Chicago: Regnery, 1965.

Rifelj, Carol de Dobay. *Word and Figure: The Language of Nineteenth-Century French Poetry*. Columbus: Ohio State UP, 1987.

Riffaterre, Michael. "Compulsory Reader Response: The Intertextual Drive." *Intertextuality: Theories and Practices*. Ed. Michael Worton and Judith Still. Manchester: Manchester UP, 1990. 56–78.

———. *Semiotics of Poetry*. Bloomington: Indiana UP, 1978.

Rincé, Dominique. *Baudelaire et la modernité poétique*. Paris: PUF, 1984.

Robb, Graham. *La Poésie de Baudelaire et la poésie française, 1838–1852*. Paris: Aubier, 1993.

Le Robert and Collins French-English, English-French Dictionary. 1979.

Ronsard, Pierre de. *Œuvres complètes*. Paris: Gallimard, 1994.

Ruff, Marcel A. *Baudelaire*. Paris: Hatier, 1967.

Ruskin, John. *The Elements of Drawing*. New York: Wiley, 1865.

Russell, Jeffrey Burton. *Mephistopheles: The Devil in the Modern World*. Ithaca: Cornell UP, 1986.

Saint-Amant, Marc-Antoine Gérard de. *Œuvres*. Vol. 1. Paris: Nizet, 1971.

Sartre, Jean-Paul. *Baudelaire*. Paris: Gallimard, 1946. Trans. Martin Turnell. New York: New Directions, 1950.

Saussure, Ferdinand de. *Course in General Linguistics*. La Salle: Open Court, 1986.

Schmeck, Ronald R., ed. *Learning Strategies and Learning Styles*. New York: Plenum, 1988.

Schofer, Peter, Donald Rice, and William Berg. *Poèmes, pièces, prose: introduction à l'analyse de textes littéraires français*. New York: Oxford UP, 1973.

Schwab, Carlos. *Spleen et idéal*. Collection of Gérard Lévy, Paris. (Cover illustration of *Baudelaire: Selected Poems*, trans. and ed. Joanna Richardson [New York: Penguin, 1975].)

Shattuck, Roger. *The Innocent Eye*. New York: Washington Square, 1984.

Staël, Germaine de. *Delphine*. 2 vols. Geneva: Droz, 1987.

Starkie, Enid. *Baudelaire*. Norfolk: New Directions, 1958.

Stephenson, Katherine. "Luce Irigaray." *French Women Writers: A Bio-biographical Source Book*. Ed. Eva Martin-Sartori and Dorothy Wynne-Zimmerman. New York: Greenwood, 1991. 229–43.

Stevenson, Rosemary J., and Jay A. Palmes. *Learning Principles, Processes, and Practices*. New York: Cassell, 1994.

Terdiman, Richard. "Baudelaire's 'Le Cygne': Memory, History, and the Sign." Terdiman, *Present Past* 106–47. Rpt. in *Home and Its Dislocations in Nineteenth-Century France*. Ed. Suzanne Nash. Albany: SUNY, 1993. 169–89.

———. *Present Past: Modernity and the Memory Crisis*. Ithaca: Cornell UP, 1993.

Thellot, Jérôme. *Baudelaire: violence et poésie*. Paris: Gallimard, 1993.

Toga, Arthur, and John C. Mazziotta, eds. *Brain Mapping: The Methods*. San Diego: Academic, 1996.

Turnell, Martin. *Baudelaire: A Study of His Poetry*. New York: New Directions, 1972.

Vapereau, Gustave. *Dictionnaire universel des contemporains*. Paris: Hachette, 1858.

Verlaine, Paul. "Art Poétique." *Œuvres poétiques complètes*. Ed. Yves Le Dantec. Rev. Jacques Borel. Paris: Gallimard, 1962. 326–27.

Vigny, Alfred de. "Eloa, ou la sœur des anges." *Œuvres complètes*. Ed. Fernand Baldensperger. Paris: Gallimard, 1948. 60–80.

Vivien, Renée. *Poésies complètes*. Paris: Deforges, 1989.

Weber, Max. "The Social Psychology of the World Religions." *From Max Weber: Essays in Sociology*. Trans. and ed. H. H. Gerth and C. Wright Mills. New York: Oxford UP, 1958. 267–301.

Weil, Simone. *Attente de Dieu*. Paris: Aubier, 1950.

Whitford, Margaret. *Luce Irigaray: Philosophy in the Feminine*. London: Routledge, 1991.

Wing, Nathaniel. "Exile from Within, Exile from Without." *A New History of French Literature*. Cambridge: Harvard UP, 1989. 737–43.

———. *The Limits of Narrative: Essays on Baudelaire, Flaubert, Rimbaud and Mallarmé*. Cambridge: Cambridge UP, 1986.

Wright, Gordon. *France in Modern Times: From the Enlightenment to the Present*. 5th ed. New York: Norton, 1995.

Zeldin, Theodore. *France, 1848–1945*. 2 vols. Oxford: Oxford UP, 1973.

Zimmermann, Eléonore. "Expression et répression chez Baudelaire." *Repression and Expression*. Ed. Carrol F. Coates. New York: Lang, 1996. 223–29.

———. *Poétiques de Baudelaire dans Les Fleurs du Mal: rythme, parfum, lueur*. Situation 51. Paris: Lettres Modernes Minard, 1998.

Further Reference Materials

The list of works cited precedes this list.

Books by Baudelaire

Art in Paris 1845–1862: Salons and Other Exhibitions. Trans. and ed. Jonathan Mayne. London: Phaidon, 1965. (Paperback, 1970; also New York: Da Capo, 1986. Companion to Baudelaire's *The Painter of Modern Life*.)

L'Art romantique. Paris: Garnier, 1931.

Baudelaire as a Literary Critic. Ed. Lois B. Hyslop and F. E. Hyslop. University Park: Pennsylvania State UP, 1964.

The Mirror of Art. Trans. and ed. Jonathan Mayne. London: Phaidon, 1955. (Also Garden City: Doubleday, 1956. Later expanded as *Art in Paris*.)

"The Painter of Modern Life" and Other Essays. Trans. and ed. Jonathan Mayne. London: Phaidon, 1995. (Paperback, 1970; also New York: Da Capo, 1986.)

Anthology

Leggewie, Robert, comp. *Anthologie de la littérature française*. 3rd ed. Oxford: Oxford UP, 1990.

Works about Baudelaire and His Background

Anderson, Jean. "Baudelaire misogyne: vers une lecture féministe des *Fleurs du Mal*." *New Zealand Journal of French Studies* (1987): 16–28.

Austin, Lloyd James. *Poetic Principles and Practice: Occasional Papers on Baudelaire, Mallarmé and Valéry*. Cambridge: Cambridge UP, 1987.

———. *L'Univers poétique de Baudelaire: symbolisme et symbolique*. Paris: Mercure de France, 1956.

Babuts, Nicolae. "Baudelaire et J. G. F." *Bulletin baudelairien* 14 (1979): 3–6.

———. "Baudelaire in the Circle of Exiles: A Study of 'Le Cygne.'" *Nineteenth-Century French Studies* 22.1–2 (1993–94): 123–38.

———. *The Dynamics of the Metaphoric Field: A Cognitive View of Literature*. Newark: U of Delaware P, 1992.

———. "Structure and Meaning in Baudelairean Images of Immersion." *Symposium* 31.3 (1977): 185–95.

Bandy, W. T. "Baudelaire et Edgar Poe: vue rétrospective." *Revue de littérature comparée* 41 (1967): 180–94.

Bassim, Tamara. *La Femme dans l'œuvre de Baudelaire*. Neuchâtel: La Baconnière, 1974.

Bataille, Georges. *L'Erotisme*. Paris: Minuit, 1992.

———. *La Littérature et le mal*. Paris: Gallimard, 1957. Trans. as *Literature and Evil*. London: Boyars, 1990.

Baudelaire. Spec. issue of *Revue des sciences humaines* 127 (1967): 337–496.

Benamou, Michel. *Pour une nouvelle pédagogie du texte littéraire*. Paris: Hachette, 1971.

Benjamin, Walter. "Paris, capitale du XIXième siècle." *Gesammelte Schriften*. Vol. 5. Ed. Rolf Tiedemann. Frankfurt: Suhrkamp, 1982. 60–78.

Bermann, Sandra. *The Sonnet over Time: Petrarch, Shakespeare, Baudelaire*. Chapel Hill: U of North Carolina P, 1988.

Blin, Georges. *Baudelaire*. Paris: Gallimard, 1939.

———. *Le Sadisme de Baudelaire*. Paris: Corti, 1948.

Bloom, Harold. *The Anxiety of Influence: A Theory of Poetry*. New York: Oxford UP, 1973.

———, ed. *Charles Baudelaire*. New York: Chelsea, 1987.

Brombert, Victor. "'Le Cygne' de Baudelaire: douleur, souvenir, travail." *Etudes baudelairiennes* 3 (1973): 254–61.

———. *The Hidden Reader: Stendhal, Balzac, Hugo, Baudelaire, and Flaubert*. Cambridge: Harvard UP, 1988. (See pp. 90–96 on "La Chevelure," 97–102 on "Le Cygne.")

Buci-Glucksmann, Christine. *La Raison baroque: de Baudelaire à Benjamin*. Paris: Galilée, 1984. Trans. as *Baroque Reason: The Aesthetics of Modernity*. London: Sage, 1994.

Bulletin baudelairien (Vanderbilt U). 1965– .

Cargo, Robert T. *Baudelaire Criticism 1950–67: A Bibliography with Critical Commentary*. University: U of Alabama P, 1968.

———. *A Concordance to Baudelaire's* Fleurs du Mal. Chapel Hill: U of North Carolina P, 1965.

Carrier, David. *High Art: Charles Baudelaire and the Origins of Modernist Painting*. University Park: Pennsylvania State UP, 1966.

Cassagne, Albert. *Versification et métrique de Charles Baudelaire*. Geneva: Slatkine, 1972.

Caws, Mary Ann, and Michael Riffaterre, eds. *The Prose Poem in France: Theory and*

Practice. New York: Columbia UP, 1983.

Cellier, Léon. "'Les Phares': étude de structure." *Revue des sciences humaines* 121 (1966): 97–103.

Citron, Pierre. *La Poésie de Paris dans la littérature française de Cazotte à Baudelaire*. Paris: Minuit, 1961.

Clark, Timothy J. "Delacroix and Baudelaire." *The Absolute Bourgeois*. Greenwich: New York Graphic Soc., 1973. 124–77.

———. *The Painting of Modern Life: Paris in the Art of Manet and His Followers*. London: Thames, 1985.

Clements, Patricia. *Baudelaire and the English Tradition*. Princeton: Princeton UP, 1985.

Cobban, Alfred. *A History of Modern France*. 3 vols. 3rd ed. New York: Penguin, 1963–65.

Cooper, Barbara T., and Mary Donaldson-Evans, eds. *Modernity and Revolution in Late-Nineteenth-Century France*. Newark: U of Delaware P, 1992.

Cousin, Victor. *The Philosophy of the Beautiful*. London: Pickering, 1848.

Crow, Christine. "'Le Silence au vol de cygne': Baudelaire, Mallarmé, Valéry and the Flight of the Swan." *Baudelaire, Mallarmé, Valéry: New Essays in Honour of Lloyd Austin*. Ed. Malcolm Bowie, Alison Fairlie, and Alison Finch. Cambridge: Cambridge UP, 1982. 1–23.

Culler, Jonathan. *Structuralist Poetics*. London: Routledge, 1975.

Delacroix, Maurice, and Walter Geerts, eds. *"Les Chats" de Baudelaire: une confrontation de méthodes*. Paris: PUF, 1980.

Deloffre, Frédéric. *Le Vers français: stylistique et poétique françaises*. Paris: SEDES, 1970.

de Man, Paul. *The Rhetoric of Romanticism*. New York: Columbia UP, 1984.

Dijkstra, Bram. *Idols of Perversity: Fictions of Feminine Evil in Fin-de-Siècle Culture*. New York: Oxford UP, 1986.

Etudes baudelairiennes. 1969– .

Fischer, Michael. *Does Deconstruction Make Any Difference? Poststructuralism and the Defense of Poetry in Modern Criticism*. Bloomington: Indiana UP, 1985.

Fiser, Emeric. *Le Symbole littéraire: essai sur la signification du symbole chez Wagner, Baudelaire, Mallarmé, Bergson, et Proust*. Paris: Corti, 1941.

Fournel, Victor. *Paris nouveau et Paris futur*. Paris: Lecoffre, 1865.

Freud, Sigmund. "Mourning and Melancholia." Freud, *Standard Edition* 14: 237–58.

———. *Totem and Taboo: Some Points of Agreement between the Mental Lives of Savages and Neurotics*. Trans. James Strachey. New York: Norton, 1950.

Gale, J. E. "De Quincey, Baudelaire, and 'Le Cygne.'" *Nineteenth-Century French Studies* 5 (1977): 296–307.

Gans, Eric. "Mon semblable, mon frère." *Stanford French Review* 8.1 (1984): 75–88.

Gasarian, Gérard. *De loin tendrement: étude sur Baudelaire*. Paris: Champion, 1996.

Genette, Gérard. *Figures II*. Paris: Seuil, 1969.

Gilman, Margaret. *Baudelaire the Critic*. New York: Octagon, 1971.

Guerlac, Suzanne. *The Impersonal Sublime: Hugo, Baudelaire, Lautréamont*. Stanford: Stanford UP, 1990.

Hampton, Timothy. "Virgil, Baudelaire and Mallarmé at the Sign of the Swan: Poetic Translation and Historical Allegory." *Romanic Review* 73 (1982): 438–51.

Hannoosh, Michèle. *Baudelaire and Caricature*. University Park: Pennsylvania State UP, 1992.

Hanson, Anne. *Manet and the Modern Tradition*. New Haven: Yale UP, 1977.

Hiddleston, James. *Baudelaire and* Le Spleen de Paris. Oxford: Oxford UP, 1987.

Holland, Norman N. *The Critical I*. New York: Columbia UP, 1992.

Irigaray, Luce. *Je, tu, nous, vous*. Paris: Grasset, 1990.

———. *Speculum of the Other Woman*. Trans. Gillian C. Gill. Ithaca: Cornell UP, 1985.

Jackson, John E. *La Mort Baudelaire*. Neuchâtel: La Baconnière, 1982.

Jakobson, Roman. *Questions de poétique*. Paris: Seuil, 1973.

Jauss, H. R. "On the Question of 'Structural Unity' of Older and Modern Lyric Poetry." *Aesthetic Experience and Literary Hermeneutics*. Trans. Michael Shaw. Minneapolis: U of Minnesota P, 1982. 221–62.

———. "The Poetic Text within the Change of Horizons of Reading: The Example of Baudelaire's 'Spleen III.'" *Toward an Aesthetic of Reception*. Minneapolis: U of Minnesota P, 1982. 139–85, 214–18(nn).

Johnson, Barbara. "The Dream of Stone." *A New History of French Literature*. Ed. Denis Hollier. Cambridge: Harvard UP, 1989. 743–51.

Kamuf, Peggy. "Baudelaire's Modern Woman." *Qui parle* 4.2 (1991): 1–7.

Kant, Immanuel. *Analytic of the Beautiful*. Indianapolis: Bobbs, 1963.

Kaplan, Edward. "Baudelaire's Portrait of the Poet as Widow: Three 'Poèmes en prose' and 'Le Cygne.'" *Symposium* 34 (1980): 233–48.

———. "Solipsism and Dialogue in Baudelaire's Prose Poems." Cooper and Donaldson-Evans 88–98.

Kempf, Roger. *Dandies, Baudelaire et Cie*. Paris: Seuil, 1977.

Kerbrat-Orecchioni, Catherine. *La Connotation*. Lyon: PU de Lyon, 1977.

Knight, Philip. *Flower Poetics*. Oxford: Oxford UP, 1986.

Lacan, Jacques. *Ecrits*. Paris: Seuil, 1966. Partial trans. as Ecrits: *A Selection*. New York: Norton, 1977.

Lalou, René. *Les Etapes de la poésie française*. "Que sais-je?" Paris: PUF, 1977.

Leakey, Felix. "Baudelaire and Mortimer." *French Studies* 7 (1953): 101–15. Leakey, *Baudelaire: Collected Essays* 111–23.

———. *Baudelaire and Nature*. Manchester: Manchester UP, 1969.

———. *Baudelaire: Collected Essays, 1953–1988*. Cambridge: Cambridge UP, 1990.

———. *Baudelaire:* Les Fleurs du Mal. Cambridge: Cambridge UP, 1992.

———. "The Originality of Baudelaire's 'Le Cygne': Genesis as Structure and Theme." Leakey, *Baudelaire: Collected Essays* 92–107.

Lewis, Roy. *On Reading French Verse: A Study of Poetic Form*. Oxford: Clarendon, 1982.

Lloyd, Rosemary. *Baudelaire's Literary Criticism*. Cambridge: Cambridge UP, 1981.

———. "Un Peintre et ses critiques: Dominique Papety." *Romantisme* 50 (1985): 104–10.

Loncke, Joycelynne. *Baudelaire et la music*. Paris: Nizet, 1975.

MacFarlane, Keith M. "'Le Cygne' de Baudelaire: 'Falsi Simoentis ad undam.'" *L'Information littéraire* 27.3 (1975): 139–44.

Magraw, Roger. *France, 1815–1914: The Bourgeois Century*. London: Fontana, 1983.

Marriage, Anthony. "Whitman's 'This Compost' and Baudelaire's 'A Carrion': Out of Decay Comes an Awful Beauty." *Walt Whitman Review* 27.4 (1981): 143–49.

Marx, Karl. *The Communist Manifesto*. Harmondsworth: Penguin, 1984.

Mauron, Charles. *Le Dernier Baudelaire*. Paris: Corti, 1966.

———. *Des métaphores obsédantes au mythe personnel*. Paris: Corti, 1963.

McLees, Ainslie Armstrong. *Baudelaire's Argot Plastique*. Athens: U of Georgia P, 1989.

———. "Baudelaire's 'Une Charogne': Caricature and the Birth of Modern Art." *Mosaic* 21.4 (1988): 111–22.

Milner, Michael, ed. Les Fleurs du Mal: *l'intériorité de la forme*. Paris: SEDES, 1989.

Nelson, Lowry, Jr. "Baudelaire and Virgil: A Reading of 'Le Cygne.'" *Comparative Literature* 13 (1961): 332–45.

New History of French Literature. Ed. Denis Hollier. Cambridge: Harvard UP, 1989.

Nuiten, Henk, W. T. Bandy, and Freeman G. Henry, comps. Les Fleurs *expliquées: bibliographie des exégèses des* Fleurs du Mal *et des* Epaves *de Baudelaire*. Amsterdam: Rodopi, 1983.

Nurnberg, Monica. "Animated Sculpture: A Paradox of the *Transposition d'Art* from Chénier to Hérédia." *Parnasse* 1.4 (1983): 41–48.

Olson, Janet. *Envisioning Writing: Toward an Integration of Drawing and Writing*. Portsmouth: Heinemann, 1992.

Peyre, Henri, ed. *Baudelaire: A Collection of Critical Essays*. Englewood Cliffs: Prentice, 1962.

———. *Connaissance de Baudelaire*. Paris: Corti, 1951.

Pia, Pascal. *Baudelaire: études et témoignages*. Neuchâtel: La Baconnière, 1967.

———. *Baudelaire par lui-même*. Paris: Seuil, 1975.

Pilkington, A. E. "Baudelaire's 'Les Phares.'" *Forum for Modern Language Studies* 25.2 (1989): 95–106.

Poe, Edgar Allan. "The Poetic Principle." *Edgar Allan Poe: Essays and Reviews*. Ed. G. R. Thompson. New York: Lib. of Amer., 1984. 71–94.

Pommier, Jean. *La Mystique de Baudelaire*. Geneva: Slatkine, 1967.

Porter, Laurence M. "The Invisible Worm: Decay in the Privileged Moments of Baudelaire's Poetry." *L'Esprit Créateur* 13.2 (1973): 100–13.

Poulet, Georges. *La Poésie éclatée: Baudelaire-Rimbaud*. Paris: PUF, 1980.

Pour le centenaire des Fleurs du Mal. Spec. issue of *Revue des sciences humaines* 85 (1957): 5–110.

Proust, Marcel. "A propos de Baudelaire." *Contre Sainte-Beuve: précéde de* Pastiches et mélanges *et suivi de* Essais et articles. Ed. Pierre Clarac. Paris: Gallimard, 1971. 618–39.

Quatrème de Quincy, Antoine-Chrysostome. *An Essay on the Nature, the End, and the Means of Imitation in the Fine Arts.* New York: Garland, 1979.

Quesnel, Michel. *Baudelaire, solaire et clandestin: les données singulières de la sensibilité et de l'imagination dans* Les Fleurs du Mal. Paris: PUF, 1987.

———. *La Création poétique.* Paris: Colin, 1996.

Ransom, Amy. "'Mon semblable, ma mère': Woman, Subjectivity, and Escape in *Les Fleurs du Mal.*" *Paroles gelées* (1993): 11+.

Revue d'histoire littéraire de la France 67 (1967): 225–460. Spec. issue, untitled.

Richard, Jean-Pierre. *Poésie et profondeur.* Paris: Seuil, 1955.

Ruwet, Nicolas. "Sur un vers de Charles Baudelaire." *Linguistics* 17 (1965): 76–77.

Saignieux, J. *Les Danses macabres de France et d'Espagne.* Lyon: Vitte, 1972.

Schlossman, Beryl. *The Orient of Style: Modernist Allegories of Conversion.* Durham: Duke UP, 1991.

Schofer, Peter. "You Cannot Kill a Cloud: Code and Context in [Baudelaire's] 'L'Etranger.'" Cooper and Donaldson-Evans 99–107.

Scott, Clive. "A Privileged Syllable: The Articulated *e* in *Les Fleurs du Mal.*" *A Question of Syllables: Essays in Nineteenth-Century French Verse.* Cambridge: Cambridge UP, 1986. 86–116.

Sedgwick, Eve Kosofsky. *Epistemology of the Closet.* Berkeley: U of California P, 1990.

Sharpe, William Chapman. *Unreal Cities: Urban Figuration in Wordsworth, Baudelaire, Whitman, Eliot, and Williams.* Baltimore: Johns Hopkins UP, 1990.

Soupault, Philippe. *Baudelaire.* Paris: Rieder, 1931.

Starobinski, Jean. *La Mélancholie au miroir: trois lectures de Baudelaire.* Paris: Julliard, 1989.

Thompson, William, ed. *Understanding* Les Fleurs du Mal: *Critical Readings.* Nashville: Vanderbilt UP, 1997.

Turner, M. B., and George Lakoff. *More than Cool Reason: A Field Guide to Poetic Metaphor.* Chicago: U of Chicago P, 1989.

Valéry, Paul. "Situation de Baudelaire." *Paul Valéry: Œuvres.* Ed. Jean Hytier. Vol. 1. Paris: Gallimard, 1960. 598–613.

Weinberg, Bernard. "Baudelaire's 'Le Cygne.'" *The Limits of Symbolism.* Chicago: U of Chicago P, 1966. 8–36.

Weinberg, Kerry. "Women of Eliot and Baudelaire: The Boredom, the Horror, and the Glory." *Modern Language Studies* 14.3 (1984): 31–42.

Wieser, Dagmar. "Témoignage de Baudelaire: du fétischisme dans 'Une Martyre.'" *Versants* 25 (1994): 97–115.

Wilson, Emma. *Sexuality and the Reading Encounter: Identity and Desire in Proust, Duras, Tournier, and Cixous.* Oxford: Clarendon, 1996.

Wund, Jo Ann S. *Teacher's Guide to the Advanced Placement Course in French Literature*. Princeton: ETS, 1994.

Zimmermann, Eléonore. *L'Evolution de la poétique de Baudelaire dans* Les Fleurs du Mal. Paris: Minard, 1997.

Original Works by Other Authors

Balzac, Honoré de. La Recherche de l'absolu, *suivi de* La Messe de l'athée. Paris: Gallimard, 1976.

Desbordes-Valmore, Marceline. *Les Œuvres complètes*. 2 vols. Grenoble: PU Grenoble, 1973.

Flaubert, Gustave. *L'Education sentimentale, histoire d'un jeune homme*. Ed. Edouard Maynial. Paris: Garnier, 1964.

Gautier, Théophile. *Emaux et camées*. Paris: Lettres Modernes, 1968.

Goethe, Johann Wolfgang von. *Faust*. Trans. Walter Arndt. Ed. Cyrus Hamlin. New York: Norton, 1976.

Lamartine, Alphonse de. "Le Lac." *Œuvres poétiques complètes*. Ed. Marius-François Guyard. Paris: Gallimard, 1963. 38–40.

Mallarmé, Stéphane. "L'Après-Midi d'un faune." Mallarmé, *Œuvres* 50–53.

———. "Crise de vers." Mallarmé, *Œuvres* 360–68.

———. *Œuvres complètes*. Ed. Henri Mondor and G. Jean-Aubry. Paris: Gallimard, 1970.

Maupassant, Guy de. "La Chevelure." *Contes fantastiques complètes*. Ed. Anne Richter. Paris: Marabout, 1990. 185–92.

Milton, John. *Paradise Lost*. New York: Norton, 1975.

Nerval, Gérard de. "Fantaisie." *Œuvres*. Vol. 1. Ed. Henri Lemaître. Paris: Garnier, 1958. 20.

Wilde, Oscar. *The Picture of Dorian Gray*. New York: Oxford UP, 1981.

Zola, Emile. *Les Rougon-Macquart, histoire naturelle et sociale d'une famille sous le Second Empire*. 4 vols. Paris: Gallimard, 1960–67.

Audiovisual Aids

CD-ROMS in Print. Westport: Meckler, annual.

The Multimedia and CD-ROM Directory. Stockton, annual.

Art

Baudelaire et les peintres. Winterthur: Kunstmuseum, 1989.

Courbet, Gustave. *L'Atelier, Portrait de Baudelaire*.

Delacroix, Eugène. *The Bride of Abydos, The Death of Sardanapalus, The Fire, Jacob Wrestling with the Angel, The Jewels, Liberty Leading the People, The Massacre* at Chios, Ovid in Exile among the Scyths, Piétà, Woman with a Parrot, Woman with White Stockings, Women of Algiers in Their Apartment.

Goya, Francisco. Los Caprichos: The Bewitched, Clothed Maja, Naked Maja, Old Woman at the Mirror, Satan Devouring His Son.

Leonardo da Vinci. Angel Musicians, The Mona Lisa, Portrait of Ginevra de' Benci, Saint John, Virgin and Child with Saint Anne, The Virgin of the Rocks.

Manet, Edouard. La Musique aux Tuileries.

Michelangelo Buonarroti. The Dying Captive, Hercules, The Heroic Captive, Last Judgment, The Piétà, The Risen Christ.

Puget, Pierre. Faun, Hercules and Cerberus, Milos of Croton.

Rembrandt. The Anatomy Lesson of Doctor Nicolas Tulp, The Apostle Paul in Prison, Christ on the Cross, Christ the Healer, Three Crosses.

Rubens, Peter Paul. The Erection of the Cross, Samson and Delilah, Self-Portrait with His Wife Isabella Brant.

Watteau, Antoine. The Elysian Fields, The Embarkation for Cytherea, Venetian Fêtes.

Music

Berlioz, Hector. Symphonie fantastique.

Debussy, Claude. L'Après-midi d'un faune, La Mer.

Hylan, Bryan. Devil or Angel.

Wagner, Richard. Der fliegende Holländer, Lohengrin, Tannhäuser.

Weber, Carl Maria von. Der Freischütz.

Photography and Iconography

Baudelaire, Charles. Les Fleurs du Mal. Texte de 1861. Ed. Jean Pommier and Claude Pichois. Paris: Club des libraires de France, 1959.

Baudelaire. Petit Palais, 23 novembre 1968–17 mars 1969. Paris: La Réunion des Musées Nationaux, 1968.

Recorded Readings of Baudelaire's Poems

For current availability, price, and supplier, see the most recent issue of the annual Bowker Words on Cassette.

Beauclair, Claude, perf. Les Fleurs du Mal. Olivia and Hill, Box 7396, Ann Arbor, MI 48107.

Beauclair, Claude, and Françoise Mojeret, perfs. Panorama de la poésie française. Paralogue, 93 rue de Maubeuge, Paris 75010.

Leakey, F. W., perf. Les Fleurs du Mal. Sussex Video, 1989, FCIA.

Le Gallienne, Eva, and Louis Jourdan, perfs. Les Fleurs du Mal. Harper Audio, HarperCollins, 10 East 53 St., New York, NY 10022.

Pichois, Claude, with Yves Bonnefoy and Pierre Emmanuel, perfs. Trois Paris de Baudelaire. 3 cassettes. Olivia and Hill. n.d.

Videocassettes

For price and supplier, see *The Video Source Book*, ed. Julia C. Furtaw, 15th ed. (Detroit: Gale, 1994).

Delacroix, 1798–1863. 1967. Prod. Anthony Roland. Roland Collection, n.d.

Delacroix, the Restless Eye. 1987. Dir. Colin Nears. Home Vision Cinema.

Madame Bovary. 1949. Dir. Vicente Minelli. MGM/UA Home Video.

Madame Bovary. 1991. Dir. Claude Chabrol. Columbia Pictures Home Video.

Paris in the Time of Balzac. Films for the Humanities and Sciences, 1989.

Paris in the Time of Zola. Films for the Humanities and Sciences, 1989.

INDEX OF WORKS BY BAUDELAIRE

---

*A section of *Les Fleurs du Mal*.

INDEX OF NAMES

Modern Language Association of America

Approaches to Teaching World Literature

Joseph Gibaldi, series editor

Achebe's Things Fall Apart. Ed. Bernth Lindfors. 1991.
Arthurian Tradition. Ed. Maureen Fries and Jeanie Watson. 1992.
Atwood's The Handmaid's Tale *and Other Works*. Ed. Sharon R. Wilson,
    Thomas B. Friedman, and Shannon Hengen. 1996.
Austen's Pride and Prejudice. Ed. Marcia McClintock Folsom. 1993.
Baudelaire's Flowers of Evil. Ed. Laurence M. Porter. 2000.
Beckett's Waiting for Godot. Ed. June Schlueter and Enoch Brater. 1991.
Beowulf. Ed. Jess B. Bessinger, Jr., and Robert F. Yeager. 1984.
Blake's Songs of Innocence and of Experience. Ed. Robert F. Gleckner and
    Mark L. Greenberg. 1989.
British Women Poets of the Romantic Period. Ed. Stephen C. Behrendt and
    Harriet Kramer Linkin. 1997.
Brontë's Jane Eyre. Ed. Diane Long Hoeveler and Beth Lau. 1993.
Byron's Poetry. Ed. Frederick W. Shilstone. 1991.
Camus's The Plague. Ed. Steven G. Kellman. 1985.
Cather's My Ántonia. Ed. Susan J. Rosowski. 1989.
Cervantes' Don Quixote. Ed. Richard Bjornson. 1984.
Chaucer's Canterbury Tales. Ed. Joseph Gibaldi. 1980.
Chopin's The Awakening. Ed. Bernard Koloski. 1988.
Coleridge's Poetry and Prose. Ed. Richard E. Matlak. 1991.
Dante's Divine Comedy. Ed. Carole Slade. 1982.
Dickens' David Copperfield. Ed. Richard J. Dunn. 1984.
Dickinson's Poetry. Ed. Robin Riley Fast and Christine Mack Gordon. 1989.
Narrative of the Life of Frederick Douglass. Ed. James C. Hall. 1999.
Eliot's Middlemarch. Ed. Kathleen Blake. 1990.
Eliot's Poetry and Plays. Ed. Jewel Spears Brooker. 1988.
Ellison's Invisible Man. Ed. Susan Resneck Parr and Pancho Savery. 1989.
Faulkner's The Sound and the Fury. Ed. Stephen Hahn and Arthur F. Kinney. 1996.
Flaubert's Madame Bovary. Ed. Laurence M. Porter and Eugene F. Gray. 1995.
García Márquez's One Hundred Years of Solitude. Ed. María Elena de Valdés and
    Mario J. Valdés. 1990.
Goethe's Faust. Ed. Douglas J. McMillan. 1987.
Hebrew Bible as Literature in Translation. Ed. Barry N. Olshen and
    Yael S. Feldman. 1989.
Homer's Iliad *and* Odyssey. Ed. Kostas Myrsiades. 1987.
Ibsen's A Doll House. Ed. Yvonne Shafer. 1985.
Works of Samuel Johnson. Ed. David R. Anderson and Gwin J. Kolb. 1993.
Joyce's Ulysses. Ed. Kathleen McCormick and Erwin R. Steinberg. 1993.
Kafka's Short Fiction. Ed. Richard T. Gray. 1995.
Keats's Poetry. Ed. Walter H. Evert and Jack W. Rhodes. 1991.
Kingston's The Woman Warrior. Ed. Shirley Geok-lin Lim. 1991.

Lafayette's The Princess of Clèves. Ed. Faith E. Beasley and Katharine Ann
    Jensen. 1998.
Lessing's The Golden Notebook. Ed. Carey Kaplan and Ellen Cronan Rose. 1989.
Mann's Death in Venice *and Other Short Fiction*. Ed. Jeffrey B. Berlin. 1992.
Medieval English Drama. Ed. Richard K. Emmerson. 1990.
Melville's Moby-Dick. Ed. Martin Bickman. 1985.
Metaphysical Poets. Ed. Sidney Gottlieb. 1990.
Miller's Death of a Salesman. Ed. Matthew C. Roudané. 1995.
Milton's Paradise Lost. Ed. Galbraith M. Crump. 1986.
Molière's Tartuffe *and Other Plays*. Ed. James F. Gaines and
    Michael S. Koppisch. 1995.
Momaday's The Way to Rainy Mountain. Ed. Kenneth M. Roemer. 1988.
Montaigne's Essays. Ed. Patrick Henry. 1994.
Novels of Toni Morrison. Ed. Nellie Y. McKay and Kathryn Earle. 1997.
Murasaki Shikibu's The Tale of Genji. Ed. Edward Kamens. 1993.
Pope's Poetry. Ed. Wallace Jackson and R. Paul Yoder. 1993.
Shakespeare's King Lear. Ed. Robert H. Ray. 1986.
Shakespeare's The Tempest *and Other Late Romances*. Ed. Maurice Hunt. 1992.
Shelley's Frankenstein. Ed. Stephen C. Behrendt. 1990.
Shelley's Poetry. Ed. Spencer Hall. 1990.
Sir Gawain and the Green Knight. Ed. Miriam Youngerman Miller and
    Jane Chance. 1986.
Spenser's Faerie Queene. Ed. David Lee Miller and Alexander Dunlop. 1994.
Stendhal's The Red and the Black. Ed. Dean de la Motte and Stirling Haig. 1999.
Sterne's Tristram Shandy. Ed. Melvyn New. 1989.
Swift's Gulliver's Travels. Ed. Edward J. Rielly. 1988.
Thoreau's Walden *and Other Works*. Ed. Richard J. Schneider. 1996.
Voltaire's Candide. Ed. Renée Waldinger. 1987.
Whitman's Leaves of Grass. Ed. Donald D. Kummings. 1990.
Wordsworth's Poetry. Ed. Spencer Hall, with Jonathan Ramsey. 1986.
Wright's Native Son. Ed. James A. Miller. 1997.